# TO BE FREE

## PIONEERING STUDIES IN AFRO-AMERICAN HISTORY

*BY HERBERT APTHEKER*

*Introduction by John Hope Franklin*

A CITADEL PRESS BOOK
Published by Carol Publishing Group

*To the memory of my parents and brother*

First Carol Publishing Group Edition 1991



A Citadel Press Book
Published by Carol Publishing Group
Citadel Press is a registered trademark of Carol Communications, Inc.

| Editorial Offices | Sales & Distribution Offices |
|---|---|
| 600 Madison Avenue | 120 Enterprise Avenue |
| New York, NY 10022 | Secaucus, NJ 07094 |

In Canada: Musson Book Company
A division of General Publishing Co. Limited
Don Mills, Ontario M3B 2T6



Manufactured in the United States of America

10 9 8 7 6 5 4 3 2 1

Carol Publishing Group books are available at special discounts for bulk purchases, for sales promotions, fund raising, or educational purposes. Special editions can also be created to specifications. For details contact: Special Sales Department, Carol Publishing Group, 120 Enterprise Ave., Secaucus, NJ 07094

ISBN 0-8065-1257-1

# CONTENTS

# INTRODUCTION
## by John Hope Franklin

When *To Be Free* first appeared more than forty years ago, Herbert Aptheker was one of a very small number of white historians who displayed more than casual interest in the history of African Americans. When I reviewed the volume in the *American Historical Review* in July 1948, I pointed out that essays such as those in *To Be Free* suggested the need to reexamine certain aspects of the relationship between blacks and the larger community. I also observed that with studies like these, it became more and more difficult to ignore or neglect the history of the Negro in America. Already Aptheker had written the best study of slave revolts and had remarked with supreme confidence and considerable prescience that "American life as a whole cannot be understood without knowing that history."

Through essays, general works, and as editor of documents and papers, Aptheker has contributed significantly to our knowledge of the history of a group that most historians had simply ignored. Surely, Herbert Aptheker has been one who has helped raise the study of Negro Americans to a respectable and important area of intellectual inquiry; and his works contributed much to the appreciation and, indeed, the acceptance of the field.

I first came to appreciate the extent of slaves' resistance to their status when I read Aptheker's "Slave Guerrilla Warfare." It was Aptheker, moreover, who provided us with some understanding of the role of blacks in the Civil War, especially in his studies of black casualties in that most tragic of wars. When I first heard Aptheker read a paper on that subject at the annual meeting of the Association for the Study of Negro Life and History, I was appalled not only by his graphic account of the carnage, caused in part by the lack of training of the black soldiers, but also by the fact that earlier historians of the Civil War scarcely recognized blacks as a fighting force in "their war for freedom."

It was, therefore, fortunate for students of African-American history that in 1948 Aptheker collected a number of seminal essays and brought out a volume that included, among others, his studies of slave guerrillas, Negro casualties in the Civil War, slaves purchasing their freedom, and a sketch of the life of that remarkable black leader during the reconstruction of Mississippi, Charles Caldwell. In due course *To Be Free* went out of print, and it was no longer possible to find these important studies in a single place, although the most diligent could search them out in their original versions in pamphlets and various journals.

The reappearance of *To Be Free* in this new, attractive format is an occasion to celebrate. It marks not only the availability once again of some important early studies in the history of the United States, but the affirmation of the durability of a field of study recently recognized by a large number of students but appreciated by Herbert Aptheker in the days when most of them turned their attention to other matters. Thus, this is also an opportunity to celebrate the pioneering work by one who was appreciated by no less a person than Carter G. Woodson, the founder of the Negro History Movement, who invited him to read papers at the annual meetings of the Association and published his findings in the *Journal of Negro History*. I am pleased to be not only one of Herbert Aptheker's contemporaries but one who learned much from him and was greatly stimulated by his zeal and scholarship.

November 21, 1990 John Hope Franklin

# TO BE FREE

# AUTHOR'S INTRODUCTION

The Negro's past runs through the warp and woof of the fabric that is America. His history must be understood not only because it is the history of some fifteen million American citizens, but also because American life as a whole cannot be understood without knowing that history.

This past has been clouded and obscured by distortion, omission, and, at times, by sanctimonious, patronizing sentimentality. This methodology has mirrored and simultaneously bulwarked the super-exploitation of the American Negro people. Denying them a past worthy of serious study and emulation weakens their fight for equality and freedom.

Prolonged and rigorous research is required into the still largely untapped source material from which an over-all history worthy of its subject may be obtained. Nothing can replace this basic procedure in scientific investigation, and it is only on the strength of such digging and probing, such sifting and weighing, that the discipline of Negro historical writing will be lifted above the level of fantasy, mythology, wish-fulfillment, and bigotry, into the realm of fact and reality.

This book represents an attempt to contribute in that direction. The chapters, some of which appeared in condensed form in *The Journal of Negro History, Science and Society,* and *Opportunity,* deal with hitherto neglected but nevertheless vitally important subjects and personalities.

The studies of slave guerrilla warfare and of the techniques and extent of self-purchase of freedom serve to further demonstrate the militance and deep craving for freedom that form the backbone of the Negro's past. The chapter dealing with abolitionism substantiates the same thesis and demonstrates, too, how inextricably interwoven has been the struggle for Negro liberation with that of the general effort to preserve and extend freedom for all Americans. It helps point up, in addition, how indigenous and deep-rooted have been revolutionary sentiments of the most profound and uncompromising character. It becomes clear from that study that the thinking of a man like John Brown, far from being unique, epitomizes the mental process of large segments of the American population during the pre-Civil War years.

The chapters dealing with the contributions made by the Negro in labor and in blood towards the winning of the Civil War demonstrate concretely and specifically his active and vital role in securing his own personal freedom as well as helping to maintain the existence of the United States as a nation. By employing the microcosmic method, the studies on the Reconstruction epoch try to make clear the fundamental democratic issues involved during those years and the demands, organizational activities, and types of leaders then developed by the Negro people themselves.

Throughout the work attention is centered upon the words and deeds of the Negro himself. As much as is possible within a descriptive and analytical volume, the object has been to permit the Negro to talk for himself. Because of the unfamiliar nature of the subject matter and the widely dispersed and largely unpublished character of the source material, full documentation has been offered.

It is this writer's conviction that he who studies and absorbs the history of the Negro people will face the future with supreme confidence. For this history proves that, let the despoilers of humanity do what they will, the aspirations and the struggles of mankind continue and endure.

Of the Negro it may be said as truly as of any other oppressed people that, in fighting for a better world, they had nothing to lose but their chains. This has forged within their hearts a yearning for peace and security, a knowledge of the necessity for unity, and a contempt for the oppressor which constitute a progressive potential of the utmost significance to the United States.

It is a duty and a necessity to resurrect and treasure the precious heritage that the Negro people have bestowed upon America.

# SLAVE GUERRILLA WARFARE

Some definitions of the word "maroon" are quite revealing. As a noun the word is said to refer to "One of a class of fugitive negroes living upon a West Indian island or in Dutch Guiana"; while as an intransitive verb it is defined as follows: "In the southern part of the United States, to camp out in a wild or secluded place as a recreation."[1]

The facts, however, do not justify the limited regional application given this word as a noun. On the contrary, an ever-present feature of our own slave South was the existence of groups of outlawed fugitive slaves. The existence of these American maroons not only represented a serious monetary loss to the slaveholding class but, in addition, they served as sources of insubordination. They offered, too, havens for fugitives, served as bases for marauding expeditions against nearby plantations and, at times, supplied leadership to planned uprisings.

Public notice of these maroon communities was taken only when they were accidentally uncovered or when their activities became so dangerous to the slavocracy that their destruction was felt to be necessary. Evidence of the existence of very many such communities in various places and at various times, from 1672 to 1864, has been found. The mountainous, forested, or swampy regions of South Carolina, North Carolina, Virginia, Louisiana, Florida, Georgia, Mississippi, and Alabama ( in order of importance) appear to have been the favorite haunts for these black Robin Hoods. At times a settled life, rather than a belligerent and migratory one, was aimed at, as is evidenced by the fact that these maroons built homes, maintained families, raised cattle, and pursued agriculture, but this type of life appears to have been exceptional.

The most noted of such communities was that located in

the Dismal Swamp between Virginia and North Carolina. About two thousand Negroes, fugitives, or the descendants of fugitives, lived in this area. They carried on a regular, if illegal, trade with white people living on the borders of the swamp.[2] Such settlements may have been more numerous than available evidence would indicate, for their occupants aroused less excitement and less resentment than the guerrilla outlaws.

The activities of maroons in Virginia in 1672 approached a point of rebellion so that a law was passed urging and rewarding the hunting down and killing of these outlaws. An item of November 9, 1691, notices the depredations caused by a slave, Mingoe, from Middlesex county, Virginia, and his unspecified number of followers in Rappahannock county. These Negroes not only took cattle and hogs, but, what was more important, they had recently stolen "two guns, a Carbyne & other things."[3]

In June, 1711, the inhabitants of the colony of South Carolina were kept "in great fear and terror" by activities of "several Negroes [who] keep out, armed, and robbing and plundering houses and plantations." These men were led by a slave named Sebastian, who was finally tracked down and killed by an Indian hunter.[4] Lieutenant-Governor Gooch of Virginia wrote to the Lords of Trade, June 29, 1729, "of some runaway Negroes beginning a settlement in the Mountains & of their being reclaimed by their Master." He assured the Lords that the militia was being trained to "prevent this for the future."[5]

In September, 1733, the governor of South Carolina offered a reward of £20 alive and £10 dead for "Several Runaway Negroes who are near the Congerees, & have robbed several of the Inhabitants thereabouts." The Notchee Indians offered, April, 1744, to aid the government of South Carolina in maintaining the subordination of its slave population. Three months later, July 5, 1744, Governor James Glen applied "for the assistance of some Notchee Indians in order to apprehend some runaway Negroes, who had sheltered themselves in the Woods, and being armed, had committed disorders. . . ."[6]

The number of runaways in Georgia and South Carolina in 1765 was exceedingly large. This led to fears of a general rebellion, and at least one considerable camp of maroons was destroyed that year by military force. A letter from Charleston of August 16, 1768, told of a battle with a body of maroons, "a numerous collection of outcast mulattoes, mustees, and free negroes."[7]

Governor James Habersham of Georgia learned in December, 1771, "that a great number of fugitive Negroes had committed many Robberies and insults between this town [Savannah] and Ebenezer and that their Numbers were now Considerable [and] might be expected to increase daily." Indian hunters and militiamen were employed to blot out this menace. Yet the same danger was present in Georgia in the summer of 1772. Depredations and arson were frequent, and again the militia saw service.[8] A letter from Edmund Randolph to James Madison of August 30, 1782, discloses somewhat similar trouble in Virginia. At this time it appears that "a notorious robber," a white man, had gathered together a group of about fifty men, Negro and white, and was terrorizing the community.[9]

The British had combated the revolutionists' siege of Savannah with the aid of a numerous body of Negro slaves who served under the inspiration of a promised freedom. The defeat of the British crushed the hopes of these Negroes. They fled, with their arms, called themselves soldiers of the King of England, and carried on a guerrilla warfare for years along the Savannah river. Militia from Georgia and South Carolina, together with Indian allies, successfully attacked some Negro settlements in May, 1786, with resulting heavy casualties.[10] But this by no means ended the danger. For in March, 1787, a slaveholder of Purrysburgh, S. C., informed his state legislator of repeated attacks by slave guerrillas. They had, he declared, ransacked his own plantation and wounded his overseer. The legislator was warned that unless the state immediately took suppressive measures, "the matter may become of too serious a nature, as hereafter to give ourselves farther trouble about the matter more than quietly submit our Families to be sacrificed by them & probably by our own indoor Domestics."

The recipient of this disquieting note wrote the next day to his colleague from St. Peter's Parish, Charleston, that South Carolina had to do something, "even if we follow the example of the Georgians by a Proclamation so much per head – dead or alive." By March 20, Governor Thomas Pinckney officially called the situation to the attention of the legislature and submitted pertinent letters describing its gravity. The same day a joint committee of both Houses reported, "That his Excellency the Governor be requested immediately to adopt the most decisive and effectual measures to extirpate the Runaway Negroes committing depredation in the Southern part of this State." It added its recommendation that the governor be authorized "to Issue a Proclamation offering a reward of Ten pounds sterling for each of said Negroes killed or taken in this state" and that the legislature agree to "provide for any Expence that may be incurred in the prosecution of this business."

From an "Account of expenditures attending the dispersing the Fugitive Slaves near Purrysburg" it appears that the State militia, assisted by Catawba Indians, under the command of Lieutenant Colonel Thomas Hutson, used up over two hundred and forty pounds to pay for "this business," of which forty pounds went to "Capt. Patton for scalps taken by Catawbas under his command," while a total of twenty pounds were earned by Jacob Winkler and Nathaniel Tettler for the same tasteful trophies.

Funds for this purpose were appropriated by the legislature during the end of February, 1788. In the resolution providing this special money appears the interesting information that the militia in performing their duties was "carried out of this into the State of Georgia . . ."

Evidence is present of similar proceedings in the spring of 1793. There exists a request to the legislature, dated April 19, for payment of one Captain William Harley and eighteen men who had been "employed by order of the Governor against the Negro fugitives." These men had required fifteen days for the performance of their task, and the captain received his payment. In addition, there is a receipt, of the same date, acknowledging the payment of thirty pounds to twenty-two other men (two sergeants and twenty privates), for seven days' service in "an expedition against runaway negroes."

Captain Harley was a busy man that season as was demonstrated by an order upon the state's treasurer, signed by Governor Moultrie, on May 20, 1793, to pay the captain $245 for himself and twelve men. This money was paid to compensate the labors of the thirteen individuals who "from the 29th April to the 17th May . . . were raised & sent in pursuit of a Number of armed fugitive Slaves, in the parishes of St. John, St. James, Goosecreek, & St. George."[11]

Chesterfield and Charles City counties, Virginia, were troubled by maroons in November, 1792. At least one white man was killed while tracking them down. Ten of the runaways were finally captured, with the aid of dogs.[12] The neighborhood of Wilmington, North Carolina, was harassed in June and July, 1795, by "a number of runaway Negroes, who in the daytime secrete themselves in the swamps and woods. . . . at night committed various depredations of the neighbouring plantations." They killed at least one white man, an overseer, and severely wounded another. About five of these maroons including the leader, known as the General of the Swamps, were killed by hunting parties. It was hoped that "these well-timed severities" would "totally break up this nest of miscreants —At all events, this town has nothing to apprehend as the citizens keep a strong and vigilant night guard." Within two weeks of this first report, of July 3, the capture and execution of four more runaways was reported. On July 17 it was believed that only one leader and a "few deluded followers" were still at large.[13]

Petitions for state aid presented in 1800 to the South Carolina legislature, by the widows of two overseers, Adam Culliatt and Joseph C. Brown, declare that both men were killed in October, 1799, by slave outlaws. Mrs. Culliatt stated that her husband lost his life while a member of a party commanded by a Captain Paul Hamilton, "in pursuit of a party of negroes who had recently committed a murder in the neighborhood" of Jacksonborough, while Mrs. Brown declared that her husband and another overseer were "in search of a gang of runaway negroes . . . who infested" St. Paul's parish, and that both men were shot by these fugitives.[14]

The existence of a maroon camp in the neighborhood of Elizabeth City, North Carolina, in May, 1802, is indicated by the fact that the plots and insubordination uncovered among the slave population at that time were attributed to the agitation of an outlawed Negro, Tom Cooper, who "has got a camp in one of the swamps." In March, 1811, a runaway community in a swamp in Cabarrus county, North Carolina, was wiped out. These maroons "had bid defiance to any force whatever, and were resolved to stand their ground." In the attack two Negro women were captured, two Negro men killed, and another wounded.[15]

The close proximity of the weakly governed Spanish territory of East Florida persistently disturbed the equanimity of American slaveholders. Many of the settlers in that region, moreover, were Americans, and they, aided by volunteers from the United States, raised the standard of revolt in 1810, the aim being American annexation.[16] In the correspondence of Lieutenant Colonel Thomas Smith and Major Flournoy, both of the United States Army and both actively on the side of the rebels or "patriots" in the Florida fighting, and of Governor Mitchell of Georgia, there are frequent references to the fleeing of American slaves into Florida, where they helped the Indians in their struggle against the Americans and the "patriots." A few examples may be cited.

Smith told General Pinckney, July 30, 1812, of fresh Indian depredations in Georgia and of the escape of about eighty slaves. He planned to send troops against them, for "The safety of our frontier I conceive requires this course. They have, I am informed, several hundred fugitive slaves from the Carolinas and Georgia at present in their Town & unless they are checked soon they will be so strengthened by desertions from Georgia & Florida that it will be found troublesome to reduce them." And it was troublesome. In a letter to Governor Mitchell of August 21, 1812, Smith declared, "The blacks assisted by the Indians have become very daring." In September, further slave escapes were reported from Georgia. On September 11, a baggage train under Captain Williams and twenty men, going to the support of Colonel Smith, was attacked and routed, Williams himself being killed by Indians and maroons. In January, 1813, further escapes were reported, and, in February, Smith wrote of battles with Negroes and Indians and the destruction of a Negro fort. One Georgia participant in this fighting, Colonel Daniel Newman, declared the maroon allies of the Indians were "their best soldiers."[17]

The refusal of the Senate of the United States, at the moment, to sanction occupation of East Florida, finally led to a lull in the fighting. By 1816, however, the annoyance and danger from runaway slaves again served as justification for American intervention. With southern complaints ringing in its ears[18] the administration dispatched, in July, United States troops with Indian allies under Colonel Duncan Clinch against the main stronghold of the maroons, the well-stocked Negro fort on Appalachicola Bay. After a siege of ten days a cannon shot totally destroyed the fort and annihilated two hundred and seventy men, women and children. But forty souls survived.[19]

Another major expedition against a maroon community was carried out in 1816. This occurred near Ashepoo, South Carolina. Governor David R. William's remarks concerning this in his message of December, 1816, merit quotation:

> A few runaway negroes, concealing themselves in the swamps and marshes contiguous to Combahee and Ashepoo rivers, not having been interrupted in their petty plundering for a long time, formed the nucleus, round which all the ill-disposed and audacious near them gathered, until at length their robberies became too serious to be suffered with impunity. Attempts were then made to disperse them, which either from insufficiency of numbers or bad arrangement, served by their failure only to encourage a wanton destruction of property. Their new forces now became alarming, not less from its numbers than from its arms and ammunition with which it was supplied. The peculiar situation of the whole of that portion of our coast, rendered access to them difficult, while the numerous creeks and water courses through the marshes around the islands, furnished them easy opportunities to plunder, not only the planters in open day, but the inland coasting trade also without leaving a trace of their movements by which they could be pursued. . . . I therefore ordered Major-General Youngblood to take the necessary measures for suppressing them, and authorized him to incur the necessary expenses of such an expedition. This was immediately executed. By a judicious employment of the militia under his command, he either captured or destroyed the whole body.[20]

The Norfolk *Herald* of June 29, 1818, referred to the serious damages occasioned by a group of some thirty runaway slaves, acting together with white men, in Princess Anne county, Virginia. It reported, too, the recent capture of a leader and "an old woman" member of the outlaws. In November of that year maroon activities in Wake county, North Carolina, became serious enough to evoke notice from the local press which advised "the patrol to keep a strict look out." Later an attack upon a store "by a maroon banditti of negroes" led by "the noted Andey, alias Billy James, better known by the name of Abellino," was repulsed by armed citizens. The paper believed that the death of at least one white man, if not more, might accurately be placed at their hands.[21] The Raleigh *Register* of December 18, 1818, printed Governor Branch's proclamation offering $250 reward for the capture of seven specific outlaws and $100 for Billy James alone. There is evidence that, in this same year, maroons were active in Johnston county, in that state, and one expedition against them resulted in the killing of at least one Negro.[22]

Expeditions against maroons took place in Williamsburg county, South Carolina, in the summer of 1819. Three slaves were killed, several captured and one white was wounded. Similar activities occurred in May, 1820, in Gates county, North Carolina. A slave outlaw, Harry, whose head had been assessed at $200, was killed by four armed whites. "It is expected that the balance of Harry's company [which had killed at least one white man] will very soon be taken."[23]

Twelve months later there was similar difficulty near Georgetown, South Carolina, resulting in the death of one slaveholder and the capture of three outlaws.[24] The activities of considerable maroon groups in Onslow, Carteret, and Bladen counties, North Carolina, aided by some free Negroes, assumed the proportions of rebellion in the summer of 1821. There were plans for joint action between these outlaws and the field slaves against the slaveholders. Approximately three hundred members of the militia of the three counties saw service for about twenty-five days in August and September. About twelve of these men were wounded when two companies of militia accidentally fired upon each other. The situation was under control by the middle of September, although the militia men "did not succeed in apprehending all the runaways & fugitives [still] they did good by arresting some, and driving others off, and suppressing the spirit of insurrection."[25] A newspaper item of 1824 discloses that the "prime mover" of this trouble, a Negro called Isam, "alias General Jackson," was among those who escaped at the time, for he is there reported as dying from lashes publicly inflicted at Cape Fear, North Carolina.[26]

In the summer of 1822 activity among armed runaway slaves was reported from Jacksonborough, South Carolina. Three were executed on July 19. In August Governor Bennett offered a reward of two hundred dollars for the capture of about twenty maroons in the same region. It is possible that these Negroes had been enlisted in the far-flung conspiracy of Denmark Vesey, uncovered and crushed in June, 1822.[27]

The Norfolk *Herald* of May 12, 1823, contains an unusually full account of maroons under the heading "A Serious Subject." It declares that the citizens of the southern part of Norfolk county, Virginia,

> have for some time been kept in a state of mind peculiarly harassing and painful, from the too apparent fact that their lives are at the mercy of a band of lurking assassins, against whose fell designs neither the power of the law, or vigilance, or personal strength and intrepidity, can avail. These desperadoes are runaway negroes (commonly called outlyers). . . . Their first object is to obtain a gun and ammunition, as well to procure game for subsistence as to defend themselves from attack, or accomplish objects of vengeance.

Several men had already been killed by these former slaves; one, a Mr. William Walker, very recently. This aroused great fear. "No individual after this can consider his life safe from the murdering aim of these monsters in human shape. Every one who has haply rendered himself obnoxious to their vengeance, must, indeed, calculate on sooner or later falling a victim" to them. Indeed, one slaveholder had received a note from these amazing fellows suggesting it would be healthier for him to remain indoors at night—and he did.

A large body of militia was ordered out to exterminate these outcasts and "thus relieve the neighbouring inhabitants from a state of perpetual anxiety and apprehension, than which nothing can be more painful." During the next few weeks there were occasional reports[28] of the killing or capturing of outlaws.

culminating June 25, 1823, in the capture of the leader himself, Bob Ferebee, who, it was declared, had been an outlaw for six years. He was executed on July 25. In October of this same year runaway Negroes near Pineville, South Carolina, were attacked. Several were captured, and at least two, a woman and a child, were killed. One of the maroons was decapitated, and his head stuck on a pole and publicly exposed as "a warning to vicious slaves."[29]

In December, 1825, at a cost of $700, the state of South Carolina purchased, from a Mrs. Perrin of Richland County, her slave Royal, and freed him. This action was taken as the result of a petition of the previous year from eighty-one planters of the lady's neighborhood.

It may be assumed that only extraordinary services to the master class would evoke two such tributes and this assumption is correct. The planters' petition reveals, "It is now some years since Mr. Ford, a highly worthy and respected citizen of our State, was murdered somewhere not far from Georgetown, So[uth] Ca[rolina], by a negroe belonging to Mr. Carroll of Richland District named Joe (or Forest)." A reward was offered by the relatives of the deceased and by the Governor of the State, but the rebel was not taken. The petition continues:

> He was so cunning and artful as to elude pursuit and so daring and bold at particular times when no force was at hand as to put everything at defiance. Emboldened by his successes and his seeming good fortune he plunged deeper and deeper [into] wild crime until neither fear nor danger could deter him from threatening and then from executing a train of mischiefs we believe quite without parallel in this country.
>
> Most of the runaways flew to his Camp and he soon became their head and their life. He had the art and the address to inspire enthusiasm. Such was his cunning that but few of the enterprises for mischief planned by himself failed of success. We believe that nearly four years have now elapsed since the murder of Mr. Ford, the whole of which time, until his merited death, was marked by Crimes, by Mischiefs and by the desemination of notions the most dangerous among the blacks in our Sections of the County (such as were calculated in the end to produce insubordination and insurrection) . . . We were compelled as we conceived from the necessity of the case to associate together for the purposes of domestic safety and for the object of impressing our blacks with proper fear by the power of wholesome ex-

ample. . . .We organized several companies of Infantry from among our Association. . . .

Yet, as the planters state, this force was unable to cope with "Joe (or Forest)," and his followers. Here entered Mrs. Perrin's favorite slave, Royal, who recommended strategy and offered to trick the partisan and his band into an ambush for slaughter by the planters. And, indeed, Royal "managed to decoy those who, we had long sought . . . Soon perceiving their mistake and the danger of all before them, they instantly attempted to defend themselves with well charged musquets but at a single well directed fire from the party of whites in the Boat Joe with three of his party fell dead. The rest of the gang of runaways were subsequently either killed in pursuit, hung for attempts to murder or were frightened to their respective homes."

Thus did Royal gain his own freedom—of body, if not of mind.[30]

A maroon community consisting of men, women, and children was broken up by a three-day attack made by armed slaveholders of Mobile county, Alabama, in June, 1827. The Negroes had been outlaws for years and lived entirely by plundering neighboring plantations. At the time of the attacks the Negroes were constructing a stockade fort. Had this been finished it was believed that field slaves thus informed would have joined them. Cannon would then have been necessary for their destruction. The maroons made a desperate resistance, "fighting like Spartans." Three were killed, others wounded, and several escaped. Because of the poor arms of the Negroes but one white was slightly wounded.[31]

In November, 1827, a Negro woman returned to her master in New Orleans after an absence of sixteen years. She told of a maroon settlement some eight miles north of the city containing about sixty people. A drought prevailed at the moment so it was felt that "the uncommon dryness . . . has made those retreats attainable . . . and we are told there is another camp about the head of the bayou Bienvenu. Policy imperiously calls for a thorough search, and the destruction of all such repairs, where-ever found to exist."[32]

In the summer of 1829 "a large gang of runaway negroes, who have infested the Parishes of Christ Church and St. James

[S. C.], for several months, and committed serious depredations on the properties of the planters" was accidentally discovered by a party of deer hunters. One of the Negroes was wounded and four others were captured. Several others escaped, but the Charleston *Mercury* hoped the citizens would "not cease their exertions until the evil shall be effectually removed."[33]

In the same year twenty-three planters of the parish of Christ Church in South Carolina presented a petition to the state legislature which is an illuminating document in many respects and is particularly revealing as to the incessant activities of maroons.

The specific prayer of the petitioners was for the repeal of a law enacted by the state in December 1821, entitled "An Act to increase the punishment inflicted on persons convicted of murdering any slave." This provided that if any person did "wilfully, maliciously, and deliberately murder any slave [he] on conviction shall suffer death without the benefit of clergy," while if the killing were done "on sudden heat and passion," the penalty was to be a fine of not over $500, and imprisonment for not over six months.

These slaveholders declared that "from the vicinity of their property to Charleston, from their parish being surrounded by navigable water leading directly to it, and occasioning much intercourse with that City, and from the great Northern road passing through their parish in its whole length [they] are peculiarly exposed to the great evil of absconding slaves and their ruinous depredations." They went on to say that they were

> . . . aware that these Causes have long combined to produce this evil, but they have within these latter Years only, found it operate to an extent producing great irregularity and disorder among their Slaves, and now leading directly to a state of insubordination and danger affecting the lives of individuals and the security of property.
>
> This state of things is operating, your Memorialists believe, in every part of the lower and middle divisions of the State as they are informed by the inhabitants of other parishes and it cries aloud for the interference of your Honourable House. They think it unnecessary to say anything of the unceasing efforts made by enthusiasts out of Carolina, to poison the minds of our domestic people, these must be met in a different way, and cannot hurt us if the Southern States are true to

themselves; but they would distinctly state their conviction, that great mischief has been already done, and is daily increasing by the misguided zeal and unguarded movements, acts and conversation of persons within our own State, owning little or none of the property they so earnestly and so unceasingly crave to meddle with, yet living and supported by the agriculture of the country.

In developing this interesting allusion to anti-slavery feeling among the poorer folk of South Carolina, the planters went on to state that its danger had been accentuated by the then current economic depression. They pointed out that "large bodies of negroes" had been sold to traders in Charleston because of this depression, and that there followed an "unrestrained intercourse of these [slaves] with free blacks and low and worthless white people [and this] infused into the minds of negroes ideas of insubordination and of emancipation, which they carry with them when sold into every part of the State . . ."

Returning to the law of 1821 the memorialists held that those who enacted it

. . . were not practical Southern planters . . . [nor] Southern legislators [!] for if they had been, they would have known that *changing the nature of the penalties in the case of negroes*—that inflicting the punishment of death on a white man for killing a slave, *who is a property, instead of exacting a fine* for the loss of that property [emphases in original—H.A.] was placing the white inhabitants on a footing which would not be admitted by Juries of our Countrymen, and hence that the penalty would never be inflicted in any case however enormous. . .

These planters asserted their beliefs that "the very effect of the law . . . is to produce upon the part of the negro, such acts of violence, as call immediate vengeance down upon him." Let us have, they begged, the undiluted laws of our forefathers, "for the old laws were practical, reasonable and therefore carried into execution." This act of 1821 with its "peculiar fitness to impress upon the minds of Slaves (to whom it is too often read), that they are now on a different footing as regards their owners and the whites, from what they formerly were; a footing approaching nearer to a State of emancipation from their authority," leads "of course to a State of unrestrained liberty and licentiousness," while its provisions tend to restrain the whites from dealing with this "State" in a befitting fashion!

This alleged condition "of security in crime" brings about

> . . . greater and yet greater atrocities, hence the depredations upon our property, crops and cattle, have been enormous. . . Such negroes as have in consequence of this combination of fatal circumstances remained out for Years, at length cease to respect the whites, become reckless of consequences and choosing their opportunities during the sickly season of the Year when individuals are alone and supposed to be defenseless, attack them with a view to destroy them.

Let us, continued the petitioners, cite a few examples to demonstrate these facts:

> In 1822 a negro belonging to the Estate of Spring, . . . absconded and came into the parish [of Christ Church] as a runaway. In 1824 a fellow belonging to Mr. Legare joined him as a runaway was Shot and killed in his company—In 1825 a family five in number purchased at the sale of A. Vanderhorst, absconded and joined the same ringleader. They continued out until October last [1828], when the Children surrendered (one having been born in the woods) the father and mother having been both shot and killed—In 1827 three Negroes belonging to a Parishioner's Estate returned in like manner after the sale of his effects as runaways. One of them in January last [1829] snapped a gun heavily loaded with Slugs at one of your Memorialists, who met him in the woods and immediately shot the negro. Another of these three negroes in October last attacked another of your Memorialists with a knife fifteen inches long, stabbed him in the hand, and would have cut his throat, but for assistance rendered in time to save him. In 1828, runaway slaves were collected from various parts of the Parish, one was killed upon the spot, and another severely wounded for the second time and taken, in January last eighteen slaves the property of your Memorialists went off under their driver and of these one fellow has been shot and killed, while the house of the owner has been pillaged by his own Slaves, ten of whom are still out in a neighboring parish. . . . [This condition is] no longer to be tolerated or borne with—one negro taken some months ago, declared on his trial, that he had in three weeks destroyed Forty head of Cattle, and many of your Memorialists are altogether prevented from keeping Stock of any Kind, from these causes, after having had large gangs of cattle, sheep and hogs destroyed.[34]

Maroons were important factors in causing slave insubordination in Sampson, Bladen, Onslow, Jones, New Hanover and Dublin counties, North Carolina, from September through December, 1830. Citizens complained that their "slaves are becoming almost uncontrollable. They go and come when and where they please, and if an attempt is made to correct them they immediately fly to the woods and there continue for months and years committing grievous depredations on our Cattle, hogs and Sheep."[35] One of these fugitive slaves, Moses, who had been out for two years, was captured in November. From him was elicited the information that an uprising was imminent, that the conspirators "had arms & ammunition secreted, that they had runners or messengers to go between Wilmington, Newbern & Elizabeth City to 'carry word' & report to them, that there was a camp in Dover Swamp of 30 or 40—another about Gastons Island, on Price's Creek, several on Newport River, several near Wilmington." Arms were found in the place named by Moses

> in possession of a white woman living in a very retired situation—also some meat, hid away & could not be accounted for—a child whom the party [of citizens] found a little way from the house, said that his mamy dressed victuals every day for 4 or 5 runaways, & shewed the spot. . . where the meat was then hid & where it was found—the place or camp in Dover was found, a party of neighbours discovered the camp, burnt 11 houses, and made such discoveries, as convinced them it was a place of rendezvous for numbers (it is supposed they killed several of the negroes).[36]

Newspaper accounts referred to the wholesale shooting of fugitives. In 1830 the Roanoke *Advertiser* stated: "The inhabitants of Newbern being advised of the assemblage of sixty armed slaves in a swamp in their vicinity, the military were called out, and surrounding the swamp, killed the whole party." A later item, dated Wilmington, January 7, 1831, declared, "There has been much shooting of negroes in this neighborhood recently, in consequence of symptoms of liberty having been discovered among them." It is of interest to note that Richmond papers, on receiving the first reports of Nat Turner's slave revolt of August, 1831, asked, concerning the rebels, "Were they connected with the desperadoes who harassed N. Carolina last year?"[37]

In June 1836, there was mention that "a band of runaway negroes in the Cypress Swamp" near New Orleans "had been committing depredations." The next year, in July, was reported the killing of an outlaw slave leader, Squire, near the same city, whose band, it was felt, was responsible for the deaths of several white men. Squire's career had lasted three years. A guard of soldiers was sent to the swamp for his body, which was exhibited for several days in the public square of the city.[38]

The year 1837 also saw the start of the Florida or Seminole War which was destined to drag on until 1843. This war, "conducted largely as a slave-catching enterprise for the benefit of the citizens of Georgia and Florida" was, before its termination, to take an unknown number of Indian and Negro lives together with the lives of fifteen hundred white soldiers and the expenditure of twenty million dollars. The Indians had at the beginning of hostilities about 1,650 warriors and 250 Negro fighters. The latter, it was reported, were "the most formidable foe, more blood-thirsty, active, and revengeful, than the Indian."[39]

Armed runaways repulsed an attack near Wilmington, North Carolina, in January, 1841, after killing one of the whites. A posse captured three of the Negroes and lodged them in the city jail. One escaped, but two were taken from the prison and lynched.[40] Late in September two companies of militia were dispatched in search of a body of maroons some 45 miles north of Mobile, Alabama. "It is believed that these fellows have for a long time been in the practice of theft and arson, both in town and country . . . A force from above was scouring down, with bloodhounds, &c, to meet the Mobile party." A month later frequent attacks upon white men were reported from Terrebonne Parish, Louisiana.[41]

In the summer of 1841 serious difficulty arose in what is now Oklahoma and was then known as Indian Territory. A contemporary source declared that "some 600 negroes" formerly from Florida, as well as additional runaways from among the slaves of Choctaws, Cherokees and white planters, uniting "with a few Indians, and perhaps a few white men" had associated themselves together "in the fastnesses west of Arkansas." They were engaged in hunting buffalo.

[They] built a very tolerable fort with logs, surrounded with a ditch, to protect themselves from all dangers! They caught but few buffalo, and therefore to supply their wants, invaded the possession of the Choctaws and carried off cattle, poultry, grain &c. The Choctaws followed, but finding their numbers and fortifications an overmatch, they retired and sent to Fort Gibson for the U. States dragoons. . . three companies of dragoons [were sent] but after arriving upon the Red river, he [their commander] found their entrenchments too strong, and their number too great to venture an attack. He accordingly sent to Fort Towson and was reinforced with a fine company of infantry and a couple of pieces of cannon.

The cannon were shortly brought to bear upon the works and soon made the splinters fly and the log move *so queerly,* that the refugees, at a signal rushed outside of their fortifications and began to form upon the prairie in front of their works. . . [The] gallant dragoons charged upon them at full gallop. The carnage that ensued is represented as terrific—the dragoons routed them in all directions, and, after putting large numbers to the sword, succeeded in capturing the *whole body!* The conduct of the dragoons is represented as worthy of all commendation as regards both skill and bravery. The bravery and numbers of the refugees availed absolutely nothing against the irresistible charge of the mounted dragoons.

This decisive blow will give security to that exposed portion of our frontier and convince the refugee negroes and Indians that our dragoons may not be trifled with. The loss of the dragoons was unknown to our informant—he said an express brought the news to the fort.

Notwithstanding this, however, the next year in the same area, according to the statement of two visiting Friends, about two hundred fugitive slaves of Creek and Cherokee masters were causing "much excitement, and a posse was sent after them. . . ."[42]

Several armed planters near Hanesville, Mississippi, in February, 1844, set an ambush for maroons who had been exceedingly troublesome. Six Negroes, "part of the gang," were trapped, but three escaped. Two were wounded and one was killed. In November, 1846, about a dozen armed slaveholders surprised "a considerable gang of runaway negroes" in St. Landry Parish, Louisiana. The maroons refused to surrender and fled. Two Negroes, a man and a woman, were killed, and two Negro women were "badly wounded." The others escaped.[43]

Joshua R. Giddings, the famous fighting Ohio Congressman, referred to the flight in September, 1850, of some three hundred former Florida maroons from their abode in present Oklahoma to Mexico. This was said to have been accomplished after the

Negroes had driven off Creek Indians sent to oppose their exodus. Somewhat later the Houston, Texas *Telegraph* reported that fifteen hundred former American slaves were aiding the Comanchee Indians of Mexico in their fighting. Five hundred of these Negroes were from Texas. Giddings referred, too, to unsuccessful expeditions by Texas slaveholders in 1853 into Mexico for the purpose of recovering fugitive Negroes, and declared that at the time he was writing (1858) maroons in southern Florida were again causing trouble. Frederick Law Olmsted, one of the best known journalists of this period, cited evidence of maroon troubles in the 1850's in Virginia. Louisiana, and northern Alabama.[44]

A letter of August 25, 1856, to Governor Thomas Bragg of North Carolina, signed by Richard A. Lewis and twenty-one other citizens, informed him of a "very secure retreat for runaway negroes" in a large swamp between Bladen and Robeson counties. There "for many years past, and at this time, there are several runaways of bad and daring character—destructive to all kinds of Stock and dangerous to all persons living by or near said swamp." Slaveholders attacked these Negroes on August 1, 1856, but accomplished nothing and saw one of their own number killed. "The negroes ran off cursing and swearing and telling them to come on, they were ready for them again." The Wilmington *Journal* of August 14 mentioned that these runaways "had cleared a place for a garden, had cows, &c in the swamp." Mr. Lewis and his friends were "unable to offer sufficient inducement for negro hunters to come with their dogs unless aided from other sources." The Governor suggested that magistrates be requested to call for the militia, but whether this was done or not is unknown.[45]

A runaway camp was destroyed, and four Negroes, including a woman, captured near Bovina, Mississippi, in March, 1857. A similar event, resulting in the wounding of three maroons, occurred in October, 1859, in Nash County, North Carolina. An "organized camp of white men and negroes" was held responsible for a slave conspiracy, involving whites, which was uncovered in Talladega County, Alabama, in August, 1860.[46]

The years of the Civil War witnessed a considerable accentuation in the struggle of the Negro people against enslavement. This was as true of maroon activity as it was generally. There were reports of depredations committed by "a gang of runaway slaves" acting together with two whites along the Comite River, Louisiana, early in 1861. An expedition was set "on foot to capture the whole party." A runaway community near Marion, South Carolina, was attacked in June, 1861. There were no casualties, however, the slave-hunters capturing but two Negro children, twelve guns, and and one axe.[47]

The appearance of Federal troops always resulted in Negroes flocking to their lines. Among these people contemporaries noticed that some had lived for years as fugitive denizens of the surrounding countryside. Brigadier-General Burnside, for instance, informed Secretary of War Stanton, early in 1862, after having just entered Newbern, North Carolina, that the Negroes

> seem to be wild with excitement and delight . . . The city is being overrun with fugitives from the surrounding towns and plantations. Two have reported themselves who have been in the swamps for five years. It would be utterly impossible, if we were so disposed, to keep them outside of our lines, as they find their way to us through the woods and swamps from every side.[48]

Confederate Brigadier-General R. F. Floyd asked Governor Milton of Florida on April 11, 1862, to declare martial law in Nassau, Duvar, Clay, Putnam, St. John's and Volusia Counties, "as a measure of absolute necessity, as they contain a nest of traitors and lawless negroes."[49] In October, 1862, a scouting party of three armed whites, investigating a maroon camp containing one hundred men, women, and children in Surry County, Virginia, were killed by these fugitives.[50] Governor Shorter of Alabama commissioned J. H. Clayton in January, 1863, to destroy the nests in the southeastern part of the state of "deserters, traitors, and runaway Negroes."[51] Colonel Hatch of the Union Army reported in August, 1864, that "500 Union men, deserters, and negroes were . . . raiding towards Gainsville," Florida. The same month a Confederate officer, John K. Jackson, declared that:

> Many deserters. . .are collected in the swamps and fastnesses of Taylor, La Fayette, Levy and other counties [in Florida], and have organized,

with runaway negroes, bands for the purpose of committing depredations upon the plantations and crops of loyal citizens and running off their slaves. These depredatory bands have even threatened the cities of Tallahassee, Madison, and Marianna.[52]

A Confederate newspaper noticed similar activities in North Carolina in 1864. It reported:

[It is] difficult to find words of description . . . of the wild and terrible consequences of the negro raids in this obscure . . . theatre of the war. . . . In two counties of Currituck and Camden, there are said to be from five to six hundred negroes, who are not in the regular military organization of the Yankees, but who, outlawed and disowned by their masters, lead the lives of banditti, roving the country with fire and committing all sorts of horrible crimes upon the inhabitants.

This present theatre of guerrilla warfare has, at this time, a most important interest for our authorities. It is described as a rich country. . . and one of the most important sources of meat supplies that is now accessible to our armies. . . .

This account ends with a broad hint that white deserters from the Confederate Army were fighting shoulder to shoulder with these self-emancipated Negroes.[53]

The story of America's maroons is of interest not only because it is an important part of the history of the South and of the Negro, but also because of the evidence it provides to help demonstrate that the conventional picture of slavery as a more or less delightful, patriarchal system is fallacious. The corollary of this distortion—docile, contented slaves—is also, of course, seriously undermined.

The ancient cliché, still reiterated, that American Negro slavery was characterized by placidity is a colossal hoax anticipating fascism's technique of the "big lie" by several generations.[54]

# BUYING FREEDOM

Through the fabric of the American Negro people's history there runs like a bright thread their yearning for liberation. This yearning evoked various and numerous forms of struggle in the ante-bellum slave South: from shamming illness to destroying tools; from poisoning masters and assassinating overseers to self-mutilation and suicide; from flight and guerrilla warfare, conspiracy and rebellion, to enlistment, when possible and when liberty was the reward, in the armies and navies of the states and the Federal government; from destroying single buildings and entire communities by fire to the purchase of their own bodies—to buying freedom.

This last mode of struggle, while usually unobtrusive and rarely spectacular, nevertheless required great perseverance and a deliberate, cool courage. Evidence establishes the fact that thousands of Negro slaves managed to buy their freedom, or to have it bought for them by relatives and friends. The former case naturally provokes the question: how was a slave, another person's property, able to accumulate the wherewithal to purchase himself?

For this to occur four conditions, besides, of course, the Negro's own desire, had to be present: the owner had to express a willingness to permit the slave to buy himself; it had to be possible for the slave to earn and to retain the money required; it was necessary that the owner, having made possible the first two conditions, accept in good faith from his slave the money involved and in return present him with papers of manumission; and, finally, the possibility of manumission, in a legal sense, and particularly manumission by self-purchase, had to exist.

To obtain permission to attempt this undertaking and for the slave to retain possession of his earnings once it was launched were not easy. Nor was it unheard of that, after having agreed to terms and having struggled and accumulated all or a large part of the purchase price, the slave was compelled to suffer the torture of seeing these earnings appropriated by the master, the agreement denied or disavowed, and the extra labor gone for nought. Again, it sometimes happened that the work and hope of years turned to ashes with the death of the master; or sometimes the master, for any of a number of reasons, decided to sell the slave prior to the consummation of the agreement.[1]

In certain areas the right of a slave to enter into a contract with his master for the working out, or the purchase of, freedom and the binding quality of this instrument upon both parties, were legally recognized. This was true, for example, in New England during the seventeenth and eighteenth centuries when agreements were entered into stating the number of years the Negro slaves were to labor without compensation prior to manumission.[2]

This was true, also, of Virginia, both as a colony and as a state. Thus, in the seventeenth century, a Negro named Tony Bowze entered into a written agreement with his master, Major-General Bennett, providing that he was to pay eight hundred pounds of tobacco yearly to the General "and be at Liberty." The death of the master brought an attempt to re-enslave the Negro, but the latter "producing a note under his said Master's hand," providing as above specified, the Court decided that Bowze was to remain at liberty so long as he could "Give Security for payment of 800 lb. [of tobacco] per Annum dureing his life. . . ."[3]

Other cases involving the validity of a contract for manumission by self-purchase repeatedly reached Virginia's highest court and this ruled, in principle, in favor of the Negroes. In 1844, for example, one John D. Miles drew up the following document:

> I . . . for the sum of four hundred dollars . . . paid and contracted to be paid to me by my negro man named Felix Smith, have, and by these presents do manumit and set free my said negro man Felix, he serving me faithfully for the space of six years and at the expiration of that period he is to be and go absolutely free . . . if . . . Felix shall, before the expiration of said six years, have well and fully paid . . . the sum

of four hundred dollars, with interest . . . his period of service shall expire, and he is manumitted and set free by these presents, at the time of such full payment.

When the highest court of Virginia was asked to rule on this agreement it not only recognized its legality but declared it to represent "an immediate, and not a future manumission."[4]

Kentucky's courts ruled in a manner similar to that of Virginia. Occasionally, too, in that state, contracts for the purchase of freedom were made on the part of the Negro by white agents. Suits against these agents by Negroes were not unknown and at times resulted in verdicts favorable to the plaintiff.[5]

Tennessee and Louisiana endowed the slave, by law, with the power to enter into a contract for the purchase of his freedom. The law of Tennessee, enacted in 1833, was repeatedly referred to by that state's Supreme Court in upholding the validity of such contracts. This formed the occasion for one of the most remarkable pronouncements in the history of American Negro slavery. In 1846 Judge Green, of Tennessee's Supreme Court, declared in rendering a decision:

> A slave is not in the condition of a horse . . . he is made after the image of the Creator. He has mental capacities, and an immortal principle in his nature, that constitute him equal to his owner, but for the accidental condition in which fortune has placed him . . . the laws . . . cannot extinguish his high born nature, nor deprive him of many rights which are inherent in man . . . he can make a contract for his freedom, which our laws recognize, and he can take a bequest of his freedom, and by the same will he can take personal or real estate.[6]

Under two articles of the Louisiana code slaves were "vested with the same right of contracting as to their emancipation as freemen are as to any other species of property," and contracts and suits based upon these provisions existed.[7]

Everywhere in the ante-bellum United States the right of a slave to accumulate, with his master's permission, his own personal property—or peculium—was recognized, either by law, judicial decision, or custom. Evidence concerning this is implicit in the material already presented on the slave's right to contract for his own purchase, but even where this right was not acknowledged, or specifically denied, the right to personal property was, in fact, granted.

In South Carolina, for example, not only was this right explicitly enunciated by its Supreme Court, but, in 1792, Chief Justice Rutledge declared that a slave might use this personal wealth to buy and free another slave.[8] In Maryland and the District of Columbia courts denied the slave's right to contract for his own purchase, but they heard many cases in which the possession of personal property by slaves was taken for granted.[9] And in North Carolina where an act of 1830 required that one who petitioned for the manumission of a slave swear that he had "not received in money or otherwise the price or value, or any part thereof, of said slave," the fact of slaves possessing, or being able to possess, such money is assumed.[10]

Certainly throughout the slave era and area (particularly in urban communities) the hiring out of slaves, or permitting them to drive their own bargains and requiring only the payment by them of a fixed weekly sum, or allowing them to retain tips and gratuities, or rewarding them with "wages" for particularly good work, or providing them with payments for "overtime" labor were all fairly common practices.[11] By these means, and in other ways,[12] Negroes in bondage were able, from time to time, to accumulate the resources to emancipate themselves. And it is a fact that hundreds of slaves did buy their own, or some loved one's freedom, and that hundreds of others were bought and liberated by free relatives and friends.

There are several references to large groups of Negroes who in this way became free. It is known, for example, that up to 1826 at least two hundred and cighty-one Negroes obtained their freedom by self-purchase or by being bought and emancipated by relatives, in Kent and Baltimore counties, Maryland, while the same source adds that "considerable numbers" likewise gained their freedom in Anne Arundel, Frederick, Harford, Dorchester, Queen Anne's and Talbot counties in this state.[13]

In 1829 about eighty slaves belonging to John McDonogh of New Orleans agreed to perform extra work for him providing this labor was credited towards earning their freedom. Within twelve years all these Negroes thus became free.[14] Again, of the 7,836 Negroes sent to Africa by the American Colonization

Society from 1817 to 1852, two hundred and four had purchased their freedom.[15] Documentary evidence establishes the fact that in the three Virginia towns of Richmond, Petersburg, and Fredericksburg, the freedom of at least sixty-one Negroes was obtained, between 1831 and 1860, by direct bargaining between master and slave and subsequent self-purchase by the latter. Moreover, in Richmond alone, from 1830 to 1860, free Negroes liberated a minimum of thirty-three relatives—children, mothers, wives, husbands—whom they had bought for that purpose.[16]

A contemporary account tells us that of the eleven hundred and twenty-nine Negroes in Cincinnati, Ohio, sometime in the 1830's, who had once been slaves, four hundred and seventy-six had purchased themselves at an average cost of over $450, representing a total expenditure of almost a quarter of a million dollars.[17] Another contemporary estimate of this same phenomenon for the same city is contained in the very moving letter which the great Abolitionist, Theodore D. Weld, wrote to a comrade, Lewis Tappan, in 1834. It merits extensive quotation:

> Of the almost 3,000 blacks in Cincinnati more than three-fourths of the adults are emancipated slaves, who worked out their own freedom. Many are now paying for themselves under large securities. Besides these, multitudes are toiling to purchase their friends, who are now in slavery.
>
> I visited this week about 30 families, and found that some members of more than half these families were still in bondage, and the father, mother and children were struggling to lay up money enough to purchase their freedom. I found one man who had just finished paying for his wife and five children. Another man and wife had bought themselves some years ago, and have been working night and day to purchase their children; they had just redeemed the last and had paid for themselves and children 1,400 dollars! Another woman had recently paid the last instalment of the purchase money for her husband. She had purchased him by taking in washing, and working late at night, after going out and performing as help at hard labor. But I cannot tell half, and must stop. After spending three or four hours and getting facts, I was forced to stop from sheer heartache and agony.[18]

Some Negroes, it is clear, devoted their entire lives to the purchasing and liberating of others. Examples of these heroic people may be offered. Samuel Martin, of Mississippi, who had bought his own freedom, purchased, freed, and transported to Ohio six other Negroes in 1844. John B. Meachum, a Negro Baptist minister of St. Louis, liberated twenty of his people in this way by 1836.[19]

A remarkable Negro woman, Aletheia Turner, who had been a domestic servant for Thomas Jefferson, devoted practically all her earnings to this glorious work. In 1810 she had bought and purchased herself for $1400, and by 1828 she had bought and liberated her sister (at $850) and ten children and five grandchildren (at a total cost of $5250), while by 1837 she freed two more women and four more children.[20] Another Negro woman, Jane Minor of Petersburg, Virginia, almost equaled the record of Mrs. Turner by freeing nineteen individuals during her lifetime.[21] The honor of being the individual who bought and emancipated more human beings than any other person seems to belong to John C. Stanly, a free Negro farmer and barber of New Bern, North Carolina. The record of this man's selflessness and doggedness reads as follows: in 1805 he bought and freed his own wife and two children; in 1807, his brother-in-law; in 1812, a friend; in 1813, another friend; in 1815, a man, a woman and five children; in 1816, a woman and six children; and between 1817 and 1818, three more women, or a total of twenty-three emancipated people![22]

It is likely that in some of these cases a portion of the money, if not all, required for the purchase was provided the free Negro by the slave involved. An actual paper of manumission may be quoted to make clear the explicit and contractual nature of such transactions. In a deed book for the city of Petersburg, the Negro scholar, Professor Luther P. Jackson, found the following entry:[23]

> Whereas I, Armistead Harwell (a free Negro) of the county of Prince George did in the year 1843 purchase from William W. Wynn, a Negro named Jones Mitchell, with money furnished for that purpose by said Jones, and upon agreement with said Negro to emancipate him, Now therefore in pursuance of said agreement, I Armistead Harwell do hereby manumit and set absolutely free the said Negro man slave by name Jones Mitchell, as witness my hand and seal this 26th day of September, 1846.

The purchasing of the freedom of members of one's immediate family occurred frequently. A few examples, culled more or less at random, may be offered. Isaac Hunter, of Raleigh, North Carolina, purchased his own freedom and that of his wife and four children. For Virginia, Rosetta Hailstock thus liberated herself, two daughters, and a son; Albert Brooks, himself, wife, and three children; Jesse Green, wife, and four children; Benjamin Belberry, himself and wife; a Negro known merely as Frank, himself, wife, and three children; Samuel Johnston, wife, and two children; and the grandfather of Monroe Work, the late director of research at Tuskegee, purchased the freedom of his wife and ten children.[24]

At times Negroes raised this ransom money by public appeals and lecture tours throughout the North and Mid-West. Noah Davis, for example, a shoemaker of Fredericksburg, Virginia, having succeeded in buying himself, set out to liberate his wife and five children. He accomplished this not only by twelve years of hard labor at his craft, but also by appearances before public gatherings in Philadelphia, New York, and Boston. Peter Still, a brother of the director of the Underground Railroad in Philadelphia, purchased his own liberty and that of his wife and three children (at a total cost of $5,500) by three years of hard work and addresses delivered throughout New England, New York, and Pennsylvania. Lunsford Lane of North Carolina similarly obtained the freedom of himself, wife and seven children (at a cost of $3,500) through his own work and mass subscriptions obtained in Massachusetts and Ohio.[25]

The records of a single newspaper, the Cleveland, Ohio, *Leader,* for a brief period of time, 1855-1857, will convey some idea of the frequency of this type of activity. In June, 1855, this paper told its readers that a Negro named Handy Mobley had finally succeeded in purchasing his wife and seven children. Mr. Mobley, then in New York, asked the *Leader* to convey his thanks to the citizens of Cleveland where he had "raised $55 . . . for the above purpose." The next month there was reported the holding of a public meeting in Jefferson, Ohio, to devise means to help a Negro resident of Youngstown, one Elick Wood, purchase the freedom of his seven children. The citizens appointed a committee to collect the ransom and to enter into negotiations with the owner. Somewhat later the same month the sum of $23.60 was raised at a meeting of residents of Cleveland to help Thomas Long free his family. In October, it was announced that a lady of Cleveland, Ellen Wills, was seeking to obtain sufficient funds to free her mother, a slave in Mississippi. The next month readers of the *Leader* learned that: "The Rev. George Brents, formerly a slave in Paducah, Ky., is the father of 7 children, and is now in the city seeking means to liberate his son, Anderson. Anderson's master has agreed to take $1,100. In other cities he's raised $260."

The next year, in August, the editor reported that a Negro woman, formerly a slave, had called on him and had explained that she had purchased her own freedom and was now attempting to raise funds with which to buy her husband. She had already secured half the needed sum in Cincinnati, Dayton, and Columbus. The editor concluded: "A collection in all the churches of the city tomorrow will help lift a load from this woman's heart." The same month, in 1857, another editorial told of the efforts of one Alfred Johnson to raise money to free his wife in Alabama, and two weeks later another editorial referred to the arrival in Cleveland of a Mrs. Charlotte Ashe of Washington, D. C., seeking money to rescue two of her children from bondage in Mississippi.[26]

Cases of individuals purchasing only their own freedom occurred frequently—too frequently for any attempt at enumeration.[27] Note should be taken, however, of the fact that several outstanding figures in Negro history, in addition to those already mentioned, became free in this manner. Among others may be noted the great religious leaders, Andrew Bryan, Richard Allen, and Absalom Jones; the educator, Fanny J. Coppin; a brother of the Abolitionist, James W. C. Pennington (who held the degree of Doctor of Divinity from Heidelberg University); a sister-in-law of the militant fighter, Henry Highland Garnet; the distinguished eighteenth century physician, James Derham, and such state representatives and senators of Virginia as Samuel P. Bolling, Joseph P. Evans, and Peter G. Morgan.[28]

The record of this particular method of fighting against enslavement is not complete without mention of the fact that many Negroes bought loved ones and were compelled to hold them in a nominal type of slavery. This occurred because in certain states at particular times laws were passed making emancipation or manumission extremely difficult.[29] One way to evade these laws was by free Negroes purchasing slaves and, while exercising none of the prerogatives of a master, still maintaining the legal fact of enslavement. Thus may one account for the vast majority of cases of Negro slaveholders listed in census reports.[30] This fine example of sacrifice and condemnation of slavery has actually been seized upon by ignorant or vicious writers and distorted into a defense of the institution of human bondage!

This practice of purchasing freedom is of importance not only as an interesting and revealing phase of the history of the American Negro people, and as a method by which many among them obtained a basic human right, but also because it was a factor in the stimulation of the entire movement against chattel slavery.

The activities of the Negro people themselves were fundamental to that movement—their flights, their newspapers, their societies, their speakers, their individual outbreaks, their revolts and plots were the spring and the fountain of the Abolitionist cause. Each of these actions and agencies demonstrated the iniquities of bondage, and the deep desire of the Negro for liberation. And added to them is this story of courage, persistence, and devotion that enabled thousands to buy their freedom.

Such individuals were a living, fearful condemnation of the whole evil system of enslavement. And when these individuals took their cause to the public, as sometimes happened, few were unmoved by their appeals. As Levi Coffin, the famous "President" of the Underground Railroad, remarked, when one was asked to contribute to a fund to purchase the liberty of a dear one "it was hard to refuse, almost impossible if one brought the case home to himself."[31] Again, James Russell Lowell wrote his friend, Sydney H. Gay, that though short of funds and though opposed, in principle, to compensated emancipation, yet "if a man comes and asks us to help him buy a wife or child, what are we to do? . . . Such an appeal" he could not refuse.[32]

Cries such as these—"Help me *buy my mother!*" "Help me *buy my children!*"—rang in the ears of many Americans a few generations ago. They were not easily denied and not quickly forgotten, and surely they must have helped move some to vow that the system responsible for such pleas must be extirpated.

# MILITANT ABOLITIONISM

The crusade against chattel slavery in the United States was one of the most profound revolutionary movements in the world's history. It was permeated by three major schools of thought, one of which insisted that the only proper and efficacious instrument for change was moral suasion; another held that moral suasion had to be buttressed by political action; and the third expressed a belief in the necessity for resistance in a physical sense, in direct, militant action. Members of the last school adopted, at times, the methods of the first two as well.[1]

Among the earliest protests against American slavery may be found the kernel of this militancy: the righteousness of the cause for which slaves conspired and fought was acknowledged. In the famous Germantown Quaker Protest against slavery of 1688, the authors put this question: Suppose the slaves rebel here and now, as they have frequently done elsewhere at other times, "will these masters and mastrisses take the sword at hand and warr against these poor slaves, licke, we are able to believe, some will not refuse to doe; or have these negers not as much right to fight for their freedom, as you have to keep them slaves?" Ten years later, again in Pennsylvania, this time Concord, another Quaker protest[2] against slavery, signed by Robert Pyle, asked a similar question: Suppose our slaves do rebel, and blood is shed? The Friend wondered "whether our blood will cry innocent whether it will not be said you might have let them alone."

The Grand Jury of Charles Town, South Carolina, made the

We present as a Public Grievance a certain book or Journal sign'd by Hugh Brian, directed to ye Honble, the Speaker, and the rest of the members of the Commons house Assembly in Charles Town, wch we have perused and find in general, contains sundry enthusiastic

Prophecys, of the destruction of Charles Town, and deliverance of the Negroes from their Servitude, and that by the Influence of ye said Hugh Brian, great bodys of Negroes have assembled to gether on pretence of religious worship, Contrary to ye laws, and destructive of ye Peace. . . .

Other whites, Jonathan Brian, William Gilbert, and Robert Ogle, were also declared to possess opinions inimical to the security of a slave society. Mr. Brian's work was suppressed but what punishment, if any, was meted out to the individuals is not known.[3]

Some of the literature produced just before and during the Revolutionary War contained, as one might expect, passages justifying, if not actually urging, attempts on the part of the Negroes to liberate themselves by violence. The writings of James Otis, for example, particularly his famous pamphlet published in Boston in 1764, *The Rights of the British Colonies Asserted and Proved,* excoriated the institution of slavery, and affirmed the Negro's inalienable right to freedom.[4] The logical deduction was plain, and did not pass unnoticed, as John Adams testified:

> Young as I was, and ignorant as I was, I shuddered at the doctrine he taught and I have all my life shuddered, and still shudder, at the consequences that may be drawn from such premises. Shall we say, that the rights of masters and servants clash, and can be decided only by force? I adore the ideal of gradual abolitions. But who shall decide how fast or how slowly these abolitions shall be made?[5]

Another popular pamphlet of this year, that by the Reverend Isaac Skillman, *An Oration upon the Beauties of Liberty, or the Essential Rights of the Americans* (published in Boston in 1772 and in its fourth printing by 1773), vehemently attacked the enslavement of the Negroes, demanded their immediate liberation, and affirmed, "Shall a man be deem'd a rebel that support his own rights? it is the first law of nature, and he must be a rebel to God, to the laws of nature, and his own conscience, who will not do it."[6] Very much the same point was made by the Reverend Samuel Hopkins of Newport, Rhode Island, in a work first published in 1776.[7]

From then on the action of the American colonists in waging

war for political and economic freedom was often referred to by militant abolitionists in order to support their own views justifying or urging Negro rebellion. One of the earliest writings of this type was produced by a "Free Negro," who denounced slavery, denied the oft-repeated idea concerning his people's "inferiority," and demanded,[8] "Do the rights of nature cease to be such, when a Negro is to enjoy them? Or does patriotism, in the heart of an African, rankle into treason?"

In this same period Thomas Paine wrote from Paris to an anonymous friend in Philadelphia concerning anti-slavery efforts then in progress. His concluding remarks were: "We must push this matter [Negro slavery] further on your side of the water. I wish that a few well instructed could be sent among their brethren in bondage; for until they are enabled to take their own part, nothing will be done."[9]

A physician, Dr. George Buchanan, delivered a very militant speech on July 4, 1791, at Baltimore, before a public meeting of the Maryland Society for Promoting the Abolition of Slavery. In the course of it occur these passages, spoken six weeks before the outbreak of the great Haitian Revolution:

> What then, if the fire of Liberty shall be kindled amongst them? What, if some enthusiast in this cause shall beat to arms, and call them to the standard of freedom? Would they fly in clouds, until their numbers become tremendous, and threaten the country with devastation and ruin?. . .
>
> Led on by hopes of freedom, animated by the aspiring voice of their leader, they would soon find, that "a day, an hour of virtuous liberty, was worth a whole eternity of bondage."[10]

With the eruption of the Haitian Revolution many people felt called upon to declare their attitudes towards it, and some, who gloried in the American and French Revolutions, found it but consistent and logical to welcome that which occurred in the West Indies. Typical of this group was the Bostonian, J. P. Martin, who wrote in an article entitled "Rights of Black Men":

> We believe that freedom is the natural right of all rational beings, and we know that the blacks have never voluntarily resigned that freedom. Then is not their cause as just as ours? . . . Let us be consistent, Americans, if we justify our own conduct in the late glorious revolution, let us justify those who, in a cause like ours, fight with equal bravery.[11]

A delegate to the Kentucky Constitutional Convention of 1792, the Reverend David Rice, argued against the establishment of slavery, declaring it to be "a perpetual war, with an avowed purpose of never making peace," and an institution which would weaken the home front and strengthen an enemy. He pointed to the events then taking place in the West Indies, and declared:

> There you may see the sable, let me say the brave sons of Africa, engaged in a noble conflict with their inveterate foes. There you may see thousands fired with a generous resentment of the greatest injuries, and bravely sacrificing their lives on the altar of liberty.[12]

A prominent resident of Connecticut went even further in a public speech delivered two years later, for he applied the case to the United States, itself. Warning of coming plots and rebellions, he went on:

> And when hostilities are commenced, where shall they [the slave-holders] look for auxiliaries, in such an iniquitous warfare? Surely, no friend to freedom and justice will dare to lend them his aid . . . Who then can charge the negroes with injustice, or cruelty, when "they rise in all the vigour of insulted nature," and avenge their wrongs. What American will not admire their exertions, to accomplish their own deliverance?[13]

Like sentiments were occasionally printed in the press, as the Hartford *Connecticut Courant* in 1796 and 1797.[14] In the latter year, too, a Massachusetts Negro, Prince Hall, a veteran of the Revolutionary War, a fighter against his people's enslavement, and a leader in the Masonic movement, expressed admiration for the militant activities of his brothers in Haiti.[15]

Early in the year 1804 a judge for the eastern district of Georgia, Jabez Brown, Jr., created a sensation by his "inflammatory" charge to the grand jury of Chatham. The jury refused to have this charge published and bitterly condemned the judge. A resident of Savannah wrote shortly afterwards that "Judge Bowen's charge related to the emancipation of the Negroes; and that he went to the length of declaring, that if the Legislature did not, their first session, pass a law liberating all slaves, he would put himself at the head of the Negroes and effect it, though at the expense of the lives of every white inhabitant of the State." In May the Judge was dismissed from office and imprisoned on a charge of inciting servile insurrection, but early in June he was released into the custody of his father, on condition that he be sent out of the state. He was—to Rhode Island—but, "he still swears vengeance against the white people of this place."[16]

A white Missourian, one Humphrey Smith, was indicted by the Howard County grand jury in 1819 for inciting servile insurrection, but the outcome of this case is not clear.[17] In October, 1822, four white men were arrested and convicted of having encouraged the Negroes involved in the Vesey plot. These residents of Charleston represented four different nationalities, Andrew S. Rhodes, English; William Allen, Scotch; Jacob Danders, German; and John Igneshias, Spanish. Only Allen's motives were suspect since he was accused by a free Negro named Scott of expecting to reap a financial reward from the successful rebels. The others, however, hated slavery, and their crime consisted in letting the Negroes know this and in telling them, as the German put it, "they had as much right to fight for their liberty as the white people." All were sentenced to prison terms ranging from three to twelve months and to fines from one hundred to one thousand dollars, which had to be paid prior to release from jail.[18]

In 1829 alone, there appeared three works produced by Negroes which contained more or less open calls for, or justifications of, outright revolt.

The least open of these is the remarkable book of poems, called *The Hope of Liberty,* written by George Moses Horton, a slave of Chatham County, North Carolina, and published by Joseph Gales, editor of a leading newspaper, the Raleigh *Register.*[19] Occasional lines were fairly militant, as for example:

*Oh, Liberty, thou golden prize*
*So often sought by blood—*
*We crave thy sacred sun to rise,*
*The gift of Nature's God!*
*Bid slavery hide her haggard face,*
*And barbarism fly:*
*I scorn to see the sad disgrace*
*In which enslaved I lie.*

A truculent note of foreboding and militance was struck by the peculiar mystical pamphlet issued in February, 1829, by a New York Negro, Robert Alexander Young.[20] This appears especially in the prophecy of the coming of a Negro saviour who, by his invincibility, will lead his people to freedom.

David Walker's work, written in clear, unmistakable prose and containing no far-fetched allusions, appeared in the closing months of that year. Not much is known of this very interesting man, but these facts appear well-established: He was born, of a free mother, in Wilmington, North Carolina, on September 28, 1785.[21] The enslavement of his fellow men disgusted and enraged him. In 1828 he had written:

> If I remain in this bloody land, I will not live long, as true as God reigns, I will be avenged. This is not the place for me, no, I must leave this part of the country. It will be a great trial for me to live on the same soil where so many men are in slavery, certainly I cannot remain where I must hear their chains continually, and, where I must encounter the results of their hypocritical enslavers. Go I must.

Walker went to Boston where he earned his bread by dealing in old clothes. Here he became active in anti-slavery work, making at least one speech before the Colored Association of the city in December, 1828. He served as Boston agent for the fighting New York anti-slavery newspaper edited and published by Negroes, *Freedom's Journal,* and occasionally contributed to it.

In September, 1829, he published his *Appeal,*[22] and from then until his mysterious death[23] sometime in 1830, supervised the distribution and reprinting of this booklet, which during the last year of his life went into its third edition.

It is certain that copies of this pamphlet were sent south with the object of getting them into the hands of slaves. And it reached them at a moment when they were displaying great unrest. Note of this is made by Governor John Forsyth, of Georgia, in a communication to the State legislature on December 21, 1829, in which he referred to a recent conspiracy in Georgetown, South Carolina, and "the late fires in Augusta and Savannah" set by the slaves.[24] These occurrences, said the Governor, added to the importance of a letter he had just received from W. T. Williams, the Mayor of Savannah, "informing me that sixty pamphlets of a highly seditious and insurrectionary character had been seized by the police of the city." The description that follows identifies this as the work of Walker, and then appears the information that they had been "carried to Savannah by the Steward of some vessel (a white man), and delivered by him to a negro preacher for distribution."

In January, 1830, the Mayor of Richmond, Virginia, reported the finding of a copy of the same pamphlet in the home of a recently deceased free Negro, and in the same year and city another free Negro, Thomas Lewis, was found to possess thirty copies of the fearful pamphlet.[25]

A printer in Milledgeville, Georgia, Elijah H. Burritt, brother of Elihu, the famous "learned blacksmith," was accused in February, 1830, of introducing this work within the state[26] and "was finally forced to flee for his life in the middle of the night when a hostile mob attacked his dwelling."[27] Some copies were also discovered early in 1830 in New Orleans. In May, a Mr. James Smith of Boston (whether Negro or white is not stated) was convicted of circulating the *Appeal,* fined one thousand dollars and sentenced to a year's imprisonment in that city.[28]

The pamphlet's appearance in Walker's native state, where slave disaffection was rife at the time, created much excitement. First mention of it came from Wilmington in August, 1830, when a free Negro brought a copy to the police. A slave, unnamed, who had acted as distributor of the disconcerting booklet, was arrested, but refused—although it is a good guess that very persuasive tactics were used—to implicate others or to tell how many he had distributed.[29] Spies were used in Fayetteville in order to discover whether the pamphlet had appeared there, but, said a report to the Governor of September 3, "altho this plan has been sometime in operation, it has yet developed nothing that ought to excite our alarm."[30]

The stirring contents of Walker's *Appeal* justified the fears of the slavocracy. He used the Declaration of Independence with telling effect, flinging its immortal words into the teeth of those who upheld slavery. He denounced the colonizationists and affirmed the Negro's right to the title of American. He excoriated the traitors among his own people, finding it difficult to find words damning enough with which to express his contempt for them. He waxed sarcastic and exuded bitterness as he contemplated the prevalent hypocrisy, with everyone *talking* about liberty and equality:

> But we (coloured people) and our children are *brutes!!* and of course are, and *ought to be* Slaves to the American people and their children forever!! to dig their mines and work their farms; and thus go on enriching them, from one generation to another with our *blood* and our *tears!!!* [Rebel, he said, rebel and] if you commence, make sure work—do not trifle, for they do not trifle with you—they want us for their slaves, and think nothing of murdering us in order to subject us to that wretched condition—therefore, if there is an *attempt* made by us, kill or be killed.[31]

At only one point did David Walker leave the immediate and the practical, and this he did in order to utter the prophecy:

> . . . for although the destruction of the oppressors God may not effect by the oppressed, yet the Lord our God will bring other destruction upon them—for not infrequently will he cause them to rise up one against another, to be split and divided, and to oppress each other, and sometimes to open hostilities with sword in hand.

The ensuing years witnessed a sharply accelerating growth in militant abolitionism as the struggle between pro- and anti-slavery forces became more acute. In 1831 William Lloyd Garrison expressed his opinion on this subject and maintained it throughout his long devotion to the cause. He wrote Le Roy Sunderland on September 8 of that year that he did not advocate servile rebellion, since he believed in non-resistance to evil, but, "Of all men living, however, our slaves have the best reason to assert their rights by violent measures, inasmuch as they are more oppressed than others."[32]

His newspaper, in line with its editor's belief in freedom of expression, did occasionally print material that bore no signs of non-resistance, as, for example, a poem "supposed to be sung by slaves in insurrection," contributed by "V" and published one month before the Turner uprising. Portions of this work went as follows:

*See, tyrants see; your empire shakes;*
*Your flaming roofs the wild wind fans;*
*Stung to the soul, the Negro wakes:*
*He slept, a brute—he wakes, a man!*
*His shackles fall,*
*Erect and tall*
*He glories in his new found might,*
*And wins with bloody hand his right.*

*Up, Afric, up; the land is free*
*It sees no slave to despot bow.*
*Our cry is Liberty—*
*On; strike for God and vengeance now*
*Fly, tyrants fly,*
*Or stay and die.*
*No chains to bear, no scourge we fear;*
*We conquer, or we perish here.*[33]

Once a revolt started Garrison could not help wishing it success and the bitterness of his language condemning the hypocrisy of the slaveholders who habitually expressed sympathy with rebels in Greece or France or Belgium or Poland, but contempt for those on their very plantations, could not be exceeded. Thus, following the Turner uprising, Garrison, in his inimitable style, wrote:

> Ye patriotic hypocrites! ye panegyrists of Frenchmen, Greeks, and Poles! ye fustian declaimers for liberty! ye valiant sticklers for equal rights among yourselves! ye haters of aristocracy! ye assailants of monarchy! ye republican nullifiers! ye treasonable disunionists! be dumb! Cast no reproach upon the conduct of the slaves, but let your lips and cheeks wear the blisters of condemnation![34]

A visitor to the city of Petersburg, Virginia, a Mr. Robinson, was indiscreet enough to remark in the course of a private talk, at the height of the terror evoked by Nat Turner in September, 1831, that, while he deprecated the rebellion yet he felt compelled to acknowledge that "black men have, in the abstract, a right to their freedom." When his opinion became known, a mob of over one hundred persons ("some of them . . . men of fortune") dragged him from his residence, lashed and stripped him and, in this condition, drove him from the town. A Mr.

Carter, who was the victim's host, was also compelled to leave. "Not the least disgraceful feature in the case was, that the civil authorities, though applied to, declined interfering."[35]

At about this time James Forten, the well-to-do and courageous Philadelphia Negro reformer, congratulated Garrison for having withstood unflinchingly the campaign of intimidation let loose against him, particularly after Turner's attempt. Forten asserted that the cause of servile rebellion was in the South, not in Garrison's *Liberator,* and that the latest revolt would strengthen the anti-slavery movement by "bringing the evils of slavery more prominently before the public . . . Indeed we live in stiring [sic] times, and every day brings news of some fresh effort for liberty, either at home or abroad—onward, onward, is indeed the watchword."[36]

Others were moved to write, print, and send into the South letters such as the following, dated Albany [N. Y. ?] September 15, 1831:

> Sir—As our Constitution says that all men are created equal; and as God has made of one flesh all the nations of the earth; and as the Negroes are no worse when born than the Whites; and as there is no good prospect that a voluntary release of the slaves will be effected to any (great) degree, I hereby make known that for these and other reasons, I will, as an individual, use all honorable means to sever the iron band that unites the slave to their masters. And as long as this national ulcer (slavery) remains upon a part of the republic, a disunion is highly desirable. It is a disgrace to the United States. It is looked upon as such by most of Europe. What? a republic, boasting its equal rights, when a worse system of slavery is hardly (if at all) to be found. It is a shame.
>
> Yours Respectfully,
>
> Sherlock P. Gregory[37]

An even more militant letter was sent, anonymously, from Boston, at about the same time, to the postmaster of Jerusalem, the seat of the Virginia county, Southampton, which had witnessed the Turner Rebellion. The length of this as yet unpublished letter—it comes to about 6,000 words—precludes its full quotation here.

The author states he is a Negro, and affirms the existence of an extensive secret organization of his fellows whose object is the forcible liberation of their enslaved brethren. He declares that its agents were, and had been, touring the South and planting seeds of rebellion, and that men in the North—Negro and white—had contributed and would continue to contribute money and supplies for this work. "We prefer," he writes, "to see every person of colour headless and their heads on poles, if you please, than to see them servants to a debauched and effiminate [sic] race of whites. Oh, my blood boils, when I think of the indignities we have suffered, and I long for the scene of retribution." The letter closes with these words: "Till you hear from us in characters of blood, I remain your humble, attentive, watchful, and the Public's obedient servant, Nero."[38]

In April, 1835, at a Boston anti-slavery meeting the question, "Would the slaves be justified in resorting to physical violence to obtain their freedom?" was submitted for discussion. The position generally adopted was very much like that held by Garrison.[39] The Reverend Samuel J. May and George Thompson, the British Abolitionist, declared that if any human being could justly employ violence it would be the slave in an endeavor to gain freedom, but both agreed that pacifism was right, in all cases, even for the slaves, and thus replied to the question in the negative. A Mr. Parker, of the Newton Theological Institution, came around to an agreement with this predominant feeling, although early in the discussion he had felt differently. He had permitted himself to say: "If the masses of the slaves would occasionally rise, like men and patriots, and assert their rights, would not these attempts hasten the day of total and complete emancipation?" He had, moreover, declared that to the vast majority of the slaves the message of true Christianity had not been brought, and the Bible remained a closed book. "As heathens, then, would they not be justified in revolting against their oppressors, especially as their object would be to obtain an immense good—liberty and the Bible?"

Only one man, a Mr. Weeks, expressed and maintained disagreement with the accepted philosophy, and even he opposed violence. He did this, however, merely on the ground of expediency, and argued that the Bible could be used as easily to sanction the rising of the slaves as not.[40]

Following the slave plots of the summer of 1835 and the

accusations leveled against the Abolitionists, there appeared, as already noted, denials on their part of advocacy of rebellion. It is, nevertheless, interesting to observe that the disavowals were not considered complete or satisfactory by some connected with the movement. This appears, for example, in a letter from William Oakes to Samuel Sewell.

> I have looked with great anxiety to see under the signatures of the most respectable & best known abolitionists in Boston, a statement of their principles, and especially a *full,* & not to be misunderstood denial in general & particular, of insurrectionary doctrines, or practices of any kind. Let it be fully understood that ¾ of the Abolitionists do not believe in defensive war, much less in the "sacred right of insurrection."[41]

There was much thinking, talking, and writing among Abolitionists in 1837 concerning this perplexing question of non-resistance. It arose in the annual meeting of the Massachusetts Anti-Slavery Society held in Boston in January. A Negro, identified merely as a Mr. Johnson who had once been a slave, spoke at this meeting and informed the audience that he had read Walker's pamphlet. He went on to express similar convictions, remarking that the white people in the United States had fought for liberty and were revered as heroes for doing so. Moreover, said Mr. Johnson, in his sparkling style, even a bug will try to bite when stepped upon.

William Lloyd Garrison followed, and conceded that when Mr. Johnson pointed to the inconsistency of white Americans in denouncing slave rebellion and glorying in their own Revolution, his argument was unanswerable. Garrison also noted the fact that several of the state constitutions, as those of Maryland and Tennessee, contained the words, "The doctrine of non-resistance to oppression is absurd, slavish, and destructive of the good and happiness of mankind." Yet, he said, this was not his opinion and he could but reiterate his belief in the evil of violence and the duty of non-resistance.

This appeared to be the dominant sentiment of the meeting. Indeed, a Negro Abolitionist of Boston, the Reverend Hosea Easton, offered the following resolution, meant in a complimentary sense, and it was adopted—though its statement of fact is open to grave doubt: "Resolved, That the spirit of insurrection and insubordination of the slave population of this country, is restrained more by the influence of the free colored people thereof, than by all the oppressive legislative enactments of the slave-holding states."[42]

The determined resistance to mob attack offered by the anti-slavery editor, Elijah Lovejoy, and his friends (Lovejoy himself being killed at Alton, Illinois, November 7, 1837), and the fact that the Abolitionist societies did not deprecate the resistance then offered aroused considerable comment. The famous radical ladies from South Carolina, Sarah and Angelina Grimké, wrote a joint letter to Theodore Weld referring to the use of violence in this episode and to the absence of an expression of regret over this on the part of the American Anti-Slavery Society.[43] "Surely to be consistent," said these earnest young women, "abolitionists sh'd go South and help the slaves to obtain their freedom at the point of the bayonet."

Charles Marriott, a Hicksite Quaker whose anti-slavery agitation was to lead to his disownment, wrote an illuminating letter, headed "private," to Garrison in December. Marriott declared:

> I & some other of my friends called soon after [the Lovejoy tragedy] at the A.S. office to urge the necessity of disavowing this resort to arms—all the satisfaction we could obtain was that Abolitionists were divided on the subject of defensive war, and that they could not say what they did not believe in. A division on this point, seems almost inevitable. *Fighting* & *pacific* Abolitionists! Your Mass. Society has done nobly, as also has Benja. Lundy, Wm. Goodell, H. C. Wright, and some other individuals, but from the spirit manifested by not a few abolitionists, Slavery is not likely to be terminated by a *moral* conflict *only*.[44]

A communication from Putnam, Ohio, of a little later date revealed growing uncertainty as to the wisdom of pacifism and appealed to Garrison for philosophic ammunition to hurl at the doubters.[45] The subject of force was discussed at the town's lyceum, and it was discovered that while about half the inhabitants of the community opposed slavery, only some three or four individuals were non-resistants.

The same question was discussed in 1837 in a Negro newspaper, the *Colored American*, published in New York City, in a series of articles by William Whipper. Mr. Whipper's essay took a pacifist stand, yet it is interesting to observe that the editor, Samuel E. Cornish, in introducing the series, wrote: "But we honestly confess that we have yet to learn what virtue there would be in using moral weapons, in defense against kidnappers or a midnight incendiary with a torch in his hand."[46]

An early militant Abolitionist who actually discussed details of a plan for putting his ideas into practice was Jabez D. Hammond of Cherry Valley, New York. In the spring of 1839 he told Gerrit Smith (who did not then agree) of this belief in the justice of the use of force in this case, and suggested the establishment of military schools for young Negroes in Canada and Mexico. "I believe that young men thus educated . . . would be the most successful Southern missionaries."[47]

By 1841, however, Gerrit Smith had moved to the point of urging slaves to flee and to take whatever they needed and to blast away all obstacles in order to succeed in their effort at self-liberation. The organization which heard his words, the American Anti-Slavery Society, while not committing itself to an approval of them, did feel impelled to go on record as declaring that its members would not aid in suppressing Negro insurrection.[48]

David Ruggles, a leading New York Negro Abolitionist, headed an open letter announcing an anti-slavery convention with the motto, "Know ye not who would be free, Themselves must strike the first blow!" In the text of the letter itself were these words: "Our condition is everywhere identical. Rise, brethren, rise! Strike for freedom, or die slaves!"[49]

An exceedingly severe note of bitterness enters the writings of the great Theodore Weld at about this time. Thus, in a letter to his wife in the midst of a severe economic depression in the South, and threats of war against Great Britain (which, should they materialize might culminate, he thought, in freedom of the Negroes), Weld wrote:

> The slaveholders of the present generation, if cloven down by God's judgments, cannot plead that they were *unwarned.* Warnings, reproofs, and the foreshadows of coming retribution have for years frightened the very air, and should sudden destruction come upon them at last, well may the God of the oppressed cry out against them, "because I have called and ye have refused. . . . Therefore will I laugh at your calamity and mock when your fear cometh."[50]

The rebellion in October, 1841, of the slaves aboard the domestic slavetrader, *Creole,* while en route from Hampton Roads, Virginia, to New Orleans, the sterling character displayed by the Negroes, their success in getting the ship to Bermuda, and the resulting international complications brought the question of pacifism among Abolitionists once more to the fore.

One of the country's most eminent fighters against slavery, the Ohio Congressman, Joshua R. Giddings, made his position clear in a resolution introduced in the House of Representatives in 1842 opposing the treatment of the rebellious slaves as common criminals. The resolution maintained that slavery existed only by positive, local law, not by a Federal statute. Once the ship, therefore, had reached the high seas and left the jurisdiction of any slave state, the Negroes were no longer slaves, and they had but reasserted a natural right in rebelling against those who pretended to own them. In attempting to secure their freedom, said Congressman Giddings, the Negroes did what was commendable and proper. For daring to introduce such a resolution Mr. Giddings was censured by his colleagues, by a vote of 126 to 69, and immediately resigned. But, and this marked an important milestone in the Abolitionist movement, the determined gentleman was promptly re-elected by his constituents.[51]

The year 1843 is marked by the flaming speech made by one of the best known Negroes of that day, the Reverend Henry Highland Garnet, before a Negro convention held in Buffalo, New York. Garnet had been born a slave in Kent County, Maryland, in 1815, and had, with his parents, escaped to New Hope, Pennsylvania, in 1824. That same year, however, his sister was retaken by slave-catchers. The Garnets moved to New York City in 1825. And here Garnet studied at elementary and high schools, and met and was greatly influenced by the Negro radical, the Reverend Theodore S. Wright. Together with Alexander Crummell, he then attended a school at Canaan, New Hampshire. Both, however, were driven out by a mob, at which time Garnet seems to have lost any faith he may have had in the efficacy of non-resistance, for he used a shotgun in his own defense.

From there Garnet went to Oneida Institute at Whitesboro, New York, and studied under Beriah Green. Completing his work, he taught in Troy from 1840 to 1842, and later became pastor of the Negro Presbyterian Church in that city. He was holding that position when he delivered "An address to the slaves of the United States of America" before a convention of colored citizens in Buffalo.

Henry Highland Garnet's speech advanced ideas beyond which the Abolitionist movement was never to go. He said to his brethren, "If you must bleed, let it all come at once." He reminded them of their martyrs, men like Denmark Vesey and Nat Turner, and affirmed, "It is your solemn and imperative duty to use every means, both moral, intellectual, and physical, that promises success." He was specific:

> Brethren, arise, arise! Strike for your lives and liberties! Now is the day and the hour! Let every slave throughout the land do this, and the days of slavery are numbered. You cannot be more oppressed than you have been; you cannot suffer greater cruelties than you have already. *Rather die freemen than live to be slaves.*

Should these sentiments be broadcast throughout the land as coinciding with those of the convention itself? This question was debated, with the comparative newcomer to the ranks of the Negro Abolitionists, Frederick Douglass, taking, at this stage of his career, the negative, and carrying the convention with him. But this was done by a vote of 19 to 18, the closeness of which is indicative of the fact that militancy developed earlier and was more widespread among the Negro Abolitionists—so many of whom had themselves felt the lash—than among their white fellow-workers.[52]

Desperation rather than philosophic conviction sometimes led to the expression of militant views. The difficulties of the struggle and the weakness and splits that plagued the Abolitionists led some among them to doubt that verbal or even political action would bring essential improvement. This mood was expressed by William Birney in a letter to his father, James, dated Cincinnati, June 14, 1843: "When I witness these ill-considered movements on the part of the friends of the Slave,

I do feel that our hope is not in man or in political action but in the flames of insurrection, or of foreign war."[53]

It has been asserted that in 1844 a Negro, the Reverend Moses Dickson, of Cincinnati, together with eleven other Negroes, founded an "international Order of Twelve of the Knights and Daughters of Tabor" for the purpose of accomplishing the overthrow of slavery in any and every way possible. In 1846 the same individual is supposed to have started another secret organization, called the Knights of Liberty, which used St. Louis as its headquarters and aided hundreds of slaves to flee, but whether it was active in aiding or provoking conspiracies and rebellions is not clear.[54]

A comment made early in 1844 by the Presidential candidate of the political Abolitionists, in defending his position, is indicative of a developing school of thought. James G. Birney asked, rhetorically, whether it was not a fact that all just men rejoice "when they hear that the oppressed of any land have achieved their liberty, at whatever cost to their tyrants?"[55] And while this former slaveholder did not actually express the deduction that logically followed from his words, the conclusion could hardly have been made more plain even if specifically drawn.

From the wing of the non-political Abolitionists during the same year came the blast against the Constitution delivered by the Bostonian, Francis Jackson, on the Fourth of July. Mr. Jackson publicly renounced his allegiance to this expression of the fundamental law, and he did so particularly because of its fourth article guaranteeing Federal aid for the suppression of domestic violence

> which [as he saw it], pledges to the South the military force of the country, to protect the masters against their insurgent slaves, and binds us, and our children, to shoot down our fellow-countrymen, who may rise, in emulation of our revolutionary fathers, to vindicate their inalienable "rights to life, liberty, and the pursuit of happiness"—this clause of the Constitution, I say distinctly, I never will support.[56]

Mr. Jackson's position was adopted at a convention of the New England Workingmen's Association held in January, 1846, at Lynn, Massachusetts. These laborers resolved, "That while we are willing to pledge ourselves to use all means in our power, consistent with our principles, to put down wars, insurrections and mobs, and to protect all men from the evils of the same, we will not take up arms to sustain the Southern slave-holders in robbing one-fifth of our countrymen of their labor." They urged, moreover, that "our brethren speak out in thunder tones, both as association and individuals, and let it no longer be said that Northern laborers, while they are contending for their rights, are a standing army to keep three million of their brethren and sisters in bondage at the point of the bayonet."[57]

An individual who was soon to put his philosophic convictions into practice and thereby attract the attention of the world and help precipitate the Second American Revolution, John Brown, had by this period arrived at those convictions. In the year 1847 Frederick Douglass visited Brown in his humble Springfield, Massachusetts, home. The two men spoke of means wherewith to eradicate slavery. Brown, with perfect confidence in the discreetness and integrity of Douglass, did not hesitate to tell him that, in his opinion, nothing but force could overthrow the institution of human bondage. And he told him, too, of his plan for the most effectual use of force, the employment of small units of men, Negro and white, to penetrate the slave area, establish themselves in the Appalachian Mountains and there serve as bases from which marauding expeditions against nearby slave plantations might set out, and to which slaves might flee.[58]

Douglass thought the plan had "much to commend it," but was not yet convinced that moral suasion might not convert the nation as a whole, even the slaveholders, to the anti-slavery viewpoint.[59] Nevertheless, Brown's arguments, that slavery was a state of war, and that the owners of human property would never voluntarily relinquish it, impressed Douglass so that, as he said, "My utterances became more and more tinged by the color of this man's strong impressions."

The House of Representatives heard strange words in 1848—words such as even he who now uttered them, Joshua R. Giddings, had not hitherto used. That Ohio Congressman praised Captain Drayton of the *Pearl* who, for attempting to carry to freedom a group of Washington slaves, had been caught and jailed. Mr. Giddings thought it right for an American Representative to visit such a man in his cell and to congratulate him personally on his courage. This raised a whirlwind of protest. Mr. Haskell of Tennessee asked his interesting colleague whether he actually felt it to be proper for a slave to flee from his master. Mr. Giddings said "yes," and more than yes, for he declared "that it was not only the right of the oppressed to obtain their liberty if they could do so, even by slaying their oppressors, but it was their unquestionable duty, even to the taking of the life of every man who opposed them."[60]

As the weeks and months wore on these thoughts were becoming less and less strange and more and more frequently expressed. Frederick Douglass, by 1849, was moving towards Garnet's position which he had, six years before, opposed. In Faneuil Hall, Boston, this striking individual, who bore the marks of enslavement upon his back, and whose four sisters and one brother were still in chains, denounced the oppression of his people, cited the revolutionary heritage of America, and declared:

> In view of these things I should welcome the intelligence tomorrow, should it come, that the slaves had risen in the South, and the sable arms which had been engaged in beautifying and adorning the South were engaged in spreading death and destruction there.[61]

Meanwhile, the same year the Liberty Party resolved that it was preferable to send the slaves compasses and pistols rather than Bibles.[62]

During the next decade such militant ideas were so frequently expressed that one is justified in declaring that, among anti-slavery folk, they became commonplace. It is a moot question whether the hitherto dominant pacifist or non-resistance wing in the movement (so far, at least, as its articulate members were concerned) was not overshadowed and outweighed, in the decade of crisis, by activists and believers in resistance.

A convention of Negro adherents of the Free Soil Party which met in Boston in 1852 heard the Reverend J. B. Smith of Rhode Island, whose own father had been killed while attempting to flee, declare:

> He believed that resistance to tyrants was obedience to God, and hence, to his mind, the only drawback to the matchless Uncle Tom of

Mrs. Stowe was his virtue of submission to tyranny—an exhibition of grace which he (the speaker) did not covet.[63]

In the same year, another Negro, Martin R. Delany, ended a letter to Garrison with these lines:

*Were I a slave, I would be free,*
*I would not live to live a slave;*
*But boldly* strike *for LIBERTY—*
*For FREEDOM or a Martyr's grave.*[64]

The New York Abolitionist and correspondent of Gerrit Smith, Jabez D. Hammond, whose militancy was observed as early as 1839, retained the same views and let Mr. Smith hear them again in 1852. He affirmed the righteousness of the forcible overthrow of slavery and maintained, with great optimism, that, "An organized army of 10,000 men with an able commander, and arms munitions of war and provisions for 50,000 men would march through the Southern States and liberate every slave there in six months."[65]

At about this time the Reverend George W. Perkins wrote an article entitled, "Can Slaves Rightfully Resist and Fight?" in which he warned that quick emancipation alone would spare future bloodshed. And, while himself inclining towards the non-resistant school, he confessed, as did Garrison, that,

> *If* it was right in 1776 to resist, fight, and kill to secure liberty, it is right to do the same in 1852. *If* three millions of whites might rightfully resist the powers ordained by God, then three millions of blacks may rightfully do the same.[66]

The Reverend J. W. Loguen, the Syracuse Negro who gained fame for his public defiance of the Fugitive Slave Act of 1850 and his prominence in the Jerry Rescue in 1851, wrote Garrison a letter early in 1854 concerning his own attitude, which seemed to be most prevalent among Negroes, generally:

> I want you to set me down as a *Liberator* man. Whether you will call me so or not, I am with you in heart. I may not be in hands and head—for my hands will fight a slaveholder—which I suppose THE LIBERATOR and some of its good friends would not do. . . . I am a fugitive slave, and you know that we have strange notions about many things.[67]

Charles Francis Adams, also, at this time, made an interesting generalization when he asserted that while personally he opposed rebellion on the part of the slaves, yet he believed that, "Probably few of them [Abolitionists] entertain any doubt of the abstract *right* of the slave to free himself from the condition in which he is kept against his own consent, in any manner practicable."[68]

Among a series of conventions of free Negroes called for the purpose of battling Jim-Crowism and aiding the Abolitionist movement was one held in Philadelphia in the spring of 1854. This convention adopted a most radical resolution declaring that "those who, without crime, are outlawed by any Government can owe no allegiance to its enactments;—that we advise all oppressed to adopt the motto, 'Liberty or Death.' "[69]

A widely read work issued simultaneously in 1855 by four publishers—in London, Boston, New York, and Cleveland—opened with sentences modeled after those of the manifesto of 1776, but specifically applied to the American Negro:

> When in any State, the oppression of the laboring portion of the community amounts to an entire deprivation of their civil and personal rights; when it assumes to control their wills, and to punish with bodily tortures the least infraction of its mandates, it is obvious that the class so overwhelmed with injustice, are necessarily, unless prevented by ignorance from knowing their rights and their wrongs, the enemies of the government. To them, insurrection and rebellion are primary, original duties.[70]

The Kansas war stimulated the spread and acceptance of these ideas, so that while in 1849 only a rather restricted group like the Liberty Party would resolve that pistols were more important to the southern slaves than Bibles, by the years of the Kansas excitement a minister who earnestly strove to say what he felt people wanted to hear, Henry Ward Beecher, was sending pistols into the troubled territory and calling them his Bibles. Gerrit Smith, too, exemplifies the trend. "Hitherto," he declared, "I have opposed the bloody abolition of slavery. But now, when it begins to march its conquering bands into the Free States, I and ten thousand other peace men are not only ready to have it repulsed with violence, but pursued even unto death, with violence."[71]

The influential Frederick Douglass also committed himself to the same side at this time. While affirming that it was still one's duty to use "persuasion and argument" and any other instrumentality that offered promise of ending slavery without violence,

> we yet feel that its peaceful annihilation is almost hopeless . . . and contend that the slave's right to revolt is perfect, and only wants the occurrence of favorable circumstances to become a duty. . . . We cannot but shudder as we call to mind the horrors that have marked servile insurrections—we would avert them if we could; but shall the millions for ever submit to robbery, to murder, to ignorance, and every unnamed evil which an irresponsible tyrant can devise, because the overthrow of that tyrant would be productive of horrors? We say not. The recoil, when it comes, will be in exact proportion to the wrongs inflicted; terrible as it will be, we accept and hope for it.[72]

John Henry Hill, a slave who had escaped from Richmond in 1853, expressed the opinion of one who had himself worn the chains. "Our Pappers," he wrote, "contain long details of insurrectionary movements among the slaves at the South. . . I beleve that Prayers affects great good, but I beleve that the fire and sword would affect more good in this case."[73]

At a time when old John Brown had fully matured his plans for an invasion of the slave area, another Abolitionist, Lysander Spooner of Boston, developed, quite independently, put into writing, and finally into print, a proposal strikingly similar to the ideas of Brown. Spooner printed a long circular, one side of which contained an appeal "To the Non-Slaveholders of the South" calling upon them to overthrow the domination of the Bourbons and thus assure their own well-being and advancement, as well as the liberation of the slaves. The other side contained "A Plan for the Abolition of Slavery" which envisaged the sending of money and arms to the slaves, the inciting of rebellion, the use of arson, flogging, and kidnapping to destroy the property and morale of the slaveholders, the formation throughout the nation of Leagues of Freedom, the members of which, finally, were to descend upon the slave-holding area, declare freedom for all, and, if necessary, wage a war of liberation. Moreover, said Spooner, should such a war be necessary, the property of the slave-owners was to be confiscated and given to the slaves as some compensation for their years of unrequited toil, and in order to make certain that their rights as free men would be retained after the war.[74]

Some copies of this amazing document were distributed,[75] but John Brown learned of it, and upon his informing Spooner that continued publicity and distribution would injure the possibilities of the successful carrying out of his own plan (of which Spooner heard for the first time) its distribution was stopped.[76]

Spooner sent copies of his circular (in manuscript form) to several anti-slavery leaders and received and preserved the answers from nine of them. Only one, J. R. French, writing from Painesville, Ohio, utterly and completely repudiated the idea. He felt it to be "*Quixotic* in the extreme" and found it hard to believe that a "sober man of reason," as he knew lawyer Spooner to be, would have "any faith in such a scheme," fit for "the crased [sic] brain of *S. S. Foster*."[77]

Three others, Lewis Tappan, Hinton Rowan Helper, and Francis Jackson, felt that they could not go along with Mr. Spooner. Lewis Tappan acknowledged that the Negroes had every right to their freedom, and would be as justified in obtaining it by violence as any people, including those who engineered the American Revolution, but, as for himself, he was "a Christian, and a peace-maker, and abjure all resort to deadly weapons to secure our rights."[78]

Francis Jackson, a seventy-year-old veteran of the crusade, told Spooner he could not "accept your 'Plan,' or join your 'League.'" He had, he wrote, been laboring with the Garrisonians for twenty-five years and was "loaded down to the gunwales with their apparatus" and believed their "doctrine of Non-Resistance is true." Yet, he declared, "I shall neither encourage, [n]or discourage you, because I know your motives are true to your own light, and conviction of duty," and ended, "I have but little strength left, but if I had ever so much, I could not ask, or encourage others to go, where I was not ready and willing to go myself."[79]

Hinton Rowan Helper preceded the salutation of his letter with the words, "*Immature–Impractical–Impolitic*" which, he went on, succinctly expressed his "candid criticism of the circular in regard to which you did me the honor to request my opinion." He urged that it be not distributed, "or, to say the least, that you will withhold it from the public until after the next Presidential campaign."[80] His closing paragraphs are interesting enough to warrant full quotation:

For several months past I have had it in contemplation to issue a circular especially designed to reach the South in the right way; and if I am not failed or prejudiced in my aims and efforts, I think I shall, in connection with other Southerners, who are willing and anxious to cooperate with me, be successful in accomplishing more in that direction within the next two or three years than has been accomplished within the last fifty.

My friend, Prof. Hedrick, has seen your circular, and fully concurs in the opinion which I have expressed in reference to the same. Neither the Professor nor myself, however, desire to be taken as criterions to go by. Probably it would be well for you to consult others.[81]

Wendell Phillips, Theodore Parker, Thomas Wentworth Higginson, Stephen S. Foster, and Dr. Daniel Mann expressed agreement in principle, and the last two very largely in detail, with Spooner.

The earliest reply in the whole series came from Wendell Phillips, whose letter was dated July 16, 1858. His idea is summarized in the sentence, "Your scheme would be a good one if it were only *practicable*." He doubted, however, that enough men would enlist "to save the attempt from being ridiculous," and added that if the opposite were true and a fairly "considerable number did rally round you it would be treason & the Govt. would at once move & array all its power to crush the enterprise—before it made head enough to be able to compete with an organized despotism like ours. In such circumstances I cannot see any present availability & use in the proposal."

Yet Phillips did not completely shut the door for he ended by remarking that he always heard Spooner's elaboration of his own plans "with interest & respect & sometime we will steal an hour & talk it over."

Theodore Parker's letter, written some months later, said much the same thing.

Your paper is very well thought & expressed as indeed are all your writings. If it were widely circulated at the South, it would strike a panic terror into those men, whose 2,000,000,000 is invested neither in land nor things. But I think you can't get a Corporal's Guard to carry your plan into execution. When I am well enough I will come & talk with you about it.[82]

On the same day Thomas Wentworth Higginson, who had demonstrated his resistance philosophy in fugitive slave rescues, wrote Spooner from Worcester a very long and highly informative letter of approval. The circular had his "general approbation." He felt that "the increase of interest in the subject of Slave Insurrection is one of the most important signs of the time," and was convinced "that, within a few years, the phase of the subject will urge itself on general attention, and the root of the matter be thus reached. I think that this will be done by the action of the slaves themselves, in certain localities, with the aid of *secret* co-operation from the whites." This, he believed, was "greatly to be desired" as it would terrorize the slaveholders, force them to the defensive in the national struggle and stimulate thinking in the North "on the fundamental question of Liberty."

He reaffirmed, then, his sympathy with Spooner's aim. "My only criticism on your *plan* is, that I think in Revolutions the *practical end* always comes first & and the *theory* afterwards; just as our fathers, long after the Battle of Bunker Hill, still disavowed the thought of separation—and honestly." There followed a sentence whose truth John Brown's exploit was soon to confirm:

> For one man who would consent to the *proposition* of a slave insurrection, there are ten who would applaud it, when it actually came to the point. People's hearts go faster than their heads. . . . In place therefore of forming a Society or otherwise propounding insurrections as a *plan,* my wish would be to assure it as a *fact.*

Higginson hinted at the coming Brown attempt, in which he was already deeply involved, by remarking, "Were I free to do it, I could give you assurance that what I say means something, & that other influences than these of which you speak are even now working to the same end. I am not now at liberty to be more explicit." He closed by affirming that Spooner's work had considerable value in preparing the public mind for servile rebellion, something that he always did in his speeches and had urged other agitators to do.

Another Worcester man, Stephen S. Foster, whose contempt for compromise and expediency had led even sympathetic folk to think him, at best, eccentric, though opening his letter with remarks concerning a severe rheumatic attack, proceeded to give his opinion in an essay of some one thousand words.[83] He had long seen, he declared, the need for new methods among the friends of freedom.

> The grand defect in our policy is that it sets our practice in direct conflict with our principles & teachings. We proclaim the great truth of the equality of the races, & maintain with words the equal right of the slaves with ourselves to liberty & personal protection: but in practice, with few exceptions we essentially ignore these theories, & either unite politically with their masters in active measures for the destruction of their loyalty, or fold our arms, & refuse them the protection we demand for ourselves.

In typical unyielding fashion Foster said that if we claim the products of our own labor, we must assert the slaves' right to the property of their owners, and help them to get possession of it. And if we believe in taking life,

> under any circumstances, we must teach him to cleave down his tyrant master, & aid him in the work. If we refuse allegiance to a government which tramples upon our own liberty, we must put our heel upon the government which yokes him with the brute. That abolitionism which comes short of this is essentially defective; & if persisted in when properly enlightened, is shown to be tainted & spurious.

While, according to Foster, the ultimate solution resided in the formation of a national party gaining mass support and power in order to put these principles into action, yet concerning Spooner's proposal he wrote:

> Entertaining these views I cannot but regard your plan of action, in the main, as a step in the right direction. . . . To aim at such a result is to quicken the nation's sense of justice; & thus to pave the way to the final overthrow of the whole system. . . . Every supporter of the government must be held responsible for the entire slave system, & made identical in moral turpitude with the master, & both must be outlawed.

A physician friend of Spooner's, Daniel Mann, who had recently moved to Painesville, Ohio, wrote the most enthusiastic letter of all those preserved.[84] He thanked Lysander Spooner for himself and "in behalf of the cause, for which you have done a great work, in making a *great beginning.*" He referred to America's revolutionary history, and the audacity of the slaveholders. Then came these observations:

> Truth should not disarm her champions, yet such seems to be the effect of her humanizing & elevating influences. We learn to hate fighting & therefore are not "valiant for the truth." War has been employed so long only in behalf of wrong, that the idea of its use in behalf of right has become obsolete. Yet war is wicked only when its purpose is not worthy. A war, in whatever form, & to whatever extent, however desperate & bloody against slavery would be a holy war. . . . My trust in God is stronger when I put some trust in myself & keep my powder dry. Garrisonism (which is only a new name for what Christianity once meant) would, & yet will plant the wilderness of this world with the rose of Sharon, but there needs a rough breaking up team to prepare the way. The ugly dragons heads must be cut off & their necks seared & their dens destroyed. No people are worthy of freedom who will not fight in its behalf. There may be higher truths than this, but this is as high as I can climb at present.

In 1859 a commercial publisher, A. B. Burdick of New York, who had become famous two years earlier as the publisher of Helper's *Impending Crisis,* issued a book openly advocating the inciting of servile rebellion. This was the work of a former New York *Tribune* editorial writer, James Redpath, and it was dedicated to John Brown, prior to the raid on Harper's Ferry.[85] The author had taken seriously the resolution of the Liberty Party in 1849 that pistols and compasses, not Bibles, were what the slaves most needed, and for several months in 1854 and 1855 he had traveled through Virginia, the Carolinas, and Georgia in order to put that resolution into effect.[86]

In his introductory pages Redpath boldly announces:

> I do not hesitate to urge the friends of the slave to incite insurrections and encourage, in the North, a spirit which shall ultimate in civil and servile wars. . . . What France was to us in our hour of trial, let the North be to the slave today. . . . If the fathers were justified in *their* rebellion, how much more will the slaves be justifiable in *their* insurrection? You, Old Hero! [John Brown] believe that the slave should be aided and urged to insurrection; and hence do I lay this tribute at your feet. . . . I am a Peace-Man—and something more. I would fight and kill for the sake of peace. Now, slavery is a state of perpetual war. I am

a Non-Resistant—and something more. I would slay every man who attempted to resist the liberation of the slave. I am a Democrat—and nothing more. I believe in humanity and human rights. I recognize nothing as so sacred on earth.

Similar appeals are scattered through the work and it ends on the same note. "There are men who are tired of praising French patriots—who are ready to *be* Lafayettes and Kosciuskos to the slaves."[87] Guerrilla warfare, using the mountains and swamps as bases, is the method, and the young men who gained experience in the Kansas fighting should be the leaders. "*Will you aid them—will you sustain them? Are you in favor of a servile insurrection?* Tell God in acts."

A consistent pacifist, Adin Ballou, was troubled by this swing towards militance just before John Brown crashed onto the scene. But that event, as he confessed,[88] and as Higginson had prophesied to Spooner, by turning the abstract into the concrete, dealt, for that period, a death blow to non-resistance.

Directly implicated in Brown's plans were many prominent individuals—Frank Sanborn, Theodore Parker, Thomas Wentworth Higginson, Gerrit Smith, Frederick Douglass, Harriet Tubman, Henry Highland Garnet, and others.[89] Perhaps the aspect of the affair most indicative of the turn in sentiments is the fact that two men who were with Brown at Harper's Ferry, the brothers Edwin and Barclay Coppoc, were of Quaker families, and while one of them, Edwin (hanged for his part in the raid) had earlier been disowned by the Friends for non-attendance at meetings, the other, Barclay, was still a member in good standing of the Society. This unique Quaker escaped from Virginia and returned to Iowa where he was disowned January 11, 1860, for bearing arms.[90]

Henry David Thoreau was moved to utter a "Plea for John Brown" in which he hailed the man as the possessor of a high aim and the performer of a noble act,[91] while Wendell Phillips, speaking in Brooklyn, New York, on November 1, 1859, publicly affirmed his belief that the slaves had both the right and the duty of rebelling.[92]

Striking, indeed, was the shift in attitude on the part of the Reverend Henry C. Wright. In the 'forties this man had written the "Non-Resistance" column in *The Liberator*. By 1851, however, he felt it to be the duty of Abolitionists to go into the South and aid the slaves to flee.[93] In 1859, as he wrote the imprisoned John Brown from Natick, Massachusetts, on November 21, he presided at

> a very large and enthusiastic meeting of the citizens of this town, without regard to political and religious creeds, [which] was held last evening, for the purpose of considering and acting upon the following resolution:
>
> Whereas, Resistance to tyrants is obedience to God, therefore, *Resolved,* that it is the right and duty of the slaves to resist their masters, and the right and duty of the North to incite them to resistance, and to aid them.[94]

This resolution, said Mr. Wright, was adopted "without a dissenting voice," and was mailed to the Governor of Virginia.

Lamentations by more moderate anti-slavery men also indicate the trend. This appears, for example, in a letter from David D. Bernard to Hamilton Fish complaining of the growth of militance, in the Abolitionist movement, and the spreading of the idea that for both whites and Negroes it was a duty to destroy all slaveholders.[95]

In May, 1860, James Redpath wrote to a convention of the Massachusetts Anti-Slavery Society that he would not attend as he "had no faith in conventions, but only in the sword and insurrection," and that he was "pledged to the work of inciting an armed insurrection among the slaves of the South, and therefore could have nothing to do with peaceful agitation."[96]

He did, however, organize his own meeting, but this was to be held on the anniversary of Brown's martyrdom and its dominant note was to be a rededication to the aims and purposes of the Old Man. William Lloyd Garrison, one of the founders back in 1838 of the Non-Resistance Society, was asked to speak, but declined on the grounds of indisposition. He did, however, send Redpath a long letter in lieu of his personal appearance, and while reiterating his own belief in the inviolability of human life which disarmed "alike the oppressor and the oppressed," made strong and repeated appeals to those who were not, in principle, pacifists, to aid in servile rebellions. A few examples, among many, of such passionate sentences are:

> Brand the man as a hypocrite and dastard, who, in one breath, exults in the deeds of Washington and Warren, and in the next, denounces Nat Turner as a monster for refusing longer to wear the yoke and be driven under the lash and for taking up arms to defend his God-given rights. . . . Let Hancock and Adams be covered with infamy, or the black liberators who aided John Brown be honored in history . . . were I a convert to the doctrine of '76, that a resort to the sword is justifiable to recover lost liberty, then would I plot insurrection by day and by night, deal more blows and less in words, and seek through blood the emancipation of all who are groaning in captivity at the South.[97]

As this philosophy of resistance gathered disciples, as the danger of civil war increased, and as reports of slave uprisings and plots became more and more frequent, serious consideration was given in the North to the question of its obligation to aid, if called upon, in the suppression of Negro insurrections. In September, 1860, Senator James R. Doolittle, of Wisconsin, asserted that if the slaves rose in rebellion the Constitution "binds us to put them down with ball and bayonet. The truth is, and we may as well open our eyes to the fact, that the strong arm of the federal government may be invoked to hold them for their masters to work them."[98]

He who believed this and possessed firm anti-slavery convictions was forced into the position—as were the Garrisonians—of denouncing the Constitution and advocating disunion. There were some, however, like William Jay and Lysander Spooner,[99] who professed to see no pro-slavery bias in the Constitution, and denied that it contained the obligation to suppress slave insurrections. In addition, others like John Quincy Adams, contended that the method by which the federal government ended rebellion—or, specifically, a servile rebellion—was nowhere specified.[100] And, if this might best be done by granting the demands of the insurgents—in the case of slaves, by granting them their freedom—the federal government, in the exercise of its war powers, might do that.

This, in essence, was the reply of Joshua R. Giddings to Senator Doolittle:

> If necessary to protect the people the army may be used to shoot down the slaves; but if the insurgent slaves can be pacified by having their freedom, the Executive may protect the people by giving the slaves

their liberty, or by sending them out of the State or country, as was practiced in the Florida war by Generals Scott, Jessup and Taylor.[101]

Mr. Giddings called this a "remedy" for slave revolts but it certainly was not one calculated to increase the slaveholders' devotion to the Union, nor to allay the disaffection of their victims—assuming it reached their ears.

The years of the ultimate triumph of the philosophy of resistance saw its frequent application to the slave population. In the early days of the Civil War suggestions for the provoking of Negro insurrection appeared. Thus *The Liberator* of April 26, 1861, printed a letter by "Insurrectionist" advocating servile rebellion as the quickest and surest way of conquering the slavocracy, although Garrison did not fail to record his dissent from the views of this writer. Yet a much stiffer tone of protest came from that pioneer when he learned of General Benjamin F. Butler's offer to Governor Andrew of Maryland to aid in suppressing a threatened uprising.[102]

In May, 1861, certain unnamed free Negroes of Pennsylvania offered to go down into the South for the purpose of provoking slave rebellions, but Governor Curtin refused to sanction this.[103] "A Voice from the Under Current" rising from Texas at the same time told of considerable discontent and mass flight among the slaves and advised their arming as the quickest way to end the war.[104] In subsequent months similar demands were made.[105]

Of particular interest is the letter from a Negro physician, G. P. Miller, of Battle Creek, Michigan, to Secretary of War Cameron, written October 30, 1861, offering "...from five to ten thousand free men to report in sixty days to take any position that may be assigned to us (sharpshooters preferred)... If this proposition is not accepted we will, if armed and equipped by the government, fight as guerrillas."[106]

The next year the idea of the arming of the Negroes was put forth with increasing urgency and, finally, in August, 1862, the enlistment of free Negroes as soldiers was authorized.[107] The Preliminary Emancipation Proclamation, issued September 22, 1862, promised that, on the first day of the new year, the government of the United States "will recognize and maintain the freedom" of people held in bondage by rebels and "will do no act or acts to repress such persons, or any of them, in any efforts they may make for their actual freedom."

On the designated day the President declared such persons free "and that the Executive Government of the United States, including the military and naval authorities thereof, will recognize and maintain the freedom of such persons." The great pronouncement went on to urge these individuals "to abstain from all violence, unless in necessary self-defense."

And an Abolitionist, General Rufus Saxton, commanding Negro troops in South Carolina, had the pleasure of calling his men together and fulfilling the vision of Walker and Garnet and Brown, for he told them, after reading the Proclamation:

> It is your duty to carry this good news to your brethren who are still in slavery. Let all your voices, like merry bells join loud and clear in the grand chorus of liberty "We are free," "We are free"—until listening, you shall hear its echoes coming back from every cabin in the land—"We are free," "We are free."[108]

In addition to those who wrote and spoke militantly there were some who actually entered the South and brought the message of freedom to the slaves. How much influence was thus brought to bear on the carrying out of slave plots and uprisings is not certain but it must have had some effect.[109] The activity of these people was, of course, illegal and meant great personal danger. Secrecy was, therefore, characteristic, thus making its recording very difficult, and, no doubt, fragmentary.

The names of some of these people are, however, known. Mention has already been made of John Brown and James Redpath. Other white people who carried on this type of work are Alexander M. Ross, William L. Chaplin, Charles Torrey, Calvin Fairbank, Richard Dillingham, Delia Webster, and John Fairfield.[110]

The latter, a native Virginian, whose years of activity as a liberator extended from approximately 1844 to 1856, believed that every slave was justly entitled to freedom, and that if any person came between him and liberty, the slave had a perfect right to shoot him down.[111] He always went about heavily armed himself, and did not scruple to use his weapons whenever he thought the occasion required this.

This man, who is supposed to have led hundreds of slaves to

freedom from every southern state, and to have taken part in several pitched battles, was captured only once and jailed in Bracken, Kentucky, but managed to escape within a short time. It was the belief of his friend, Levi Coffin, that Fairfield was one of the white men hanged in Tennessee in 1856 because of complicity in slave plots. This is not certain, though it is a fact that this remarkable person drops out of the picture in that year.

Free Negroes and escaped slaves were especially active in this type of endeavor. For example, Harriet Tubman, one of the most amazing women that ever lived, carried on her personal emancipation crusade in a fashion very similar to that of John Fairfield, but she, happily, lived to see emancipation a fact.[112] Others who went into the dragon's mouth were Josiah Henson, William Still, Elijah Anderson, and John Mason. The leading authority on the subject has estimated that, from Canada alone, in 1860, five hundred Negroes went into the South to rescue their brothers and carry the word of liberty among them.[113]

Some idea of the effect upon the Negro population of the mere presence of a sincere anti-slavery person, who did little more than make clear her sentiments, appears in a letter from a former resident of Massachusetts, Mrs. Louisa Leland, to her Boston friend, Mary Ann Halliburton.[114] Mrs. Leland begins by assuring her friend that her residence in the South has, far from altering her Abolitionist views, rather strengthened them, and that she has therefore refrained from using slave labor. As a servant she hired a Negro woman, Rose,

> a very intelligent black woman, who had just purchased her freedom by her own exertions. She was glad to remain in the neighborhood of her children whom she is endeavoring to free also and as we assured her of protection and high wages she gladly came to live with us. It would gladden your heart to hear her speak of the abolitionists of the North. I was reading to my husband a letter from Mrs. Childs[115] not observing that Rose was in the room until on looking up I perceived her whole countenance glowing with delight and her eyes sparkling. As soon as my husband had gone she said to me: Do you know Mrs. Childs. Do tell me about her. I wish her benevolent heart may often receive as much pleasure as I did in witnessing the gratitude and interest with which this woman heard the story of her goodness. She sat in perfect silence—but when I ceased only exclaimed fervently: God *will* bless her. The names of Garrison, Phillips and others whom we have so often heard together are often spoken of by the slaves with deepest feeling. . .

The first of August[116] is generally observed among the slaves whenever they can do it without incurring punishment. Knowing this, I told Rose to celebrate the day at our plantation[117] where they could be secure from interruption. I have heard eloquence and seen deep feeling manifested at the North on this day, but I never was so deeply moved as on witnessing this scene: They had raised a little arbor, which was decorated with flowers, where a few of the speakers stood. Never shall I forget the sight: an old man nearly eighty years old, blind and very infirm had been brought by his children to the meeting. They had succeeded in purchasing his freedom, which they preferred to their own—and now by the kind help of some Northern abolitionists, they had purchased their own and had within a few days received their free papers and were on the point of starting for the Land of Freedom. The old man took the most earnest farewell of his friends around, and then knelt in prayer. The whole assembly fell on their knees on the green turf—and a prayer ascended to Heaven, which it seemed to me must call down angels to help them. Tears streamed from his sightless eyes, as he thanked God for this day and prayed that its blessing might be extended over the whole race. Then he prayed for their masters, and with the voice and manner of a saint, he lifted his hands to heaven, and exclaimed, "Father, forgive them, for they know not what they do" —and alas! I thought have they even that excuse to plead?

The data here presented point to the conclusion that the existence of militant Abolitionism was widespread and deep-rooted. It appears to have been particularly common among the Negro people themselves, especially those who had escaped from the delights of the patriarchal paradise. In the decade of crisis, 1850-1860, the acceptance of this philosophy was fairly general among all Abolitionists.

The narrative of its development is an important part of the entire story of the anti-slavery crusade, and makes more understandable the growth of a temperament in the North necessary to a people who successfully waged a terribly bloody Civil War, and whose chosen leader, in the midst of the carnage, declared that "if God wills that it continue until all the wealth piled by the bondsman's two hundred and fifty years of unrequited toil shall be sunk, and until every drop of blood drawn with the lash shall be paid by another drawn with the sword, as was said three thousand years ago, so it still must be said 'the judgments of the Lord are true and righteous altogether.' "

# NEGRO CASUALTIES IN THE CIVIL WAR

In this chapter we shall examine one phase of the American Negro's efforts to break his chains. We shall attempt to ascertain the facts in regard to the blood he expended in the suppression of the slaveholders' counter-revolution, and in the cause of national unity and the extermination of chattel slavery.

It might well be believed that some eighty years after such a contest the victor would have compiled and preserved precise data concerning its martyrs, but the truth is otherwise. Official statistics exist but their presentation in the original sources is accompanied by qualifications and warnings which, though often unheeded in secondary works, are of a most serious character.

Thus, the War Department, in republishing, in part, the report of the Provost Marshal General to Secretary of War Stanton, made in March, 1866, added that revisions had decidedly changed the over-all casualty picture. It went on to offer corrections as of 1885, and then added: "The foregoing figures, however, are only approximative and should not be accepted as conclusive. Revision of the death record is still [*i.e.*, as of 1900] in progress."[1]

In the standard statistical study of losses during the Civil War, published a generation after the event, it was stated:

> Only a few of the regiments, comparatively, made official reports for the actions in which they were engaged . . . of the official battle reports . . . but few gave the figures for their casualties. . . . In the nominal lists of wounded men no distinction was made between the mortally, seriously, or slightly wounded; and the list of missing failed to show whether the men were captured or belonged to the class whose fate was unknown. Too often, no return whatever was made. As a result the statistics of our last war are, in many instances, meager and unsatisfactory; and, in some cases are wanting entirely.[2]

At this point but one deficiency will be particularized. Official figures state that over 29,000 Union soldiers died in the hands of the enemy, but authorities have conjectured that the correct figure for this category of deaths is probably closer to 45,000, and some have placed the number as high as 70,000. The fact is that no one can say with any assurance how many Federal soldiers died in the hands of the Confederacy because no records were obtained from fourteen of its major prisoner-of-war camps and only partial records from six others.[3]

As one would expect, the statistical picture with regard to Negro casualties in the Union Army is even less satisfactory than that for the organization as a whole. There are several reasons for this, but at this point we wish to mention but one. On the testimony of an individual who participated as an enlisted man in two different Negro regiments—serving both in the West and in the East—it was a common practice for Negro units to fail to report deaths, but rather to enlist other Negroes, assign them the names of the deceased, and carry on as before. Given the legal anonymity of the slave, the carelessness of official record-keeping in any personal sense where he was concerned, and the fact that by this process it was possible to collect the undisbursed back pay of the casualty, one can easily believe this assertion.[4]

With these precautionary remarks by way of introduction, let us present the latest revised official casualty figures for Negro troops in the service of the United States Army during the Civil War. According to these data, out of 7,122 officers and 178,975 enlisted men, or a combined strength of 186,097, a total of 324 officers and 36,523 enlisted men lost their lives, from all causes, known and unknown, making a grand total of casualties, in the form of deaths, among what were referred to as the United States Colored Troops, of 36,847.[5] Of the total number of deaths 2,870 were killed in action or mortally wounded, while 29,756 died of disease.[6]

Before analyzing these figures in some detail, it is necessary to clear up a few common misconceptions concerning them. George W. Williams, for example, in his valuable work, wrote: "From first to last there were 178,975 Negro soldiers in the United States Volunteer Army and of these 36,847 were killed, wounded and missing."[7] It will be noticed that here Williams is repeating the figure for total deaths among officers and enlisted men, but is citing the total enrollment of enlisted men only.[8] More important, however, is the fact that Williams uses the figures for deaths to cover not only the deceased, but the wounded, as well. This represents complete, though unintentional, distortion.

Statistics are available for the total number of wounded but they are not broken down in terms of Negro and white. Yet these over-all figures are helpful for they provide a ratio that may be applied, probably with fair accuracy, to the Negro troops. There was a total of 67,058 men reported as killed in action, and another 43,012 who were mortally wounded, while 275,175 were wounded other than mortally, given then a ratio of wounded to killed and mortally wounded of roughly 2.75 to 1.[9] Applying this ratio to the number of officers and enlisted men of the United States Colored Troops killed and mortally wounded (2,870), it will be seen that an addition of 7,893 must immediately be made to the *official* statistics of casualties among such troops.[10]

Let us now subject the official figures of mortalities among regiments of the United States Colored Troops to some analysis. The final Civil War report of the Provost Marshal General pointed out that total loss (that is, including the figures for deaths, desertions and discharges of all types) among white volunteer troops from the twenty-four loyal states equaled the ratio of 314.65 casualties per 1,000 men furnished, while for the Colored Troops this figure was 290.82. If, however, one adds the casualty figures for those killed in action plus those who died of disease only, in other words, if one seeks the facts as to loss of life, one finds that the ratio for white volunteers is 94.32 per thousand (*i.e.,* 35.10 killed plus 59.22 died of disease), while that for the United States Colored Troops is equal to 157.50 per thousand (*i.e.,* 16.11 killed plus 141.39 died of disease). Thus, official statistics show that the ratio of mortal casualties among the United States Colored Troops was 47.06 per thousand greater than that of the United States Volunteer Troops from the twenty-four loyal states.[11] If the Regular Army troops, comprising but 67,000, were added to the figures for the Volunteer units the discrepancy between white and Negro would be still greater, for the ratio of mortalities among them was but 72.82 per 1,000.

Putting the figures in terms of percentages we find, according to the revised official data, that of the slightly over two million troops in the United States Volunteers, over 316,000 died (from all causes), or 15.2 per cent. Of the 67,000 Regular Army (white) troops, 8.6 per cent, or not quite 6,000, died. Of the approximately 180,000 United States Colored Troops, however, over 36,000 died, or 20.5 per cent.[12] In other words, the mortality *rate* among the United States Colored Troops in the Civil War was 35 per cent greater than that among other troops, notwithstanding the fact that the former were not enrolled until some eighteen months after the fighting began!

The data then, as presented by the official figures concerning Negroes federally organized in the Army, far from substantiating the widely held belief that the Negro people were passive recipients of liberation as an incident of a civil conflict, demonstrate that, in terms of the supreme sacrifice, they expended very much more than their proportionate share, and did this in spite of the long delay on the part of the nation in accepting them into the armed services.

The disproportion is so great, in view of the circumstances, that it is incumbent upon the historian to attempt to offer some explanations for the condition. As has been shown, by far the greatest single cause of death, for all troops, was disease, and this was particularly true for the Negro troops. It has been seen that the ratio of deaths from disease per 1,000, among the Colored Troops was over 140, while for the Volunteer Troops it was under 60. Put in the words of the Surgeon-General of the Army, in his report of October 20, 1866, among white troops "the proportion of deaths, from all causes, to cases treated was one to every fifty-two," but with the Colored Troops "the mortality rate [was] one death to every twenty-nine cases treated."[13]

The facts become more dramatic when individual regiments are considered. Of the over 2,000 regiments which made up Lincoln's Army, of which about eight per cent were Negro, the one having the greatest number of mortal casualties was the 5th U. S. Colored Heavy Artillery with a total of 829 deaths (eight being officers), of which 124 occurred in battle and 697 because of disease and accidents. And the regiment having the second greatest number of deaths in the entire army was the 65th U. S. Colored Infantry, which took part in no battles, but lost from disease and accidents a total of 755 persons, six of whom were officers. Other Negro regiments stand very high on the mortality list. Thus, the regiment with the fourth highest number of deaths was the 56th U. S. Colored Infantry, with a total of 25 killed in battle (four officers), and 649 (two officers), dying of disease.[14]

It is apparent, then, that finding explanations for the heavy mortality from disease in Negro regiments will go far towards accounting for their abnormally high casualty rates. A good summarization of some of the factors involved here was presented by the Army's Provost Marshal General when he was offering reasons for the very much lower death rate from disease among officers than among enlisted men, for many of the distinctions which he makes in the conditions confronting enlisted men as compared to commissioned officers prevailed as concerns Negro and white—regardless of rank.

> Officers [wrote the Provost Marshal] are better sheltered than men; and their food is generally better in quality and more varied in kind.... They are not so much crowded together in tents and quarters. . . . They have superior advantages in regard to personal cleanliness. As prisoners of war, too, they were generally treated more leniently. . . . Another favoring circumstance, and by no means the least potential, was the superior *morale*. . . .[15]

Turning to the specific problem, we find several factors to be of great consequence in explaining the excessive Negro casualty rate. It was found difficult, for example, to find qualified surgeons to serve with Negro troops, and the War Department was not anxious to commission available Negro physicians.

According to Major General Banks, writing while in command of the Department of the Gulf:

> . . . In the organization of the colored regiments there was a serious want of Surgeons. Competent men declined to enter the service. It was impossible to get good officers to accept such commissions. In very many cases Hospital Stewards of low order of qualification were appointed to the office of Assistant Surgeon and Surgeon. Well grounded objec-

tions were made from every quarter against the inhumanity of subjecting the colored soldiers to medical treatment and surgical operations from such men. It was an objection that could not be disregarded without bringing discredit upon the Army and the Government.[16]

A less abstract objection, too, appeared at once and brought "remonstrances" from "officers of high rank" who pointed out "that in the exigencies of battle any officer might be subjected to the necessity of surgical treatment" by these untrained individuals. "Application was made to the Surgeon General at Washington, for Surgeons, but without success." Finally, a prominent physician, Dr. J. V. C. Smith, was prevailed upon to tour the nation's medical schools, particularly those in New England, and he seems to have had some success in obtaining, at long last, some fairly competent young medical graduates to serve as surgeons with Negro units.[17]

There were, of course, Negro physicians, but, to this writer's knowledge, only eight were ever appointed surgeons in the Army, and six of these were attached to hospitals in Washington, not to units, while the other two remained with Negro regiments for a very short time.[18]

The army career of one of these Negro physicians will illustrate some of the problems involved and will cast light on the conditions to which the enlisted men were subjected. On April 14, 1863, "Dr. A. T. Augusta (colored) was appointed Surgeon of U. S. Colored Troops, having been examined and found qualified."[19] He was assigned to the 7th United States Colored Infantry and went with them into garrison at Camp Stanton, near Bryantown, in Maryland. He was the senior surgeon among the Negro troops stationed there. In February, 1864, the two (white) assistant surgeons of the 7th, as well as the surgeons and assistant surgeons of the 9th and 19th regiments of Negro infantry, addressed a letter to Abraham Lincoln. It reads as follows:

> When we made application for position on the Colored Service, the understanding was universal that all commissioned officers were to be white men. Judge of our surprise when, upon joining our respective regiments, we found that the Senior Surgeon of the Command was a Negro.
>
> We claim to be behind no one, in a desire for the elevation and im-

provement of the colored race in this Country, and we are willing to sacrifice much in so grand a cause, as our present positions may testify. But we cannot in any cause willingly compromise what we consider a proper self-respect; nor do we deem that the interests of either the country or of the colored race, can demand this of us. Such degradation, we believed to be involved in our voluntarily continuing in the service, as subordinate to a colored officer. We therefore most respectfully, yet earnestly, request that this unexpected, unusual, and most unpleasant relationship in which we have been placed, may in some way be terminated.[20]

Such attitudes coming from surgeons of Negro regiments who professed to be friendly to the men they were employed to serve may go far to help explain the abnormally high mortality rate from disease which marked those regiments.

The "unpleasant relationship" was "terminated" by placing Dr. Augusta on detached service examining Negro recruits at Benedict and Baltimore, Maryland, throughout 1864, and on recruiting service in the Department of the South until the termination of hostilities. Note of one further fact connected with this Negro physician is significant. Fully a year after being commissioned, Dr. Augusta found it necessary to tell Senator Henry Wilson that the army paymaster at Baltimore had "refused to pay him more than seven dollars per month" [the pay of Negro enlisted men after clothing deduction] and that this payment had been rejected. A letter from the Massachusetts Senator to the Secretary of War, on April 10, 1864, resulted in an order, two days later, to the Paymaster General to compensate the surgeon "according to his rank."[21]

The whole concept behind, and the general practice in, the employment of Negro troops by the Union Army help explain their excessive mortality rates. The hesitancy with which the Federal government moved in employing Negroes as soldiers is an oft-repeated story. Even the law of July 17, 1862, by which Congress finally authorized the President to employ Negro troops, is highly revealing. The law stated that the President might, if he wished, receive Negroes "into the service of the United States, for the purpose of constructing entrenchments, or performing camp service, or any other labor, or any military or naval service for which they may be found competent."[22]

Similarly, the General-in-Chief of the Federal Army, Major-General Halleck, hearing, some nine months later, of a reluctance among certain officers in General Grant's command to use Negro troops, wrote him, unofficially, that the government now was committed to their use, particularly "as a military force for the defence of forts, depots, etc. . . . If they can be used to hold points on the Mississippi during the sickly season, it will afford much relief to our armies." The division in the thinking of the Commanding General revealed here as between Negro troops on the one hand and "our armies" on the other is noteworthy.[23]

Data clearly establishing the misuse of Negro troops are available. Thus, Brigadier General Q. A. Gillmore, in command of the Department of the South, issued a General Order (No. 77) on September 17, 1863, the first paragraph of which read as follows:

> It has come to the knowledge of the brigadier general commanding that detachments of colored troops, detailed for fatigue duty, have been employed in one instance at least, to prepare camps and perform menial duty for white troops. Such use of these details is unauthorized and improper, and is hereafter expressly prohibited. Commanding officers of colored regiments are directed to report promptly, to these headquarters, any violations of this order which may come to their knowledge.[24]

Eight days later, the Commissioner for the Organization of Colored Troops reported to the Secretary of War from Nashville that "the colored men here are treated like brutes; any officer who wants them, I am told, impresses on his own authority; and it is seldom that they are paid . . . one was shot."[25] From the same city, on the next day, twenty "citizens of Tennessee" wrote Mr. Stanton that Negroes were receiving the "harshest treatment . . . more that of a brute than of a human being."[26]

Notwithstanding the explicit character of General Gillmore's order, the same officer found it necessary, on November 25, 1863, to issue another General Order (No. 105) calling attention to the fact that he had

> heretofore had occasion to rebuke officers of this command for imposing improper labors upon colored troops. He is now informed that

the abuses sought to be corrected still exist. Attention is called to General Orders No. 77, current series, from these headquarters, and commanding officers are enjoined to see to its strict enforcement. Colored troops will not be required to perform any labor which is not shared by the white troops, but will receive, in all respects, the same treatment and be allowed the same opportunities for drill and instructions.[27]

The next month two officers, a captain and a brigadier-general, were sent, separately, from the adjutant general's office into the field to look into this particular phase of the handling of Negro troops. The captain was directed to investigate conditions in the Department of the South, under General Gillmore. On the twentieth he reported that excessive fatigue details were still assigned Negro troops, but that he had been told that this did not prevail in so aggravated a degree as heretofore.[28] The general was ordered to make an over-all survey of conditions, and he reported that, as a rule, Negro troops were used excessively for fatigue and labor details.[29]

At this same time the commanding officer of the 14th U. S. Colored Infantry was writing that

It behooves the friends of this movement [*i.e.,* the use of Negroes as soldiers] to secure a favorable decision from the great tribunal—public opinion. This cannot be done by making laborers of these troops. . . . [It is] degrading to single out Colored Troops for fatigue duty, while white soldiers stand by. . . .[30]

It may be pointed out that there is some evidence to show that this was precisely the reasoning of those who were anything but "friends of this movement." Thus, Brigadier-General Daniel Ullman, in command of a Negro brigade in Louisiana, told William Cullen Bryant, the editor-in-chief of the *New York Post,* in a postscript to a letter marked "Private and Confidential," that he was hearing some interesting things now that Negro troops had borne so heroic a part in the successful storming of a fortified place, as his troops had done at Port Hudson He wrote:

If it were not so serious I should be much amused at these proslavery Generals. Before the assault of the 27th May last [1863] on this place, their ridicule of the idea that the blacks would fight was constant, They then swing to the other side—forsooth they fight too well. "We must not discipline them," for if we do, we will have to fight them some day ourselves. Above all we must keep artillery out of their hands. A few pro-slavery Generals actually had the effontery to use such language to me.[31]

In September, 1863, the Commissioner for the Organization of Colored Troops complained that his work was being hindered by the "brutal" treatment accorded Negroes. Half a year later, in a letter to Senator Wilson of Massachusetts, the same individual declared that:

. . . a General Order from the War Department compelling the same Treatment to Colored as White troops, and securing Negroes from brutal treatment [was needed]; and until that is done they will be at the mercy of any officer from Colonel up, who chooses to vent his spite or air his prejudice on them. There is no use of half measures. If Mr. Stanton was as much in earnest as his Adjutant General [Lorenzo] Thomas, in this matter of protecting Colored men, one half of the abuses that are now so numerous would cease.[32]

Brigadier-General Ullman who, in March, 1864, was complaining of the misuse of his Negro unit in a "private and confidential" letter to so influential a civilian as William Cullen Bryant, some six weeks later decided to place the matter, officially, before the Army's Adjutant General. He declared:

There is a topic to which I desire to draw your attention. Doubtless you have already considered it. So far, colored troops in this Department [of the Gulf], have been used chiefly for fatigue duty. I much fear, unless there shall be a radical change, they never will be otherwise used in this Department. I have been striving for the year past to obtain an opportunity to bring my special command into shape as soldiers, not laborers. The 1st Brigade of my Division was ordered to the front some three weeks ago. I learn they are used simply on "fatigue duty." . . . I humbly suggest, then, they should not be kept in the background, and continue to be kept degraded as simply laborers. If they are thus treated in the future, as they have been in the past, we may be sure their morale will be entirely destroyed.

In January, 1863, Colonel James Montgomery was authorized to raise a regiment of Negro infantry. He proceeded to do so, but as of May, 1864, its organization was still incomplete. The

Commanding General of the Department of the South asked the Colonel to explain this deficiency, and on May 2 the latter did so. He pointed out that a considerable part of his regiment (the 34th U. S. Colored Infantry) was raised soon after authorization and that it took part, under General Gillmore, in the fighting which culminated in July, 1863, with the capture of Morris Island, South Carolina. Immediately thereafter, however, continued the Colonel:[33]

My men were then put into trenches and batteries, or detailed to mount guns, haul cannon and mortars, and were kept constantly and exclusively on fatigue duty of the severest kind.[34] To fill the heavy details which were made upon my fraction of a regiment, I frequently had to take men who had been on duty from 4 o'clock in the morning until sundown to make up the detail called for, for the night, and men who had been in the trenches in the night were compelled to go on duty again at least part of the day.

Inspections, drills, care of weapons, rest were impossible, and, "As might be expected this kind of service soon filled our hospital with broken down men. Such were my opportunities," concluded the Colonel, "from the 1st of July [1863] to the 1st of January [1864] to make soldiers of my recruits, and to complete my organization."

The blanket War Department order recommended by Major Stearns in his letter of March, 1864, to Senator Wilson seems never to have been issued, but something approximating it did appear a few months later. By order of the Secretary of War the following directive appeared on June 14, 1864:

The incorporation into the Army of the United States of Colored Troops, renders it necessary that they should be brought as speedily as possible to the highest state of discipline. Accordingly the practice which has hitherto prevailed, no doubt from necessity, of requiring these troops to perform most of the labor of fortifications, and the labor and fatigue duties of permanent stations and camps, will cease, and they will only be required to take their fair share of fatigue duty with white troops. This is necessary to prepare them for the higher duties of conflict with the enemy.[35]

The enforcement provision of this order, however, was weak for it declared that "Commanders of Colored Troops, in cases where the troops under their commands are required to perform an excess of labor above white troops in the same command, *will represent the case to the common superior, through the regular channels.*"[36]

Indeed, five months later, and but a few months before the termination of hostilities, the general who signed the above order confessed to the man responsible for it that "Where white and black troops come together in the same command, the latter have to do all the work. At first this was always the case, and in vain did I endeavor to correct it." He went on to say that since the Negro troops had thoroughly proved themselves in battle this practice had somewhat declined, but it had by no means ceased.[37]

Finally, the fact may be mentioned that several Negro regiments were specifically organized for fatigue duty, and were to be "composed of all classes of colored men capable of performing the ordinary duties of a military depot." That is to say, they were not to be composed, as were combat regiments, "of such men only as can pass the physical examination required of all men entering the military service." It was provided that as soon as these units were organized they were to be "subject to such details for fatigue duty as the Commanding General of the Department may direct."[38]

Actually, there were seven such "fatigue" Negro regiments, the 42nd, 63rd, 64th, 69th, 101st, 123rd, and 124th, but at least three of them, though composed of the type of men already indicated and though not trained for combat, did do battle with Confederate troops. Thus, the 63rd fought in Louisiana and Mississippi in April, June, and September, 1864; the 64th in the same states in May and June, 1864; and the 101st in Alabama in January, 1865.[39]

There were manifestations of this second-rate consideration of Negro troops in addition to their frequent relegation to the generally demoralizing, unpleasant and unhealthy garrison, fatigue, and labor details.

Thus, it is clear that Negro troops were not equipped as well as others. Until the equalization of pay in June, 1864, the clothing allowance for all Negroes came to $36 per year while that for the lowest ranking whites equalled $42. Moreover, frequent complaints arose from the Negroes that the hard labor and extraordinary hours of duty required of them prevented proper care of what clothing and equipment they did have.[40]

It has been pointed out that the regiment suffering the second highest number of deaths in the entire Union Army was the 65th U. S. Colored Infantry. This was true notwithstanding the fact that the unit was not sent into the field until January, 1864, and that it never engaged in combat.

The regiment was recruited throughout Missouri during the winter of 1863, and men were sent, in December of that year, to Benton Barracks, many without hats or shoes, thinly clad, and some traveling great distances with no feeding provisions having been made. There were numerous instances of frozen extremities and deaths following amputations of arms and legs, as well as many cases of disease. The regiment suffered over one hundred deaths in the less than two months spent in Missouri, prior to its use for guard, garrison, and fatigue duties along the Mississippi.[41]

As a rule, the weapons provided Negro troops were of an inferior quality. Memoranda from the Inspector General's department comment on the fact that while Negro units were usually equal to others in discipline, conduct, and bearing, their efficiency was curtailed because, for example, the arms within several regiments were of different kinds.[42] Again, early in 1864, the Adjutant-General of the Army, after having inspected a Negro regiment in New Orleans, wrote to his assistant that it, "like the other Colored Troops, is armed with the old flint lock musket altered to percussion, turned in by the white volunteers, and some of them twice condemned."[43]

Individual commanders frequently and urgently complained about this condition. Brigadier-General Ullman, for example, asserted that he had been forced to put in the hands of his Negro soldiers "arms almost entirely unserviceable, and in other respects, their equipment have been of the poorest kind."[44] Again, somewhat later, Brigadier-General J. Hawkins, commanding the 1st Brigade, U. S. Colored Troops, appealed to the War Department, for the issuance of suitable weapons. The next month the Assistant Secretary of War declared that the Department had never intended "that the colored soldiers should be armed with inferior weapons." He asserted, moreover, his belief that the foreign arms turned in by another commander, repaired by ordnance and now in the hands of Hawkins' men, could not "be properly called inferior," but, he added, that since "your officers and men" think otherwise, "new muskets" would be forwarded "as soon as they can be."[45]

There is significance, in this connection, in the remark of the heroic Colonel Robert Gould Shaw of the 54th Massachusetts Infantry, made shortly before his death, that there was serious talk at one time "of the arming of Negro troops with pikes instead of firearms. Whoever proposed it must have been looking for a means of annihilating Negro troops altogether. . . . The project is now abandoned I believe."[46] According to B. Gratz Brown, United States Senator from Missouri, it had been customary, for a time, "to prevent the Negro regiments from having any arms put into their hands until they left the State [wherein they had been raised, and, presumably, given preparatory training]; but representations in regard to this were made to the proper authorities, and the evil has been corrected."[47]

Specific contemporary references directly linking the poor arms of Negro troops with excessive battle casualties occasionally occur. This is true, for example, of the famous engagement at Milliken's Bend, Mississippi, where Negro troops predominated, and where total casualties surpassed 370 out of about 1,100 Union troops involved. Charles Dana, Assistant Secretary of War, who was in the area at the time, believed the great losses to be due in part to the inferior weapons of the Negroes, and the fact that they had received even these but "a few days before battle."[48]

Again, in reporting the engagement near Simmsport, Louisiana, of May 17, 1864, the commanding officer of the 92nd U. S. Colored Infantry declared that the enemy was forced back though, "The Regiment was and is now, armed with Springfield, smooth-bore muskets, of very inferior and defective quality; many of them becoming useless at the first fire."[49]

In terms of training for combat, Negro troops were at a serious disadvantage as compared with white soldiers. Excessive fatigue duty given Negro troops and their poorer equipment has already been indicated. The typical remark of but one commanding officer of Negro troops need be quoted on this subject: "Since

I have been in command, such has been the amount of fatigue work thrust upon the organization that it has been with the utmost difficulty that any time could be set aside for drill."[50]

Another burden borne by the Negro soldier of the Civil War was poor leadership. Available evidence forces one to the conclusion that, with a few notable exceptions (as in the Massachusetts Negro regiments, and the 1st Regiment of Kansas Colored Infantry, later the 79th U. S. Colored Infantry) the caliber of officers in Negro regiments was poorer than elsewhere. This is said with full realization of the fact that much of the criticism directed against such officers was based on bigotry, and so must be discounted in large part.[51]

Yet, solid evidence remains. Thus, for example, a brigadier-general, sent on an inspection tour of Negro units, reported in December, 1863, that the quality of their officers, though lately improved, was still poor.[52] Another general, himself commanding Negro troops, declared in the same period:

> I well know that those prophets who declare that negroes never will make soldiers are striving to force their prophecies to work out their own fulfillment, by appointing ignoramuses and boors to be officers over men who are as keensighted as any to notice the short-comings of those placed over them. Men have been made Field Officers in this section, who are not fit to be non-commissioned officers.[53]

Another reference to the alleged existence of a conspiracy to appoint incompetents as officers in Negro units occurs in a somewhat earlier letter to President Lincoln from one Major A. E. Borey, the Provost Marshal of the Norfolk-Portsmouth area in Virginia. How closely this letter approximates the actual truth, it is, of course, very difficult to say, but the position of its author and the character of its charges warrant complete presentation. Major Borey assured the President that the:

> . . . majority of our officers of all grades have no sympathy with your policy [of enlisting Negroes and emancipating slaves]; nor with anything human. They hate the Negro more than they love the Union and you would probably suppose that such men would not seek or accept positions—in the Negro Regts.; not so however. There is a regular cabal here among the very worst class of Negro hating officers, to secure & parcel out to themselves & others like themselves, all those places. . . . These men have at this moment two agents in Washington under pay—

sent there from here—to secure the appontments [sic] in this force, all the way down from Brigadier to Captain. For God's sake dont [sic] let this black Army fall into such hands. . . .[54]

Brutality – beating, bucking, gagging, hanging by thumbs – occasionally characterized the treatment of white[55] as well as Negro Union soldiers, but this appears to have been very much more common for the latter. And such refinements as pouring molasses over the naked bodies of enlisted men and forcing them to remain with arms outstretched in this manner for an entire day and night seem to have been confined to Negro troops.[56]

On the other hand, it is refreshing to note that in at least two cases white officers of Negro regiments went to very great lengths to defend their men. Thus, Colonel Isaac F. Shepard while commanding the 1st Mississippi Regiment of Colored Infantry ordered his soldiers to whip a white soldier. He did this because of the crime (unspecified) committed by the white soldier, "one calling for the severest punishment, even to the loss of life," and because "complaints to the [culprit's] commanding officer [brought] no action." A Board of Officers exonerated the Colonel, an action approved by General Grant.[57]

Of even greater interest was the case involving twenty-eight officers of the 3rd U. S. Colored Cavalry. On April 24, 1864, at Haines Bluff, Mississippi, these officers hanged a cotton trader named W. B. Wooster, after a kangaroo trial, because Wooster had praised the massacre of Southern white and Negro Federal troops by Confederate forces at Fort Pillow after its surrender. Colonel Schofield, of the Regiment, defended his officers and declared they were his best men, but the endorsement of three generals (Hawkins, Slocum, McPherson) advised dismissal. What final action was taken in this case has not been discovered.[58]

It is revealing that the headquarters charged with raising Negro troops in east and middle Tennessee found it necessary to declare in February, 1864, that:

No person is wanted as an officer in a Colored Regiment who "feels that he is making a sacrifice in accepting a position in a Colored Regiment," or who desires the place simply for higher rank and pay. . . . It can be no "sacrifice" to any man to command in a service which gives liberty to slaves, and manhood to chattels, as well as soldiers to the Union.[59]

Shortly thereafter, Major-General Rosecrans, commanding the Department of the Missouri, in referring to a Board whose duties were to enquire into the capabilities of and make recommendations concerning candidates for commissions with Negro troops, felt impelled to call

> the attention of all officers in the Department whose duty it may become to forward applications from officers or enlisted men under their command to appear before the Board to the fact that in many cases heretofore, it would appear, applicants have been recommended for no other apparent purpose than to get rid of worthless or obnoxious men, or to obtain in this way a furlough to visit St. Louis.[60]

This practice was ordered to cease, and applicants were to be forwarded, in the future, only after "due deliberation."

Negro units suffered not only from poor arms, poor equipment, poor training, and poor officers, but, in addition, their method of employment in combat seems to have been conducive, frequently, to excessive casualties. The recurrent Confederate charge that Federal forces invariably used Negro troops as breastworks and cannon fodder was exaggerated, but there were instances in which such a procedure does seem to have been followed—as at Fort Wagner, Port Hudson, Paducah, and Olustee.

It is, moreover, significant that one of the reasons for altering the original order for the Battle of the Mine at Petersburg, which called for Negro troops to lead the assault, was official concern over the charge of reckless expenditure of such units.[61] Ironically enough, the last-minute change in plans bred confusion, and helped bring on the repulse of the white troops. Following this demoralizing event Negro soldiers were required to attack over a littered battlefield, passing by defeated comrades, and to assault a well-entrenched, elated enemy. The slaughter was fearful, and Negro casualties in this engagement were much higher than that sustained by others.

In addition, attention is called to the criminal carelessness with which Negro units were at times committed. An outstanding example of this is the use of the 54th Massachusetts Infantry to storm Fort Wagner. On July 16, 1863, that regiment engaged in battle on James Island, S. C., and sustained some thirty casualties. Without rest, with very inadequate food, and many sick at its St. Helena Camp, the unit, depleted by a fatigue detail of eighty men, plus a guard detail, was sent on a forced march to Morris Island. Here, late the next day, it was assigned its lead position (though having but six hundred men in the line) for the assault, and in the afternoon of the 18th, tired and hungry, it commenced its immortal charge.

The lack of earlier planning and preparation for this assault is almost incredible: None of the company officers, let alone the enlisted men, had seen a plan of the work they were supposed to carry by the bayonet; no guide was provided the regiment advancing over unfamiliar terrain; no engineers accompanied the regiment; no provisions were made for overcoming the obstructions to be met prior to gaining the walls themselves; there was no line of skirmishers, no covering party, and no special instructions to any of the men engaged, for the first time in their lives (and having had no training in assaulting fortified works), in storming a fort. And to top it all, the starting of the assault was so timed that the approach was perfectly visible to the crews of the enemy's artillery who took full advantage of this fact. And the arrival hour was about 7:30 P.M., that is, when darkness had descended, so that the attackers were not only in completely unfamiliar surroundings, but had, in addition, absolutely no visibility!

That the 54th actually reached the parapet, and even entered the works at some points, could have resulted only from amazing determination and courage on the part of the enlisted men and officers involved. Although the regiment suffered about 42 per cent casualties in this single assault, it is surprising that any remained unharmed.[62]

Undoubtedly of importance in determining the manner of employing Negroes in combat was the low estimation in which they, as a people, were generally held. Thus, for example, early in the war, the Governor of Iowa, in arguing for the use of Negroes as soldiers, remarked to General Halleck, that, "When this war is over and we have summed up the entire loss of life it has imposed on the country I shall not have any regrets if it is found that a part of the dead are niggers and that all are not white men."[63]

Similarly, the testimony of one Nathaniel Page, a special correspondent for the New York *Tribune,* is relevant. Mr. Page spent three months at Morris Island, South Carolina, attached to General Gillmore's headquarters of the Department of the South. According to his own statement, he was present when General Gillmore and General Seymour were considering the Fort Wagner assault. General Seymour expressed the opinion that he could take the fort.

> Said General Gillmore: "Very well, if you think you can take it you have permission to make the assault. How do you intend to organize your command?" General Seymour answered: "Well, I guess we will let [General] Strong [whose brigade contained Negro troops] lead and put those damned niggers from Massachusetts in the advance; we may as well get rid of them one time as another.". . . [General Seymour] is now an ardent admirer of negro troops. These facts are personally known to me, and I am willing to swear to their truth.[64]

One condition, out of the control of military commanders, that must certainly have effected the battle casualty rate of the Negroes was the fact that they entered the war late, and so were likely to meet battlewise veterans while they themselves were still novices. There are several combat reports which emphasize this fact, and it may well have been a factor of considerable importance.[65]

The relationship between low morale and high casualties, particularly from disease, seems to be so close that note must be taken of an additional factor hurting Negro morale. This was the discrimination practiced by the government against its Negro soldiers in the matter of pay. The facts concerning this are so well known that they need but the briefest summary: All Negro troops (regardless of rank) from 1862 to 1864 were offered a monthly wage of ten dollars minus three dollars for clothing, which was three dollars less than that paid white privates. This was done notwithstanding the fact that the Negro recruits had been officially and repeatedly assured, in many instances, by high military and civil officials (including the Governor of Massachusetts and the Secretary of War)[66] that they would receive the same pay, equipment, and rations as any other United States volunteers.

What is not so well known, however, is the response of the Negro to this treatment.[67] Very briefly, one may remark that this discrimination aroused the most hostile and bitter feelings, and that it was this response, plus the resistance to enlistment on the part of the Negro, due to it and other evils, which largely accounted for the equalization of pay, retroactively, on the part of the Federal government.

Directly, though in a minute way, this affected the subject of casualties, for the issue of pay precipitated mutinies and near mutinies which, in turn, resulted in a few executions. Thus, Sergeant William Walker of the 3rd South Carolina Volunteers was shot by order of a court-martial for having led the men of his company to stack arms and to refuse to serve until the agreement under which they enlisted—equal pay—was met. At least three other Negro soldiers died for similar behavior, and over a score from one regiment alone (14th Rhode Island Heavy Artillery) were jailed.[68] The indirect effect of this crass injustice upon casualties among Negro troops, in terms of impairment of morale, cannot be determined, but was probably great.

Of some consequence in any consideration of Negro casualties during the Civil War was the policy adopted by the Confederate government in regard to Negro troops used against it. Since a good account,[69] setting forth the main facts in this regard, is readily available, here it need be but briefly mentioned. The Confederate government, until the end of 1864, did not consider Negroes as bona fide soldiers, and therefore refused to treat them, when captured, in a manner identical with that pursued with other troops.

Confederate law required that Negro prisoners be turned over to the authorities of the states wherein they had been captured for trial as incendiaries and insurrectionists. White officers of Negro units were subject to trial by courtmartial, with death as a prescribed penalty. It does not appear, however, that any were so tried.

Nevertheless, it is to be noted that James Seddon, the Confederate Secretary of War, advised Lieutenant General E. Kirby Smith that white officers of Negro troops, when captured, "had best be dealt with red-handed in the field, or immediately thereafter."[70] It is, moreover, a fact that the official casualty figures show four officers of Negro regiments as having been "killed after capture," and another as having been "executed by the enemy." Certain it is, too, that at least two white officers were murdered in cold blood and another wounded and left for dead on December 22, 1864, by Confederate troops near Lewisburg, Tennessee.[71] Occasionally, too, indignities, or what were believed to be indignities, were thrust upon such officers, and at times these resulted fatally.[72]

Evidence exists to show that a few Negroes, *who had been free prior to enlistment,* were sold into slavery by the Confederacy[73], but, by and large, they seem to have been "held in strict confinement, not yet formally recognized . . . as prisoners of war, but, except in some trivial particulars indicative of inferior consideration, are treated very much in the same manner as our other captives."[74]

It was, however, common procedure for the Confederacy to sell into slavery (theoretically to the former owners), Negroes captured by its armies and declared to have been slaves prior to enlistment. Where the masters were not found or did not appear, the armies themselves used the Negroes as laborers.[75]

But taking Negroes as prisoners was definitely discouraged by several Confederate officers,[76] and their murder after capture was not very unusual. Moreover, advance announcements that Negroes would not receive protection as prisoners of war, and, occasionally, even warnings of wholesale extermination, were not unknown.

Thus, Brigadier-General Buford, besieging Columbus, Kentucky, sent the following note to his Federal opponent on April 13, 1864:

> Fully capable of taking Columbus and its garrison by force, I desire to avoid the shedding of blood, and therefore demand the unconditional surrender of the forces under your command. Should you surrender, the negroes now in arms will be returned to their masters. Should I however be compelled to take the place, no quarter will be shown to the negro troops whatever; the white troops will be treated as prisoners of war.[77]

A somewhat similar letter went from General J. B. Hood to the Union commander at Resaca, Georgia, on October 12, 1864:

> I demand the immediate and unconditional surrender of the post and garrison under your command, and should this be acceded to all

white officers and soldiers will be paroled in a few days. If the place is carried by assault, no prisoners will be taken.[78]

One may not only find instructions advising against the taking of Negro prisoners, and warnings that none would be taken, or, if taken that they would be killed, but there is clear evidence that these instructions and warnings were realized. Examples in addition to the Fort Pillow massacre[79] exist. Even the incomplete data of the Adjutant-General show twenty-one Negro soldiers as having been "killed after capture."[80] That this is an underestimation will appear from the following material.

On September 2, 1863, the assistant adjutant-general for Confederate General Johnson wrote to a Colonel John Griffith that he had heard reports of the hanging or shooting, by members of the latter's command, of "certain federal prisoners and negroes in arms at Jackson, Louisiana, on August 3 [1863]," and ordered him to investigate and report on this matter.[81] On the same day Colonel Griffith replied:

> In reply to your note just received I would say that a squad of negroes was captured on or about the 3d of August, at Jackson, Louisiana. When the command started back, the negroes under guard, were ordered on in advance of the command, and learning that the guard had taken the wrong road, Colonel Powers and myself rode on in advance to put them in the proper route for camp. About the time we were reaching them, or shortly before, four of the negroes attempted to escape. They were immediately fired into by the guard; this created some excitement, and a general stampede among them, whereupon the firing became general upon them from the guard, and few, I think, succeeded in making good their escape. There were no federal [*i.e.* white] prisoners among them, having been separated the night previous. No further particulars remembered.

Colonel Frank Powers, mentioned above, wrote a report of remarkably similar content, adding only the detail that he gave the order to shoot down all the Negroes "and with my six shooter assisted in the execution of the order."

Colonel John L. Logan, the senior of both Griffith and Powers, in transmitting their statements the next day added, among other things, the remark: "My own opinion is that the negroes were summarily disposed of; by whom I cannot say. . . . The whole transaction was contrary to my wishes, and against my own consent." This affair seems to have died with the endorsement, dated Canton, Mississippi, September 17, 1863, by Major-General S. D. Lee, in forwarding the statements of the three colonels that:

> [I] do not consider it to the interests of the service that this matter be further investigated at present. A Court of Inquiry or a Court Martial will afford the only means of gaining correct information.[82]

An entry in the official return for February 1864, of the 1st Mississippi Volunteers of African Descent asserted that during an engagement in Arkansas a picket body was surprised and surrounded. "The men were captured and most of them brutally murdered. Fourteen were killed and six wounded." Again, the entry for March, 1864, of the 3rd U. S. Colored Cavalry reported that in a Mississippi skirmish, "The enemy captured sixteen men whom they put to death not even excepting the wounded."[83]

The commanding officer of the 8th U. S. Colored Heavy Artillery Regiment informed the Assistant Adjutant General of the Army, in August, 1864, that three men of his unit, while on advance picket duty, had been captured, and then "deliberately shot," their bodies being "left . . . in a heap . . . This fact," it was declared, "is established beyond any doubt."[84] On September 16, 1864, Confederate troops are reported to have successfully attacked the bivouac area of 125 men of the 2nd Kansas (white) Cavalry, and of the 1st Kansas Colored Infantry. But twenty men escaped. "All the white soldiers remaining there" were taken as prisoners, but the enemy killed "all the colored soldiers they could find . . ."[85]

Dalton, Georgia, was surrendered to an overwhelming force of Confederate troops under General Hood on October 13, 1864. This was done by Colonel L. Johnson of the 44th U. S. Colored Infantry who commanded, in addition to his own 600 men, about 150 other (white) soldiers from three different regiments. In his official report of the disaster, Colonel Johnson declared that, following the capitulation, one Negro soldier was shot and killed when he refused to help tear up some railroad tracks, while five others, "who, having been sick, were unable to keep up with the rest on the march" were likewise murdered.[86]

Finally, there are occasional notices of the killing after capture of individual Negro soldiers. Evidence of at least two such cases exist, one occurring in Missouri in May, 1863, the other in North Carolina in December, 1863.[87]

The announced policy of the Confederate government of refusing to treat captured Negro soldiers as prisoners of war, and its implementation of that policy in practice, provoked a desperation among these troops that seems to have increased their battle casualties. As General Ullman remarked of his Negro troops:

> They are far more in earnest than we. I have talked with hundreds of them. They understand their position full as well as we do. They know the deep stake they have in the issue—that, if we are unsuccessful, they will be remanded to worse a slavery than before. They also have a settled conviction that if they are taken, they will be tortured and hung. These impressions will make them daring and desperate fighters.[88]

An example of the effect of this upon Negro troops may be offered from the pen of a Confederate officer who had occasion to regret it. Brigadier-General L. S. Ross cut off and surrounded the Federal garrison at Yazoo City, Mississippi in March, 1864, and, on the fifth, demanded its surrender. "We squabbled about the terms of the capitulation," reported the General, "as I would not recognize negroes as soldiers, or guarantee them nor their officers protection as such." As a result, he went on, the Negroes "returned and pressed our forces so hard that we were compelled to withdraw . . . and they refused to surrender."[89]

Having attempted to account for the excessive mortality suffered by United States Colored Troops during the Civil War, we turn now to a consideration of casualties suffered by the Negro in other services.

The first item which immediately appears and which, though hitherto neglected, considerably alters the total casualty picture, is the fact that there were four combat regiments of Negroes that never were federalized, and therefore never formed part of the United States Colored Troops. The casualty figures of these units hitherto have been credited to those suffered by the states which raised them, and ultimately have come to make up part of the totals for United States Volunteer Troops, as distinguished from the Colored Troops.

These four regiments were the 29th Regiment of Connecticut Volunteer Infantry, the 5th Regiment of Massachusetts Cavalry, the 54th and 55th Regiments of Massachusetts Volunteer Infantry. The data on mortality suffered by those regiments may be observed in this table:[90]

| Regiment | Killed & Mortally Wounded | | Died from Disease | | Total |
|---|---|---|---|---|---|
| | *Officers* | *Enlisted Men* | *Officers* | *E.M.* | |
| 29th Conn. | 1 | 44 | 1 | 152 | 198 |
| 5th Cavalry | | 7 | | 116 | 123 |
| 54th Mass. | 5 | 104 | 1 | 160 | 270 |
| 55th Mass. | 3 | 64 | 2 | 128 | 197 |
| Totals | 9 | 219 | 4 | 556 | 788 |

This total of 778 is to be added to the official figure for deaths among Negro army units which thus should read 37,635 and not 36,847.

In addition there were some scattered Negro units which served for short periods of time and probably suffered some deaths, but are not included among the approximately 186,000 Negroes in the infantry, cavalry, and artillery regiments forming the body known as United States Colored Troops. Thus, there may be mentioned the formation, in July, 1864, as the result of the governor's appeal, of a company of Negro infantry, for a hundred days' service, in Philadelphia[91]; while the Provost Marshal of Alexandria, Virginia, was authorized, in October, 1864, to organize at that place, "a second independent company of colored infantry."[92]

Again, Major-General Hurlbut, commanding the Department of the Gulf, in a general order dated October 27, 1864, authorized the formation of two regiments of Negro infantry to be raised in the city of New Orleans (with no discrimination as to officers), but it appears that only one company of about eighty men, with Negro officers, was actually raised.[93] Later this year, probably in November, Major-General S. R. Curtis formed, with War Department approval, a light artillery battery of Negro men, with Negro officers, but this seems to have been unsuccessful, did not enter combat, and was mustered out in July, 1865.[94]

Of greater importance is the fact that under two different

sets of circumstances Negroes were regularly enlisted and mustered members of many of the so-called white regiments. On the one hand this was due to the ever-present phenomenon of "passing," and while no estimate of the numbers that may have been involved by the practice is possible, the evidence of its existence is conclusive.

In 1863, Governor Andrew of Massachusetts wrote that "in more than one instance, I have known 'persons of African descent' serving as volunteers in white regiments, during the present war. Only a few days since, such a person was, at his own request, transferred from his regiment belonging to a State other than Massachusetts to our 55th Regiment. . . ."[95] John Eaton, Jr. declared, before the American Freedmen's Inquiry Commission in May, 1864, that "already some old regiments of white soldiers have recruited members all their lives slaves, and not to be distinguished by any African characteristic. . . ."[96] The Negro author, Joseph T. Wilson, himself enlisted in a New York regiment, though he remained but three days. He cites, however, other instances where the Negro remained with a white unit.[97]

In August, 1862, several members of the 1st Kansas Volunteer Infantry requested the transfer of a Negro. This was approved by the Colonel, George W. Deitzler, who, with extraordinary delicacy, wrote: "He is full two thirds 'nigger,' too black to serve upon terms of equality with white soldiers. I respectfully recommend that he be mustered out of service, or transferred to Jim Lane's nigger brigade. The recommendation is not made out of disrespect for the nigger."[98] As a final example may be cited the fact that a fugitive slave enlisted in the 14th Maine Regiment of Infantry while it was stationed in New Orleans, in June, 1862, but recognition from his master brought dismissal.[99]

But the majority of Negroes who served as soldiers in the so-called "white" regiments were enlisted and mustered in as Negroes, and served as wagoners, teamsters, and, above all, as under-cooks. These men were considered and referred to as soldiers, appear on the rolls of numerous "white" regiments, and, when they died or were wounded or killed, the "white" casualty lists grew.[100]

On August 8, 1862, General Sherman, commanding the 5th Division, Army of the Tennessee, ordered that his regimental commanders might employ not over sixty-five Negroes per regiment as company cooks and teamsters, and that men so used were to "be borne on the muster-rolls," but that they were neither to be armed nor uniformed.[101] Five months later General Rosecrans, commanding the Department of the Cumberland, announced that Negroes might be employed as company cooks (2 per company), as well as laborers and nurses, by the quartermaster, engineers, and medical departments.[102] Yet, this order, too, did not actually make soldiers of the Negroes thus employed.

Shortly thereafter, however, Congress passed an act, one section of which declared that for each thirty men in a company, one cook was to be provided, while there were to be two cooks for each company of over thirty men. These cooks were to be detailed, in rotation, from the privates, each man serving ten days. In addition, the President was authorized "to cause to be *enlisted* [my emphasis—H. A.] . . . two under-cooks of African descent, who shall receive for their full compensation ten dollars per month, and one ration per day—three dollars of said monthly pay may be in clothing,"[103] *i.e.,* precisely the compensation allowed Negro soldiers in their own regiments.

Orders were issued by local commanders implementing the above act, and occasionally widening it to include Negroes serving in capacities other than that of cook. Thus, General Rosecrans ordered that, "Every cook or teamster shall be properly enrolled and mustered into service, according to law, without delay,"[104] while General Grant, in addition to ordering or permitting the hiring of Negroes for various services, authorized, in his Department of the Tennessee, the use within each of his regiments and companies of one Negro cook per fifteen men, and one Negro teamster for every wagon.[105]

The matter was clarified and standardized (at least in theory) by War Department General Order No. 323, issued on September 28, 1863. This order referred to the section of the last quoted Public Act and declared:

For a regular [army] company, the two under-cooks will be enlisted; for a volunteer company they will be mustered into service, as in the case of other soldiers. In each case a remark will be made on their enlistment papers showing that they are *under-cooks of African descent.* Their names will be borne on the company muster rolls at the foot of the list of privates. They will be paid, and their accounts will be kept, like other enlisted men. [The manner of payment was to be identical, *not* the sum disbursed.] They will also be charged in the same manner as other soldiers.[106]

Actually, records show that Negro under-cooks were *enlisted* in regiments prior to this War Department order. For example, in the 1st Kansas Volunteer Infantry there were a total of eighteen Negro soldiers. Of these one was enlisted in 1861, four in 1862, and a total of eleven prior to September, 1863.[107] On the other hand it appears that even after the War Department order, enlistments were not made out for some under-cooks. Thus, among the service records of one Private James Woods, of Company F, 121st Regiment of Ohio Volunteer Infantry, is an affidavit dated October 31, 1863, by Lieutenant Benjamin A. Banker, declaring that though Woods had been "employed as an under-cook . . . from the first day of August 1863," yet "no enlistment papers were made at the time of his employment as said under-cook or since."[108]

The clear intent of the War Department that these Negro men were to be considered as soldiers and treated as such (though paid less,[109] and permanently detailed as cooks) was realized. The enlistment papers, muster-in and muster-out documents, and other service records of these men (all filed, alphabetically, with their own regiments, precisely as other soldiers) demonstrate without any question that they were bona fide soldiers in very many regiments hitherto considered white.[110]

Some interesting points develop concerning these particular Negro soldiers. First, it may be remarked that many of their enlistment papers, notwithstanding the clear directive of the War Department, do *not* show them to have been "under-cooks of African descent," but, on the contrary, except for the description of hair and complexion, these papers are identical with that of other soldiers. On the service records themselves, under rank, one finds for these men such entries as "private," "under-cook," "cook," "colored." On the muster-out forms there is evidence, as shown in the "last-paid" column, that there was much irregularity in their payment, and occasionally one will find the remark, "never paid." It appears, too, that, in accordance with the general practice for Negro soldiers until 1864, these men were paid no bounty. Entries charging for clothing advanced, and in a few cases itemizing particular pieces of equipment lost or damaged, seem to show that these men were outfitted very much like other members of their regiments.[111]

A curious episode will show the difficulty that contemporaries had at times in dealing with these Negro soldiers of "white" regiments. This involves one Charles Danna, an eighteen year-old under-cook of Company B, 17th Regiment, Ohio Volunteer Infantry. Danna's service record shows him to have been enrolled and mustered on January 10, 1865, at Savannah, Georgia, for three years, but in April he became ill while with his unit in North Carolina, and on May 19, 1865, he died at the Foster General Hospital in New Bern. On the casualty sheet Charles Danna is listed as Private Charles Daniels, and no mention of his color appears. But on the inventory of effects submitted by the surgeon in charge of the hospital, he is listed as Private Charles Daniels of the 17th Regiment of Ohio Colored Volunteers. In due time this paper was ready for filing in the Adjutant General's office where, of course, it was discovered that no such regiment existed. In a letter of November 7, 1865, that office informed the surgeon "that no such organization is known . . . as the 17th Ohio Colored," and requested that he ascertain the correct designation "if possible."[112]

With records as they are today it would appear to be impossible to discover how many Negro soldiers were actually enlisted in "white" regiments. But that this was no inconsiderable number will appear when it is stated that a careful examination of the entire personnel roster of all Illinois regiments discloses, after elimination of duplication, that a minimum of six hundred and six Negroes were regularly enlisted members of those regiments.[113]

In terms of casualty figures for these particular soldiers, one is able to do little more than point out that they were subjected to all the hardships and dangers faced by their units. In many cases, it appears that the records of the Negroes, when kept at all, were handled with great carelessness. As an example may be mentioned the fact that out of the 606 Negroes in Illinois regiments, 57 are totally unaccounted for, with no note of even final disposition being available. However, of the remaining 549 Negroes for whom some remark is carried, there were three discharged for disability incurred in service, one missing in action, two wounded, but not mortally, three captured, seven killed in action or mortally wounded, and 26 who died of disease, making a total casualty figure of 60, or about 11 per cent.[114]

That the official records, as published by the adjutant generals of the states, are not correct as concerns casualties among these Negro soldiers, is demonstrable. As a check, the writer examined the service records of each of the thirteen under-cooks of the 69th Regiment of Ohio Volunteer Infantry. Among the papers of one of these, James Woods, appears a casualty sheet, showing that he was wounded on August 14, 1864, during the Georgia campaign, but the entry for James Woods in the printed official record does not show this.[115]

The fact of the employment by the United States during the Civil War of Negroes not enlisted as soldiers is well known, but there exists no satisfactory study of the subject. It is estimated that at least as many Negroes were hired by the government as were formally enrolled in its army's ranks; that is to say, something like 200,000 or 250,000 men and women.[116] Under the direct supervision of government agencies, they helped bring the Civil War to a successful end.[117]

A few miscellaneous data and some conclusions as to casualties among this category of Negroes may be offered. Many nonenlisted Negroes were used in military roles that brought them into proximity with the actual battleground and certainly into day-to-day relationships with soldiers.

One such type of employment that probably comprised several thousand Negroes was that of servant, or orderly, for officers. The evidence demonstrates that Negroes served in this capacity from 1861 to the close of the war,[118] and there is some indication that even government officials felt that the distinction between these Negroes and those acknowledged as soldiers was more formal than real.[119]

That these servants were involved in all the trials of war is clear. Thus, four Negro orderlies were among the 403 Federal prisoners of war delivered to Fort Monroe on February 20, 1862, by Confederate exchange officers.[120] Three days later, 372 Federal prisoners of war arrived, in exchange, at the same place, and among them were ten Negroes, probably officers' servants.[121]

Among the men of the 42nd Regiment of Massachusetts Volunteer Infantry aboard the *Harriet Lane* when it was captured at Galveston, Texas, in January, 1863, were two Negroes, both shown as "not enlisted" and both servants of the commanding Colonel.[122] And that some of these Negro servants suffered from more than capture is apparent from the circumstances affecting one of them, named Robert F. Small. He had been an officer's servant, had participated in several major battles and had lost, finally, both legs, due to over-exposure. Since he was not enlisted, he was entitled to no assistance from the government which led to a public appeal for funds.[123]

The use of Negroes by the Union Army as spies, scouts, and guides has been touched on in secondary accounts, but no thorough study has as yet been published. The activities of so well-known a Negro as Harriet Tubman have been described,[124] but they were by no means unique. Sources show that the use of Negroes in these roles was very common, and of inestimable value.

In the early weeks of the war an officer in command of an expedition in Maryland wrote: "The following reports of the force and position of the enemy opposite my positions are from negro scouts, and from appearances are nearly accurate."[125] Brigadier-General Schuyler Hamilton referred, in March, 1862, to a fugitive slave named Wallace Selvic who had recently joined his organization in Missouri and who had "with great courage and gallantry guided me in making an important reconnaissance."[126] On April 6, 1862, General Doubleday's headquarters, Military Defences North of the Potomac, ordered that fugitive slaves were not to be surrendered but rather their entry was to be encouraged because "they bring much valuable information, which cannot be obtained from any other source . . . make excellent guides . . . [and] frequently have exposed the haunts of secession spies and traitors, and the existence of rebel organizations."[127] Early in 1864 a free Negro, Tom Heath, of Goochland, Virginia, was arrested by Confederate forces for having "acted as a guide to the enemy," but the district attorney felt there was not sufficient evidence to convict Heath for treason. He noted, however, the recent suspension of the writ of habeas corpus and recommended that the Secretary of War order Heath's incarceration without trial. He did this because, "The crime with which he is charged is one of such frequent occurrence that an example should be made of Heath. It is a matter of notoriety in the sections of the Confederacy where raids are frequent that the guides of the enemy are nearly always free negroes and slaves."[128]

The best single contemporary description of this type of work yet seen is contained in the writings of a Union official in North Carolina early in 1862, and this source demonstrates that casualties were not disassociated from it. From this one learns:

> Upwards of fifty volunteers of the best and most courageous [of the Negro refugees], were kept constantly employed on the perilous but important duty of spies, scouts, and guides. In this work they were invaluable and almost indispensable. They frequently went from thirty to three hundred miles within the enemy's lines; visiting his principal camps and most important posts, and bringing us back important and reliable information . . . often on these errands barely escaping with their lives. . . . Two or three of them were taken prisoners; one of these was known to have been shot, and the fate of the others was not ascertained. The pay they received for this work was small but satisfactory. . . . They considered the work as a religious duty.[129]

The main body of non-enlisted Negroes who served the Union forces worked for army units, or for the Quartermaster, Commissary, Medical, and Engineer services in such occupations as pioneers, laborers, hostlers, teamsters, wagoners, carpenters, masons, laundresses, hospital attendants, fortification, highway and railroad builders, longshoremen, and blacksmiths.

As so-called pioneers, Negroes were actually doing the work of engineer soldiers. Thus, in the summer of 1862, in the heavy and dangerous work of felling trees, preparing gun positions and improving roads below Vicksburg, approximately twelve hundred Negroes were employed.[130] The defenses of the city of Corinth, Mississippi, built in preparation for the battle of October, 1862, was the result of the work of Negroes "organized into squads of twenty-five each" and commanded by Army personnel.[131]

The officers who had been the chief engineers of the Army of the Tennessee during its successful siege of Vicksburg officially reported:

> The labor in the trenches was done by men of the pioneer companies of divisions, by details from the lines, or by negroes. Several of the pioneer companies had negroes attached to them, who had come into our camps. These negroes were paid $10 per month in accordance with law and proved to be very efficient laborers when under good supervision. The labor performed by details from the line, as is usual in such cases, was very light in comparison with that done by the same number of pioneers or negroes.[132]

That this work entailed blood as well as sweat is clear from the following report: In the evening of July 1, 1863, the enemy exploded a huge mine, which resulted in the death of several of the besieging soldiers and "Eight negroes and the overseer in charge, working a counter-mine, were also killed."[133]

General Sherman seems to have particularly favored the use of Negro pioneers. Indeed, he reported to the Adjutant General, "I have used them [Negroes] with great success as pioneer companies attached to Divisions, and I think it would be well if a law would sanction such an organization one hundred to each Division of four thousand men. . . ."[134] A few months later, Sherman, in a Special Field Order, told his commanders that, "The organization, at once, of a good pioneer battalion for each Army Corps, composed, if possible, of negroes, should be attended to. . . ."[135]

In other types of service, too, proximity to the battleground was usual, and casualties from enemy action and from disease must have been numerous.

Some items will be cited to show the close relationship existing between the regularly enlisted soldiers and the hired Negro workers. Thus, late in 1863, Brigadier-General T. J. Boyle suggested, from Louisville, Kentucky, that it would be well to actually *enlist* two or three thousand colored teamsters, as that would be an administrative aid. The idea had the approval of the Secretary of War who instructed his Quartermaster General to draw up organizational plans for such enlisted men. The latter officer then suggested that they be organized into companies of one hundred men each, and be drilled, uniformed and armed.

It appears that this plan fell through, largely because of the opposition of the Governor of Kentucky, but in spite of this General Boyle reported on November 30, that he had ordered the Negroes "in the meantime to be employed as teamsters which was done."[136]

That Negroes generally served as teamsters directly attached (though not enlisted) to individual units is clear. Provision for this was made in January, 1863, by the Department of the Cumberland, and in August by the Department of the Tennessee. The Department of the Gulf *ordered,* in June, 1863, that, "Hereafter, negroes will be exclusively employed as teamsters in all Companies, Batteries, Regiments, and Brigades, in place of enlisted men or citizens."[137]

Some idea of the magnitude of the numbers of Negroes involved in this type of direct attachment to army units in the field may be obtained from the replies sent to the Quartermaster General's request for this information. General Meigs telegraphed top field commanders on August 4, 1863, asking for estimates of the number of Negroes employed by them in direct service with their armies. Some of the replies are available and revealing.

The Chief Quartermaster of the Army of the Potomac reported that subordinates, on a quick check, had given him figures which showed a total, as of August 15, 1863, of 4,203 Negroes employed with units of that army, but he added that he believed this figure to be a serious underestimate.[138] A telegram from the Army of the Cumberland stated "no reliable estimate" was available, but the sender expressed the belief that "not far from 6,000" Negroes were employed by it at the moment.[139] The officer in charge of the quartermaster depot at Memphis estimated that in his city "there are employed by the different staff departments . . . eight hundred negroes."[140] The analogous officer for the depot in Washington submitted a very elaborate table from which one learns that he believed there were 4,688 Negroes employed in the Quartermaster and Commissary departments in the cities of Washington, and Alexandria, Virginia.[141] Thus, it appears that, using only minimum figures, about 16,000 Negroes were directly attached to army units in the few areas from which replies are still extant.

Deaths from disease and accident among these thousands of Negroes, and particularly in the contraband camps, set aside for and usually built by themselves, which dotted the nation during the war years, must have been very numerous. A few scattered pieces of evidence concerning this are available, but from them it is impossible to even estimate, with any degree of confidence, the actual number of fatalities involved here.

Eye-witnesses condemned, in severest terms, conditions prevailing in the contraband camps at New Orleans, Carrollton, Donaldsonville, and Baton Rouge, Louisiana. They declared the Negro inhabitants of these areas were "herded together," existing under "every possible condition of misery," and "dying in large numbers."[142] A more precise, though equally incomplete, source of information, is the reports of interments performed under the supervision of the Quartermaster Department. Of these reports, the General commanding this department wrote: "These are the records of those who die in hospitals, camps, and barracks [*i.e.*, not in the field] for whose burial there is time to make decent and orderly provision under the general orders and regulations."[143] That these figures are, then, incomplete accounts of actual deaths is certain. When it is added that officers in but four of seventeen states reporting included data for contrabands interred, it is obvious that the figures represent but a fraction of their total mortalities. From this source, however, it is evident that as of 1865 Quartermaster officers in Missouri, Illinois, Virginia, and Tennessee reported the interment by this department of a total of 4,125 contrabands.[144]

There is excellent evidence of the occasional employment of these non-enlisted Negroes in actual combat with the foe. In the Department of the South it appears to have been customary to arm numbers of the contrabands, particularly on the islands dotting the coasts of South Carolina and Georgia, so that they might protect themselves from Confederate raids and incursions.

A point generally overlooked is the fact that War Department authorization of the arming of Negroes was given first in October, 1861, and not in the altered militia law of July, 1862. Thomas A. Scott, the acting Secretary of War, directed the then Brigadier-General Sherman, commanding the expedition to the Southern coast, on October 14, 1861, to avail himself "of the services of any persons, whether fugitives from labor or not, who may offer them to the National Government." These individuals were to be employed "in such services as they may be fitted for; either as ordinary employees, or, if special circumstances seem to require it, in any other capacity, with such organization, in squads, companies or otherwise, as you may deem most beneficial to the service; this however not being a general arming of them for military services."[145]

Evidence concerning Sherman's action has not been found, but it is this order which his successor, General David Hunter, cited to justify his large-scale arming of Negroes and his use of them in expeditions against the enemy. While this action was disavowed by the government, many of the men so trained, in the spring of 1862, formed the nucleus for regularly authorized infantry units that summer. The fact remains that in this department Negro guards and pickets were maintained at and around contraband centers, and that, though not enlisted, they did, at times, battle with the enemy and suffer casualties.

It is to action of this sort that Brigadier-General Rufus Saxton had reference, in his letter of August 16, 1862, in which he remarked that the island of St. Simon, off the coast of Georgia, "has been guarded for a long time by negro pickets," and that recently rebels had landed there. "They were vigorously attacked by the negro pickets," continued the General, "and during the action which ensued 2 of the latter were killed and 1 wounded. The rebels fled . . . what their loss was is not known. I think some of them must have been killed."[146] A similar event was reported by the same officer as having occurred in October, 1862, at St. Helena Island, South Carolina, when the Confederates "were fired on and driven off by the negro pickets."[147]

The report of Captain James B. Talbot, superintendent of contrabands at Pine Bluff, Arkansas, of the role played by the Negroes in the repulse of the Confederate attack upon that place on October 25, 1863, is interesting and pertinent:

When the skirmishing first commenced I received orders from you [Colonel Powell Clayton, commanding the Post] to furnish as many men as possible to roll out cotton-bales and form breastworks. I had 300 immediately brought from the camp, on double-quick, and from the short space of time in which every street opening was blockaded you may judge of their efficiency in that respect, especially when you consider that much of the work was accomplished under a heavy fire from the enemy's skirmishers.

By the time the breastworks were complete the fight had become general, and calls for water were urgent to supply the soldiers and quench the fire that had caught to the cotton-bales from our artillery. I immediately pressed every water-holding vessel within reach, and formed a chain of negroes with buckets from the top of the bank to the water's edge. At this time a galling fire that opened on them from the enemy killed 1, wounded 3, and for a moment threw them all into confusion; but they were soon rallied, and resumed their work with the most astonishing rapidity. About this time the danger was imminent of the enemy making a charge down the river under cover of the bank. Agreeably to your order, a breastwork was immediately formed under the bank, and while engaged in this work, another was wounded. Fifteen of them had arms, and were ordered to hold the point along the river; which they did throughout the action, some of them firing as many as 30 rounds, and one actually ventured out and captured a prisoner. None of them had ever before seen a battle, and the facility with which they labored and the manly efforts put forth to aid in holding the place excelled my highest expectations, and deserves the applause of their country and the gratitude of the soldiers. Their total loss is five killed and twelve wounded.[148]

When New Bern, North Carolina, was attacked, in February, 1864, its successful defense was assisted by nine hundred Negro men hurried into the trenches from a nearby contraband camp.[149] Similarly, in the attack on Frankfort, Kentucky, in June, 1864, some three hundred Negroes entered the fray with fists and knives and did good service, but their losses, which under the circumstances might well have been considerable, went unreported.[150]

There were at least two other factors producing casualties among the Negro people during the Civil War. One of these was the resistance to their masters by slaves within the borders of the Confederacy. Here the story of these activities may be summarized by pointing out that Negroes who refused to be evacuated from areas close to Federal lines were sometimes killed, others who attempted to flee to the Union forces died in the attempt, still others who waged a guerrilla warfare as members of maroon bands (at times in alliance with anti-Confederate whites) lost their lives, while deaths due to the suppression of slave uprisings or plots regularly recurred in the South during the war years.[151]

Lastly, there were casualties among the Negroes serving Confederate forces. In the vast majority of cases this service was distinctly involuntary, or the result of the status of the Negro within society. This, however, would certainly not decrease the casualties, and knowing that tens of thousands of Negroes worked for and with the Confederate Army and Navy, there can be no question but that many among them died.

In addition, free Negroes were enlisted as soldiers, or at least subject to such enlistment, in Tennessee, Alabama, and Louisiana from the early part of the war.[152] Note, too, should be taken of the fact that the Confederate Congress passed an act, on April 15, 1862, empowering payment to Negro members of army bands, and six days later authorized the use of four cooks, per company, who might be either slave or free, Negro or white. For these men a monthly wage ranging from $15 to $20 was provided, and they were to receive the same allowances, food, and *clothing* as soldiers.[153] The regular enlistment of Negroes as soldiers by the Confederacy, as its dying gasp just prior to capitulation, is well known, though it may be added that the story of how early demands for this arose, and how widespread they were, has not yet been told.[154]

No accurate figure on the number of Negroes associated in one capacity or another with the Confederate forces appears to be available, and even intelligent guesses as to casualties from battle or disease and accident are impossible. It may be mentioned, however, that authentic contemporary accounts of battle casualties suffered by Negroes in the Confederate service are exceedingly rare.[155]

The stereotyped view of the Negro as a passive onlooker during the American Civil War will not bear the light of historical investigation. Certain it is that when one writes, as did W. E. Woodward, that the Negro people "became free without any efforts of their own," he is exposing not that people's history, but rather his own ignorance. During the Civil War the American Negro contributed greatly, both on land and sea, in struggles for his emancipation.

# NEGROES IN THE UNION NAVY

So far as this writer has been able to ascertain, no study of the role of the Negro in the United States Navy during the Civil War exists. Occasionally, available literature will yield a line or two indicating some awareness of the fact that Negroes served in the Union Navy, but that is all.[1]

This void is explicable not only on the basis of the general and notorious neglect of the Negro that has marked the great body of American historiography until the past generation, but also on the basis of some quite practical considerations. The primary source for a study of any phase of the history of the Union fleet, namely the *Official Records of the Union and Confederate Navies*,[2] must be read page by page by anyone interested in the Negro, for that subject is not indexed within the individual thirty volumes.

And Massachusetts, which provided the greatest number of men for the Union fleet, has published, in one and a half volumes, the names of each of her Civil War sailors, but has not distinguished Negro from white.[3] Finally, while Congress, on February 25, 1903, authorized the publication of the complete roster of members of the Union and Confederate Armies, it did not authorize such a roster for the Navies.[4]

Still an awareness of the importance that maritime pursuits have always had in the life of the American Negro people might well lead one to expect that the story of his participation on the ships of the republic in the suppression of the slaveholders' uprising would be of sufficient interest and importance to repay overcoming these obstacles.

It is pertinent, at this point, to present, very briefly, some of the evidence establishing the close relationship that has existed, from earliest days, between the sea and the Negro.

In the seventeenth century Negroes, free and slave, were widely employed on privateers, trading vessels, and fishing boats,[5] while some of the most distinguished figures in Negro history during the following two centuries earned their livelihoods, at some point in their careers, by a maritime occupation.[6] Negroes were not uncommon in the Continental and state navies during the Revolution,[7] and they played a conspicuous part in the naval fighting of the War of 1812.[8] During that war and for several years thereafter, according to the testimony of a distinguished contemporary, Negroes formed from ten to twenty per cent of the crews, and Jim Crowism appears to have been notable by its absence. Thus, we learn that "The white and colored seamen messed together. . . . There seemed to be an entire absence of prejudice against the blacks as messmates among the crew."[9]

Available evidence makes it clear that in such cities as New York, Philadelphia, and New Orleans, and in such states as Connecticut, Virginia, and North Carolina, marine pursuits formed one of the most important types of employment for the Negro throughout the pre-Civil War period.[10] Indicative, too, is the fierce opposition displayed by northern states, and many southern merchants as well, to the enactment, following periods of acute slave unrest, of special police and tax regulations for ships carrying Negroes as crew members.[11]

Two opinions of attorneys general of the United States are relevant in presenting the seafaring background of the American Negro. In 1821 the collector of customs at Norfolk, Virginia, was faced with the problem of deciding whether or not a free Negro was qualified to command an American merchant vessel in view of the fact that the citizenship of a Negro was questionable. He requested a decision from his chief, the Secretary of the Treasury, who, in turn, asked for an opinion from William Wirt, the Attorney General. The latter decided that, "Upon the whole, I am of the opinion that free persons of color in Virginia are not citizens of the United States, within the intent and meaning of the acts regulating foreign and coasting trade, so as to be qualified to command vessels."[12]

An almost identical case reached the same office over forty years later, but changed times evoked a different opinion. Salmon P. Chase informed Lincoln's Attorney General, Edward Bates, that the schooner Elizabeth and Margaret, of New Brunswick, is detained by the revenue cutter Tiger, at South Amboy, New Jersey, because commanded by a "colored man," and so by a person not a citizen of the United States. *As colored masters are numerous in our coasting trade* [my emphasis—*H. A.*] I submit, for your opinion, . . . are *colored men citizens* of the United States, and therefore competent, according to the acts of Congress to command American vessels?

In this instance the Attorney General was of the opinion that free Negroes born in the United States are citizens thereof and "are competent, according to the Acts of Congress, to be masters of vessels engaged in the coasting trade."[13]

Additional data are available providing information on the Negro in the American Navy during the years from the termination of the War of 1812 to the commencement of the Civil War. First, the United States specifically provided for the enlistment of free Negroes in the Navy by an Act of March 3, 1813. The relevant paragraph of this act reads as follows:

That from and after the termination of the war in which the United States are now engaged with Great Britain, it shall not be lawful to employ on board any of the public or private vessels of the United States any person or persons except citizens of the United States, or persons of colour, natives of the United States.[14]

That Negroes took advantage of this enactment is apparent from the following letter written in 1839 by Acting Secretary of the Navy, Isaac Chauncey, to the Commander of the Boston Naval Office, John Downs:

Frequent complaint having been made of the number of *Blacks* and other colored persons entered at some of the recruiting stations, and the consequent undue proportion of such persons transferred to sea-going vessels it is deemed proper to call your attention to the subject and to request that you will direct the recruiting officer at the station under your command, in future, not to enter a greater proportion of free colored persons than five per cent of the whole number of white persons entered by him weekly or monthly, and in no instance and under no circumstances to enter a slave.[15]

The 5 per cent ratio appears to have been adhered to generally thereafter. Thus, when, in 1842, Congress, troubled by strained relations with Great Britain, asked the Secretary of the Navy for a report on the number of Negroes—free and slave—enlisted in the service, he replied that no slaves were enlisted in the Navy, and that since Negroes were not entered separately in the records, precise figures could not be given. He went on to say, however, that a naval regulation forbade over one-twentieth part of the crew of any ship to be Negro, and that, "It is believed that the number is generally very far within this proportion."[16]

In addition to the fact that Negroes traditionally had followed the sea, and that they had been, for generations, members of the navy, there were other forces that led many to join those already in this service during the Civil War.

In the first place, Negroes were not allowed to enlist in the Union Army until the latter part of 1862,[17] so that the only way free Negroes could get into the fight against the slaveholder was to join the navy. Secondly, fugitive slaves were enlisted by the navy many months before the army allowed any Negroes to join.

This latter action was forced by the fugitives themselves who, from the very start of hostilities, flocked in large numbers to the Federal vessels. Thus, Commander Glisson, of the *Mount Vernon,* patrolling Virginia waters, informed his superior, in July 1861, that contrabands were arriving daily, were refusing to leave, bore valuable information and were capable of performing useful work. He had provided them with rations on his own responsibility but his supplies would soon be exhausted. What was he to do?

Flag-Officer Stringham, commanding the Atlantic Blockade Squadron, sent these reports to Gideon Welles, Secretary of the Navy, adding his opinion that, "If negroes are to be used in this contest, I have no hesitation in saying they should be used to preserve the Government, and not to destroy it." He closed by putting the specific question: "These men are destitute; shall I ration them?" and by suggesting, "They may be serviceable on board our storeships."[18]

The Naval Secretary replied that while it was not the

> policy of the Government to invite or encourage this class of desertions . . . yet under the circumstances, no other cause than that pursued

by Commander Glisson could be adopted without violating every principle of humanity. To return them would be impolitic as well as cruel, and as you remark, "they may be made serviceable on board our storeships," you will do well to employ them.[19]

The flood tide continued and grew, however, and the expedient mentioned by Welles was not enough. In August came report after report of this:

. . . a small open boat [with five Negroes in it] came alongside mine demanding food and protection . . . discovered an open boat containing four negroes, with a white flag flying on the staff, and pulling for the ship. I took them on board; found them intelligent; they gave me useful information; and one of them informed me he had been as pilot to the steam tug. . . . We now have sixteen negroes on board this vessel; who are consuming our provisions and water faster than I think is desirable . . . four fine-looking negroes, contraband of war, have just arrived. . . .[20]

So it came about that on September 20, 1861, the Secretary of the Navy declared:

The Department finds it necessary to adopt a regulation with respect to the large and increasing number of persons of color, commonly known as contraband, now subsisted at the navy yard and on board ships of war.

These can neither be expelled from the service to which they have resorted, nor can they be maintained unemployed, and it is not proper that they should be compelled to render necessary and regular services without a stated compensation. You are therefore authorized, when their services can be made useful, to enlist them for the naval service, under the same forms and regulations as apply to other enlistments. They will be allowed, however, no higher rating than "boys," at a compensation of $10 per month and one ration a day.[21]

That these conditions would seem attractive to the Negro as compared to the offers of the army will appear when note is taken of the actions in this regard, and at about this period, by the headquarters of the Department of Virginia. That Department, in October, 1861, ordered that all contrabands employed as servants by officers or others were to receive their subsistence plus $8 per month ($4 for women), and that all other Negroes "under the protection of the troops," not employed as servants, were to "be immediately put to work, in either the engineer's or quartermaster's departments." No wage scale was established for the latter for two weeks, after which it was announced that boys (from 12-18 years) and infirm men were to receive $5 per month, and able-bodied men $10 plus rations. The former, however, were to receive for themselves, in actual cash, one dollar a month, the latter two dollars, while the remainder was to revert —if the laborers maintained "good behavior"—to the quartermaster's department to pay for clothing and to help support women, children and the disabled.[22]

It is no wonder, then, as an official army investigating commission reported in March, 1862, that:

> A considerable number [of Negroes] have taken service in the navy. . . . Service in the navy is decidedly popular with them. The navy rates them as boys; they get $10 a month, and are entitled to all the privileges of ships' crews, and besides, have absolute control of the earnings of their own labor, which must operate as a powerful incentive to prefer the sea to the land service, when in the latter only $2 per month is the amount they realize.[23]

The navy suffered, too, throughout the war from a chronic and serious shortage of manpower. This was due to several factors in addition to the enormous expansion of that arm from a total of seventy-six vessels in March, 1861, to six hundred and seventy-one vessels in December, 1864.[24]

Among the factors were these: enlistment in the navy, unlike that in the army, carried no bounty payment; the draft made men subject to army, but not to navy, service; and men serving in the navy were not credited to their community or state draft quotas, thus creating a serious attitude against enlistment therein.[25] Since Negroes did not receive bounties for army enlistment (with rare, minor, and local exceptions), and were not subject to the draft until the latter part of the war, these regulations adversely affected the readiness of whites to join but not that of Negroes.

These conditions, by accentuating the manpower shortage, forced the navy to encourage the enlistment of Negroes, and probably accounted for, in part, the relatively favorable conditions facing the Negro in that service. This in turn exerted influence in causing Negroes to seek enlistment in that branch.

Indeed, the army at the urgent request of the navy turned over to the latter a considerable number of Negroes. As early as the summer of 1862 the Secretary of War ordered Major-General Dix at Fortress Monroe to "turn over to Flag Officer Goldsborough such contrabands as he may select for the naval service." Twice during the month of January, 1863, Welles appealed to Stanton to let him have up to four thousand physically fit fugitive slaves in the "interests of the public service," and it is certain that considerable numbers were transferred thereafter from the army to the navy.[26]

In addition, the navy made what may be called enlistment landings. Thus, for example, Lieutenant G. B. Balch, commanding the *U.S.S. Pocahontas,* reported to Rear-Admiral Du Pont from Georgetown, South Carolina, on July 24, 1862, that he had gone ashore with the ship's surgeon where "we had a gathering of the contrabands and Dr. Rhoades proceeded to select such as were fit for the general service, in obedience to your order of the 21st instant. He has selected some ninety. . . ."[27]

Certain it is that many Negroes did enlist in the Union Navy, and while precise figures are not available it is clear that they formed a much larger proportion of the navy's personnel than they did that of the army's. The task of approximating the number of Negroes serving in the United States Navy during the Civil War is lightened considerably since it once was tackled by the Superintendent of Naval War Records. This event, so fortunate for the historian, occurred because a Congressman from Maine, Charles Edgar Littlefield, was moved—for what precise reason is not known—to write, on March 24, 1902, the following note to John D. Long, Secretary of the Navy: "I respectfully request that you furnish me with the number of colored men who enlisted in the Navy in the war of Rebellion, 1861-1865, and oblige."

On April 2, 1902, the Secretary replied. He informed Mr. Littlefield that his request had been referred to the Bureau of Navigation which reported no information on the subject, but the Superintendent of the Naval War Records Office penned the following interesting and informative response:

There are no specific figures found in this office relating to the number of colored men enlisted in the United States Navy 1861-1865. The total number of enlistments in the Navy from March 4, 1861, to May 1, 1865, was 118,044. During the War of 1812 and up to 1860 the proportion of colored men in the ships' crews varied from one-fourth to one-sixth and one-eighth of the total crew. During the Civil War the negro was enlisted in the squadrons for one year. The regular enlistments at Navy Yards were for three years. In the absence of specific data it is suggested that as several vessels report during the Civil War having a crew of one-fourth negroes that the actual number of enlistments must have been about one-fourth of the total number given above, or 29,511.[28]

As a rough check on the estimate just quoted, the muster rolls of three arbitrarily selected Civil War vessels were examined. These were the ship *New Hampshire* for June 7, 1864, the steamer *Argosy* for December 31, 1863, and the ram *Avenger* for October 1, 1864.[29] The results are tabulated as follows:

| | *Total crew* | *Negroes* |
|---|---|---|
| *New Hampshire* | 969 | 242 |
| *Argosy* | 66 | 35 |
| *Avenger* | 115 | 19 |
| Total | 1150 | 296 |
| Percentage Negroes | 26 | |

It will be observed that this offers a rather remarkable confirmation of the superintendent's estimate.

There is other evidence showing how numerous Negro sailors were. Thus, for example, the present writer checked the muster rolls of several vessels in addition to the three already cited and he has yet to find a vessel having *no* Negroes among her crew.[30]

On April 30, 1862, Naval Secretary Welles referred to "the large numbers of persons known as 'contrabands' flocking to the protection of the United States flag." He felt that this afforded "an opportunity to provide in every department of a ship, especially for boat's crews, acclimated labor." Flag officers were, therefore, "required to obtain the services of these persons for the country by enlisting them freely in the Navy, with their consent," rating them as "boys," and paying them from eight to ten dollars per month.[31]

Specific references to the frequent enlistment and use of contrabands, in addition to those already cited, recur. Thus, Welles ordered Commodore Charles Wilkes, commanding the James River Flotilla, in August, 1862, to retain his mortar vessels and to "fill up the crews with contrabands."[32] Negroes seem to have been particularly numerous aboard gunboats. Acting Rear Admiral Porter told a Lieutenant Bragg, for example, to fill up the complements of these vessels with contrabands, and occasionally one comes across reports of a gunboat such as the *Glide,* accidentally lost at Cairo in February, 1863, whose crew of thirty-eight contained thirty contrabands.[33]

In October, 1862, Porter informed Welles that four hundred sick crewmen had grievously accentuated his manpower shortage. He had "commenced substituting contrabands for firemen and coal-heavers, reducing the expenses in that way. I have so far only obtained forty, but have sent down the river to get enough for all the vessels here, and have ordered all commanders to use them hereafter in place of white men."[34]

Porter's action was adopted as a pattern by the Navy Department so that its head ordered Rear-Admiral Dahlgren "to enlist for service in the [South Atlantic Blockade] squadron as many able-bodied contrabands as you can, especially for firemen and coal-heavers."[35] At the same time Porter, himself, in a General Order, directed that, "Owing to the increasing sickness in the [Mississippi] squadron, and the scarcity of men" contrabands were to be used "to a greater extent than heretofore."[36]

Somewhat earlier the Navy Department had rescinded the regulation of April 30, 1862, and provided that contrabands might be shipped in an original rank as high as landsman (just above that of first-class boy), and that they might be promoted to coal-heavers, firemen, ordinary seamen and seamen, that is to all ranks short of petty officers.[37]

An idea of the results of such directives as those from Welles and Porter may be obtained from these words in a letter written by the latter to the Adjutant General of the army late in 1863: "All our firemen and coal heaver's [sic] are negroes, they soon learn the business, and are rated and receive pay accordingly. We have now about 814 contrabands performing the duty of coal heavers and firemen, and we have altogether (counting officer's [sic] servants, cooks &c) 1049. . . ."[38]

Negroes held all ranks in the navy, short of petty officer, while not a few occupied the technical position of pilot, normally equivalent, in many respects, to that of a commissioned officer.[39] It is noteworthy, too, that, though some reservations must be made, there was a relative absence of segregation and discrimination of Negroes in the Civil War Federal fleet.

The facts concerning positions held by Negro crew members of eight different vessels may be offered as indicative of conditions in this regard. Aboard these eight ships was a total of 364 Negroes of whom 44 were boys, 279 landsmen, four cooks, five stewards, 18 coal-heavers, one first-class fireman, one second-class fireman, five ordinary seamen, and seven seamen—a condition of affairs in fair accord with the general numerical proportion of these ratings in the Navy as a whole.[40]

In September, 1861, as has already been observed, it was ordered that while fugitive slaves might be enlisted, they were not to rank above first-class boys. This was amended in December, 1862, so that contrabands might be *shipped* in ranks up to and including landsman, and might then be promoted, aboard any particular vessel, to the rank of a seaman. Presumably these regulations governed the general practice, but that there were deviations and exceptions is demonstrable.

Thus, as early as January, 1862, a naval commander reported to (then) Flag Officer Du Pont, commanding the South Atlantic Blockade Squadron, that "I presume there will be no irregularity in shipping Isaac (as ordinary seaman), a colored refugee, or contraband, sent from U.S.S. *Savannah* on board on account of his knowledge of inlets along the coast; he is somewhat intelligent and a quiet man."[41] Again, the log of the U.S.S. *Black Hawk* for May 14, 1864, shows that two Negroes were then added to its crew, among whom was one "Taylor Cromwell (contraband) seaman," demonstrating that not all were shipped, *i.e.*, originally mustered into the crew of a particular vessel—as landsmen or lower.[42]

The use of contrabands as pilots was certainly not covered by Naval regulations, but it was, quite as certainly, commonly practiced. In 1863 a Rear-Admiral wrote to the Secretary of the Navy:

> I desire to add that I have also made use of the services of certain contraband pilots, and have authorized the payment to them sometimes of $30 and sometimes of $40 per month. May I hope that this course meets with the approval of the Department? They are skillful and competent.[43]

Note may be taken, too, of the two Negro pilots recorded as having been killed in action. One of these, unnamed, piloted the *Henry Andrew.* He took part in a landing in March, 1862, at New Smyrna, Florida, which ended disastrously with the ambushing and killing of most of the Union force. The Negro, wounded in the foot, was captured and hanged by the Confederate troops.[44] The other Negro pilot who died in action was William Ayler, of the *Coeur de Lion.* This occurred on April 17, 1863, while the vessel was engaging a Confederate battery in the Nansemond River, Virginia. A shell hit the pilot house, tore away Ayler's left leg, and he died a half hour later.[45]

There are several other references to Negro pilots in the Union fleet, though it is not clear that they were, in every case, contrabands. Some of these "employed in our gunboats on our Southern coast and off Nassau," were said, in the course of "boasting" by a prisoner of the Federals, to have betrayed important information.[46] A Union naval officer in reporting the successful accomplishment of a particular mission credited it, in large part, to information given him by the pilot of the *Paul Jones,* "a colored man and familiar with the country."[47] When the *Curlew* was assigned to survey work on the Tennessee River she was provided with two pilots, one white, and one "an old colored pilot." Of the latter Acting Rear Admiral S. P. Lee remarked: "You will please have [him] paid for his services." Finally, it may be observed that the *Dai Ching,* sunk by its own commander after being hopelessly disabled by artillery fire on the Combahee River, South Carolina, in January, 1865, was piloted by a Negro, Stephen Small.[48]

Some remarks and evidence concerning the treatment of Negro members of the Union Navy have already been offered. It is important, however, that this subject be examined in further detail. This writer has seen no evidence of any type of discrimination or segregation having been practiced upon the free Negro crewmen other than the fact that none appears to have risen above the rank of seaman, and that from about 1839 on a definite quota of five per cent for the Negro seems to have been maintained in recruiting. It appears that Negroes were messed and quartered in common with other sailors, that Negroes were frequently of superior rank to fellow crewmen of white complexion, and that even the records of the Navy Department, until the wholesale enlistment of contrabands, did not distinguish white from black.

With the enlistment of thousands of fugitive slaves a certain amount of discriminatory practice prevailed, but this was very much less sharp than that which generally prevailed in the army or in northern—not to speak of southern—civil society during the mid-nineteenth century. It is true that, by regulation, positions open to them were rather severely limited, though, even here, later provisions modified this, and, in any event, the regulations were not strictly enforced. It is also true that contrabands were employed, at times, in tasks normally required of men having a higher rating—and receiving higher pay—than that accorded them, and they were used, in disproportionate numbers, in particularly laborious, unhealthy, and dangerous work.

Moreover, certain officers, apparently more prejudiced than others, accentuated what discrimination did exist. David Dixon Porter is a good example of this type. His use of the expression "niggers" and the distinction he drew between "men" and "darkies" in written communications to a superior officer have already been cited.[49] Similarly, his instructions that contrabands were to receive no more than $9 per month, issued after the Navy Department had announced the policy of enlisting them with ratings up to landsmen (who were paid $12 per month), and in face of the fact that even first class boys received $10, would seem to have no other explanation than bigotry.[50]

Indeed, Porter, in his capacity as commander of the Mississippi Squadron, issued a general order instituting Jim Crowism. In July, 1863, he announced that "Owing to the increasing sickness in the squadron, and the scarcity of men, it becomes necessary for the efficiency of the vessels to use the contrabands to a greater extent than heretofore." He went on to remark that white men, when performing strenuous labor under a southern sun, seemed most prone to disease, and that, therefore, Negroes only were to be used under such conditions, with "every precaution being taken to keep them from being taken sick." They might be used "to defend the vessels" where a deficiency in the crew required. This policy, it was carefully explained, was "dictated by necessity," yet it was "believed that in cases of emergency the blacks will make efficient men." Porter announced that contrabands might be promoted to all ranks except that of petty officers and first-class firemen and seamen, the last two exceptions being contrary to Navy Department policy as enunciated by the secretary eight months earlier.

Moreover, said this remarkable order:

> Only clothes enough will be issued to them to make them comfortable until they are out of debt, and in all cases they must be kept distinct from the rest of the crew. They can be stationed at guns when vacancies exist, to pass shot and powder, handle handspikes, at train-tackles and side-tackles, pumps, and fire buckets; and can be exercised separately at great guns and small arms.

Porter ended this pronouncement by asserting that Negroes "are not naturally clean" and that, therefore, "great attention will be necessary" on the part of the officers to make and keep them so, and by remarking—rather late in the game—that, "The policy of the Government is to use the blacks, and every officer should do his utmost to carry this policy out."[51]

It was this same officer, as a Rear Admiral in command of the North Atlantic Blockade Squadron, who instructed one of his division commanders, late in November, 1864, to "issue an order to all the vessels of your command not to employ negroes as lookout, as they are not fit to [be] intrusted with such important duty. . . ."[52]

There is evidence, as might be expected, that other naval officers suffered from similar prejudices and in some cases there seems to have been greater eagerness among them to prevent what were referred to as "Negro excesses" than to defeat the rebels.[53]

One commodore informed a captain that conditions were "in a bad state at Ship Island [Mississippi] for the niggers have the upper hand" and the "poor whites" were suffering.[54] Revealing, too, was the report of one J. S. Watson to Porter to the effect that planters frequently complained to him of the "depredations" of Negroes, "such as killing their beeves and hogs." He asked what he was "authorized to do in such cases," though adding that he had "heretofore, when complaints have been made . . . taken on board the offenders and punished them by confinement in irons according to offense committed, and when released returned them to the place taken from." Porter's endorsement approved this procedure, declaring that "when the negroes commit these atrocities you must punish them."[55]

A year later four Union sailors were actually captured by Confederate forces at Lewisville, South Carolina, while trying to assist a planter "to restore order amongst the negroes."[56] Some evidence of an inferential nature bearing upon this same point appears in a "private and confidential" letter from Du Pont to the Assistant Secretary of the Navy in December, 1862, wherein occur these sentences: "I am working in all the contrabands I can. I am fortunate in having [Commander William] Reynolds on the *Vermont,* who is kind to them."[57]

How did the Negroes conduct themselves, or, better, how were they reported to have conducted themselves, in the Union naval service? The available evidence points clearly to a favorable reply. Indeed, this writer considers it a rather remarkable fact that he has been able to discover but two disparaging reports concerning the conduct of individual Negro sailors.

In one case, Acting Ensign M. E. Flanigan, reporting the capture of his ship, the gunboat *Petrel,* near Yazoo City, Mississippi, declared that "during the engagement the officers and men acted most gallantly with the exception of a few contrabands who were lately shipped." This, however, did not agree with the account given by the commander of the *Petrel,* in which all but two of his officers are condemned for cowardice, and mention is made of the fact that but ten of the crew were white, while "the rest were contrabands, and part of those were sick." No adverse comment as to their behavior is made.[58] The other instance, where a Negro pilot was found to have left his post under fire and so contributed to the loss of his vessel, the *Dai Ching,* has already been noticed.[59]

Favorable comments on the behavior of individuals or groups of Negroes are more numerous. One officer, reporting a successful raid upon a Confederate steamer, praised the conduct of his officers and men and added: "I was compelled by necessity to include five colored men in the party, and they behaved admirably under fire."[60]

A daring adventure culminating in the kidnapping of a postman together with much official and personal mail destined for Charleston, South Carolina, was accomplished by a white petty officer and two enlisted contrabands, with the aid of a third Negro who withdrew with the raiders and joined the Union fleet. The petty officer was promoted to the rank of Acting Ensign, while Flag Officer Du Pont remarked, "The two contrabands [never named] who went with him are also, I think, deserving of an advanced rating."[61]

There was but one Union sailor to survive and escape from the fierce hand-to-hand encounter that marked the surprise boarding and subsequent capture of the U.S.S. *Water Witch* in Ossabaw Sound, South Carolina, in June, 1864. This was a contraband named Peter McIntosh. According to the report of Admiral J. A. Dahlgren to the Secretary of the Navy it was his escape and the warnings he then gave that saved several other Federal vessels. The surgeon of the *Water Witch,* captured and later released, reported that a Negro landsman, Jeremiah Sills, who was killed in the battle, "fought most desperately, and this while men who despised him were cowering near, with idle cutlasses in the racks jogging their elbows."[62]

Pertinent, too, is the remark of the Army's Adjutant-General to the Secretary of War, early in 1863 when the army was considering the formation of Negro artillery units, that "The experience of the Navy is that the Blacks handle heavy guns well."[63]

Five Negro members of the Union Navy behaved with such outstanding gallantry that they were recommended for the nation's most coveted award, the Congressional Medal of Honor, and it is certain that at least four received this medal.

Commander William G. Temple, of the U.S.S. *Pontoosuc,* in a report to Rear-Admiral Porter, recommended that Clement Dees, a Negro of the rank of seaman, be awarded the Medal of Honor "for gallantry, skill, and coolness in action during the operations in and about Cape Fear river, which extended from December 24, 1864, to February 22, 1865, and which resulted in the capture of Fort Fisher and Wilmington."[64] The official record of recipients of the Congressional Medal of Honor, however, does not list Clement Dees, and so it must be assumed that either the record is in error, or that the recommendation was not approved.[65]

Aaron Anderson, Negro landsman of the *Wyandank,* was recommended for and awarded a Medal of Honor for bravery while serving with an expedition on Mattox Creek, Virginia, March 16-18, 1865. A launch under Acting Ensign Summers, whose "crew . . . were all black but two" was dispatched "with orders to clear that creek which [was done] most thoroughly; destroyed three schooners under a fire of musketry from 300 or 400 rebels, which fire in a few moments cut away half of his oars, piercing the launch in many places. . . ."[66]

A second Negro sailor to win the Medal was Robert Blake, listed only as "contraband," a member of the crew of the *Marblehead.* In the bitter engagement with Confederate batteries on Stono River, South Carolina, Christmas Day, 1863, Blake, "serving as a powder boy, displayed extraordinary courage, alacrity and intelligence in the discharge of his duty under trying circumstances and merited the admiration of all."[67]

John Lawson, Negro landsman aboard the flagship *Hartford,* in the battle of Mobile Bay, August 5, 1864, earned a Medal of Honor. To quote from the recommendation and citation:

> [He] was one of the six men stationed at the shell-whip on the berth deck. A shell killed or wounded the entire number. Lawson was wounded in the leg and thrown with great violence against the side of the ship; but as soon as he recovered himself, although begged to go below, he refused and went back to the shell-whip, where he remained during the action.[68]

Joachim Pease, Negro seaman aboard the *Kearsage,* earned his Medal of Honor on June 19, 1864, in the historic encounter that resulted in the destruction of the Confederate raider, *Alabama,* off Cherbourg, France. Captain Winslow of the *Kearsage,* in submitting Pease's name to the Secretary of the Navy for special attention, declared that he had "exhibited marked coolness and good conduct." His immediate superior officer, Acting Master Sumner, reported to the ship's Executive Officer, the day following the battle, that ". . . no one could be distinguished from another in courage or fortitude. . . . Among those showing still higher qualifications [was] Joachim Pease (colored seaman), loader of same [No. 1] gun. The conduct of the latter in battle fully sustained his reputation as one of the best men in the ship."[69]

At this point one may appropriately investigate the facts concerning combat casualties suffered by Negro members of the Union fleet.

The problem facing one trying to ascertain these facts is most difficult, and hope of a definitive answer is probably illusory. Once again, correspondence engendered by inquisitive folk offers some assistance.

Between 1900 and 1913 the Navy Department received letters from ten individuals asking for casualty figures. The most revealing reply was that signed by Secretary of the Navy Josephus Daniels. Mr. Daniels stated that the best official figures on casualties in the Union Navy showed a total of 3,220 killed, wounded, and missing. But this, he asserted was

> known to be a very low estimate. The total number of casualties reported after the attack on Fort Fisher was 93, but the actual number of killed, wounded, and missing was 393. The reported casualties in the Battle of Hampton Roads were 75, but 241 were killed on the *Congress* and *Cumberland* alone.[70]

On the basis of the data presented, it would appear to be safe to say that about one-fourth of the total *reported battle* casualties were suffered by Negroes, or that of the 3,220 men listed as killed, wounded, and missing, approximately 800 were Negroes.

Some details may be ascertained by a careful reading of the *Official Records of the Union and Confederate Navies,* supplemented by a study of the war year *Reports* of the Secretary of the Navy and the attached documents. These are presented in tabular form in the appendix.

It will be observed that, up to this point, mortality from disease, in the navy, has not been considered. No figure for this appears to be available, but it is practically certain that deaths from sickness far outnumbered those from shell and bullet in the navy as they did in the army. Carrying over the figures from the army, one sees that while about eleven thousand members of Negro regiments were killed *and* wounded, about thirty thousand died of disease. Thus, one has an approximate ratio between deaths from disease and *all* battle casualties of about three to one. Applying this ratio to the very approximate number of 800 battle casualties among Negroes in the Union Navy would lead to the belief that something like 2,400 Negro members of the Union Navy died of disease.

While the figures just cited are largely conjecture, there is no question whatsoever that disease was a most serious problem in the Navy.[71] Since Negroes were used, in large part, in the most dangerous and punishing types of work, and were particularly used to replace whites during the "sickly season," it may be believed that in the navy, as in the army, disease hit the Negro with greater severity than it did the white.

One may add, too, that not all the casualties incurred by Negroes in association with the navy befell those who were regularly enlisted. The deaths of others are reported from time to time, the most terrible instance being that which occurred aboard the transport, *Champion No. 3,* near the junction of the Cane and Red Rivers, on April 26, 1864. The vessel, loaded down with almost two hundred contrabands, men, women and children, while attempting to pass a Confederate fort, received a shell in the boiler, and in the ensuing explosion about one hundred and eighty-five Negroes were killed.[72]

Finally, it is to be noted that the murder of Negro naval personnel captured by the Confederacy was, as in the case of the soldier, not unknown. Thus, in March, 1862, Federal naval forces attempted a landing near New Smyrna, Florida, from the ships *Penguin* and *Henry Andrew.* Included in this landing party was the pilot of the latter ship, a Negro. He was wounded in the foot and captured in a battle that ensued when Confederate troops ambushed the invaders. Seven members of the Union force were killed in the fight, while the Negro was hanged.[73]

Another Negro, George Brimsmaid, landsman aboard the U.S. Brig *Perry,* served as the advance scout of a sixteen man reconnaissance party on Magnolia Beach, South Carolina, in December, 1863. All were captured, though one later escaped, but only fourteen prisoners survived, the other, Brimsmaid, being "officially unaccounted for," to quote a Confederate general's report. The official record flatly asserts that this Negro prisoner was hanged at Murrell's Inlet, on December 5, 1863.[74]

In June, 1864, the *Queen City* was captured. Some of the crew members perished and some escaped—including several Negroes—but among the prisoners were nine Negroes. According to the medical officer aboard the *Queen City*, a Confederate officer had remarked to him that "he supposed they [the Negro prisoners] would be treated as are the rest they had captured, kill them."[75] Generally, however, Negro naval prisoners seem to have been subjected to the same treatment as those of the Army—close confinement, hard labor, or sale into slavery.

The unique and inestimable value of the Negro to the Union navy, as to its army, was his acquaintance with the enemy and his terrain. It is impossible to study thousands of first-hand reports from army and navy officers—many of them far from sympathetic towards the Negro—without concluding that the greatest single source of military and naval intelligence, particularly on a tactical level, for the Federal government during the Civil War was the Negro. And knowing the crucial importance of information concerning the enemy for any successful military effort, these hundreds and thousands of willing and eager scouts, spies, guides, pilots, and informers, available only to the Union forces, constituted a major—albeit overlooked—source of superiority for the Union forces as opposed to their enemy.

Frequently Negroes, both enlisted and civilian, provided units of the Federal fleet with information (and at times personally guided those units) making possible the destruction or capture of valuable stores of sugar, rice, cotton, corn and salt.[76] Indeed, at times, the activities of Negroes were directly responsible for the destruction or capture of entire vessels.

Thus, in 1861, Commander Lockwood of the *Daylight*, in reporting to Flag Officer Stringham of the Atlantic Blockade Squadron the capture of a Confederate vessel in Virginia, explained that this was due to the intelligence brought him by "four fine-looking negroes—contraband of war. . . ."[77] In June, 1862, Lieutenant Braine, commanding the *Monticello,* off Wilmington, North Carolina, reported that a skiff with eight Negro men —fugitive slaves from South Carolina—had reached him. These Negroes told of two Confederate schooners being fitted to run the blockade and gave their precise location. As a result, Lieutenant Braine was ordered to attack and, if possible, capture these ships. Shortly thereafter this officer led an assaulting party which destroyed the vessels plus sixty bales of cotton and considerable quantities of turpentine and rosin.[78]

Interesting and relevant information is contained in the report of Acting Volunteer Lieutenant Couthoy, commanding the *Osage,* covering his activities from October 4 through October 8, 1863. The task of his ship was to patrol the Red River from Fort Adams to Ellis Cliffs. Lieutenant Couthoy learned from contrabands, on October 4, of river crossings being made by Confederate units. The information was specific enough to result in the capture of three ferries. The next day another fugitive arrived and informed the officer of another crossing point. Men dispatched to the point returned with several prisoners, while early on October 6, two Confederate soldiers were "brought in . . . by a party of contrabands who gave chase on their own account." Shortly thereafter Negroes told of the location of a steamer, and as a result twenty Federal sailors, with "Benjamin Williams, enlisted contraband, as guide" went to the designated spot. They found and destroyed not one but two steamers, as well as a skiff used for ferrying purposes, and captured eleven Confederate men and officers. Lieutenant Couthoy concluded: "Benjamin Williams, first-class boy, rendered important service as a guide. But for his intimate knowledge of all the short cuts to the Red River . . . the expedition would have proved a failure."[79]

On January 5, 1865, a fugitive slave came to the *Winnebago,* off Mobile Bay, and informed its commander of the location of several enemy sloops, plus valuable stores, all, according to the Negro, without armed guards. Lieutenant-Commander Kirkland promptly dispatched an expedition which returned with four captured vessels and much materiel, and reported that it had met no opposition.[80]

In discussing services rendered by Negroes resulting in the capture of entire vessels by the Union fleet mention must be made of the unique instance when Negroes personally delivered a Confederate steamer, the *Planter,* to blockading Federal ships.

This episode, of the fugitive *Planter* and his slave-capturers, which fired the imagination of the entire Union, occurred on May 13, 1862. On sunrise of that day Acting Volunteer Lieutenant J. F. Nickels, commanding the *Onward,* off Charleston, was startled to see "a steamer coming from the direction of Fort Sumter and steering directly" for his ship. He "immediately beat to quarters," sprang the ship around so as to bring her broadsides to bear, and was preparing to fire when he observed "that the steamer, now rapidly approaching, had a white flag set at the fore."[81]

Aboard were sixteen Negroes including eight men, five women, and three children, all slaves, and all acknowledging as their leader the man who had piloted the vessel to the Union fleet, Robert Smalls.[82] The *Planter,* a three hundred ton, side-wheel, wood-burning, very low draft, armed steamer was a dispatch and transportation vessel attached to the engineer department at Charleston, under Brigadier-General Ripley. It may well be believed that this officer was very much upset over the abduction of this ship especially since it followed by but a few days the disappearance of his barge which had also been brought to the blockading fleet by fugitive slaves. Adding to the general's chagrin was the fact that in delivering the *Planter* to his foe, the slaves also presented the latter with her own armament, a 32 pounder and a 24 pounder howitzer, a X inch Columbiad carriage, as well as four pieces of artillery which she was to have delivered that day to one of the forts of the city. The abduction had been long and carefully planned, the commencement coming at about 3 A.M. while the white officers were ashore. The vessel gave the proper signals while within earshot of land, and her approach at Fort Sumter was timed to coincide with that of the guard boat and so she was unchallenged.

Half the prize money of over nine thousand dollars was assigned, by Congressional act[83] to the Negroes responsible for "rescuing [the vessel] from the enemies of the Government." Robert Smalls was personally interrogated by Flag Officer

Du Pont who found him to be "superior to any [fugitive Negro] who has yet come into the lines, intelligent as many of them have been. His information has been most interesting, and portions of it of the utmost importance."

By direction of Du Pont, Smalls was employed as the pilot of the *Planter* during the four months it remained under Navy supervision,[84] and he took part with it in attacks upon Confederate positions.[85] Smalls is said to have served, thereafter, as a pilot aboard other vessels including the *Crusader, Huron, Paul Jones* and *Keokuk*.[86]

Quite fittingly and dramatically, Robert Smalls piloted the *Planter* into Charleston when that city fell in February, 1865, and he guided the ship into the city, with Henry Ward Beecher, William Lloyd Garrison, and George Thompson aboard her, when the flag of the United States was hoisted above Fort Sumter on April 15, 1865, the day Lincoln died.[87]

Information as to the location, strength, disposition, movements and activities of the enemy, both of his land and naval forces, were brought by Negroes in a constant stream to all echelons of the Union command.[88] And specific references recur as to how valuable such information was. It helped, for example, Union officers to be prepared beforehand for the actions of enemy infantry, artillery, and naval power, in ascertaining the depth of water, the existence of obstructions, the abandonment of towns or their reinforcement, as well as in obtaining specific data on enemy naval habits, schedules, and construction.[89] Indeed, at times, charts were changed, naval flotilla formations altered, areas entered, and assaults postponed on the basis, very largely, of data supplied by Negroes.[90]

The major expedition lasting from March 14 through March 27, 1863, and seeking an approach into Vicksburg from the rear in which General Grant and Admiral Porter personally participated, supported by General Sherman, was undertaken as a consequence of "information obtained from a negro." And Negroes were the eyes and ears of the *Louisville, Cincinnati, Carondelet, Mound City* and *Pittsburg,* plus four accompanying mortar vessels and four tugs while they pushed up Steele's Bayou and pressed through uncharted waters within enemy territory. They kept the commanders constantly informed of the location, strength, and activities of the enemy as well as of the terrain. Porter and Grant, upon reaching Rolling Ford, decided that enveloping Vicksburg from the rear was not practical and returned, but it is clear that neither the going nor the returning would have been possible without the intelligence provided by Negroes, both those who formed parts of the crews and those who flocked to the Yankees from within Mississippi's heart.[91]

It is to be noted that attempts were made by the Navy to systematize the obtaining of information from Negroes within Confederate areas. That this was, at times, accomplished may be seen from the fact that the commanding officer of one vessel, the *Stepping Stones,* while patrolling the Nansemond River, Virginia, regularly contacted, at night, by prearranged signals, certain free Negroes. A boat from the *Stepping Stones* would pull onto shore at a designated time and place, take aboard fugitive slaves, and carry back the latest information as to conditions and affairs within the zone of the enemy.[92]

The absence in historical literature of any consideration of the role of Negroes in the Union Navy is a serious failing. Negroes constituted some 25 per cent of the total personnel; they performed all duties required of sailors aboard mid-nineteenth century men-of-war, they conducted themselves well, and, at times, with conspicuous gallantry, under fire, and their contribution, particularly in terms of information concerning the enemy's potential, disposition, and terrain was invaluable. The role of the Federal fleet in determining the outcome of the Civil War long has been recognized as decisive. The role of the Negro members of that fleet was of primary importance.

# ORGANIZATIONAL ACTIVITIES OF SOUTHERN NEGROES, 1865

Very few studies have been made of the activities of the Negro people immediately following the Civil War.[1] Indeed, available literature forces the investigator to ask himself: Was the Southern Negro, in the midst of a situation whose revolutionary quality consisted in his own altered status, passive and inarticulate?

We shall attempt an answer to this question by narrating the facts concerning organized political and economic activities carried on by Southern Negroes during the single year, 1865.[2] In this way may be discovered something of their demands and aspirations, enunciated when gun-barrels had hardly cooled, and when the Bourbon, though defeated in battle, still retained control over what local political power then existed.

It will be well to begin this study by establishing the last point, that is, demonstrating the fact of the continuing political domination of the South by the former slaveholders in the immediately post-bellum months, the months of the Johnson-backed state governments.

This may be done most expeditiously by selecting one state as fairly typical of the entire South and by analyzing briefly its Johnsonian provisional government. For this purpose South Carolina will be used.

One month after the surrender of all Confederate forces, in June, 1865, President Johnson appointed Benjamin F. Perry, strongly pro-slavery pre-Civil War Unionist, who had held office under the Confederacy, to the position of Provisional Governor of South Carolina.

One of Governor Perry's first acts was to reinstate in public office those who had held such positions prior to May, 1865. He then conferred the suffrage upon loyal citizens who had been voters before secession, and called upon these people to elect delegates to a Constitutional Convention to be held in September, 1865.

The composition of this convention, which met in Columbia on the thirteenth, was what might be expected from such an electorate. Among the delegates were J. L. Orr, a former Confederate Senator and colonel, F. W. Pickens, the first Confederate governor of the state, S. McGowan, a Confederate major-general, and several additional generals and other high-ranking officers of the now defunct Confederate Army. In addition, among the approximately one hundred delegates, were twelve former members of the secession convention, including D. L. Wardlow who had been its president, and J. A. Inglis who had introduced therein the secession motion.[3] Such were the personnel designated, ostensibly, to remake the social order of South Carolina!

The constitution resulting from the deliberations of such individuals (which, incidentally, was not submitted to the people for ratification) dealt with the Negro in a manner that must have surprised nobody, *i.e.*, it relegated him to the lowest rung of a carefully devised system of exploitation. Governor Perry in his opening address before this convention had set the keynote by asserting, ". . . this is a white man's government, and intended for white men only. . . . The Supreme Court of the United States has decided that the Negro is not an American citizen under the Federal Constitution."[4] In the apt words of the New York *Tribune* (October 17, 1865): "Rebellion, its birthplace in Charleston, having failed to save their cause, they have carried to Columbia and seek to preserve it there."

It was a committee of this convention which drafted the notorious "Black Code" as a guide for the members of the next legislative assembly. And that legislature, composed of the members who had sat throughout the Civil War, met from October 25 to November 13, 1865, and promptly enacted that instrument of discrimination, subjugation, and attempted degradation.[5]

This, in broadest outline, was the political situation in South Carolina in 1865, and conditions, while not identical, were similar throughout the South. Immense and disheartening obstacles they were, certainly, in the path of complete Negro liberation, but a tremendous fact remained—the fact of the physical destruction of chattel slavery. With the determination and courage that have marked the American Negro, he acted, and some of the record of this remains.

On January 9, a numerously attended convention of Negroes assembled in New Orleans and adopted resolutions recommending co-operative buying and selling on the part of their newly liberated brothers as well as special assistance for the Negro veteran.[6] On the same day Negroes of Nashville petitioned the Tennessee (loyal element) Constitutional Convention, which had assembled on the eighth, for the right to vote and for protection in the courts, and urged that slavery be expressly forbidden in the new constitution. In the weeks that followed, the Houses of the reorganized Tennessee government were appealed to several times by Negroes for the rights of citizenship, but these were denied. In April, therefore, Negroes from Nashville, Memphis, and Knoxville issued a call for a statewide convention, which was held that summer.[7]

In February there began a series of remarkable meetings among the Negroes of Norfolk, Virginia. This was precipitated by an attempt on the part of certain white Unionists, in January, to oust the military and restore civilian rule to the city. The Negroes who, under General Butler, had been, as they declared, "protected in the full enjoyment of the rights and liberties of loyal men," did not object to civil rule, per se, but did object to the fact that this proposed civil rule "contemplated no representation of their rights and interests."

A committee of Negroes was formed at once and, at its call, a mass meeting was held at Mechanics' Hall on February 27, with H. F. Trimble as chairman and George W. Cook, secretary. Resolutions were adopted protesting against the restoration of civil rule on other than "a loyal and equal basis" and copies were sent to President Lincoln as well as to local military commanders.

During the following weeks further organizational efforts went forward among the Norfolk Negroes resulting, on April 4, in the holding of another mass meeting, at the same hall, with the Rev. William I. Hodges[8] in the chair. At this meeting was formed the Colored Monitor Union Club, the primary objects of which were, as stated in its constitution:

to promote union and harmony among the colored portion of this community, and to enlighten each other on the important subject of the right of *universal* suffrage to *all* loyal men, without distinction of color, and to memorialize the Congress of the United States to allow the *colored* citizens the *equal* right of franchise with other citizens; to call frequent meetings, and procure suitable speakers for the same; to form auxiliary clubs throughout the Eastern District of Virginia, to give publicity to our views all over the country, and to assist the present administration in putting down the enemies of the government, and to protect, strengthen, and defend all friends of the Union.

Two days later the organization of this club was completed with the election of officers and thereafter at regular and frequent intervals—as on April 25, May 2, and May 16—it held "large and enthusiastic meetings . . . at which much information was disseminated, respecting the movement in behalf of negro suffrage." In addition, on May 11, a mass meeting of the Negroes of Norfolk, including many not members of the Union Club, was held in a Negro Baptist Church. The building was jammed, and the participants elected as presiding officer Dr. Thomas Bayne, a dentist, itinerant preacher, and one-time fugitive slave.[9] Here nine resolutions were adopted unanimously and they merit quotation in full:

1st. *Resolved,* That the rights and interests of the colored citizens of Virginia are more directly, immediately and deeply affected in the restoration of the State to the Federal Union than any other class of citizens; and hence, that we have peculiar claims to be heard in regard to the question of its reconstruction, and that we cannot keep silence without dereliction of duty to ourselves, to our country, and to our God.

2nd. *Resolved,* That personal servitude having been abolished in Virginia, it behooves us, and is demanded of us, by every consideration of right and duty, to speak and act as freemen, and as such to claim and insist upon equality before the law, and equal rights of suffrage at the ballot-box.

3rd. *Resolved,* That it is a wretched policy and most unwise statesmanship that would withhold from the laboring population of the country any of the rights of citizenship essential to their well-being and to their advancement and improvement as citizens.

4th. *Resolved,* That invidious political or legal distinctions, on account of color merely, if acquiesced in, or voluntarily submitted to, is inconsistent with our own self-respect, or the respect of others, placing us at great disadvantages, and seriously retards our advancement or progress in improvement, and that the removal of such disabilities and distinctions are alike demanded by sound political economy, by patriotism, humanity and religion.

5th. *Resolved,* That we will prove ourselves worthy of the elective franchise, by insisting upon it as a right, by not tamely submitting to its deprivation, by never abusing it by voting the State out of the Union, and never using it for purposes of rebellion, treason or oppression.

6th. *Resolved,* That the safety of all loyal men, black and white, in the midst of the recently slaveholding States, requires that all loyal men, black or white, should have equal political and civil rights, and that this is a necessity as a protection against the votes of secessionists and disloyal men.

7th. *Resolved,* That traitors shall not dictate or prescribe to us the terms or conditions of our citizenship, so help us God.

8th. *Resolved,* That as far as in us lies, we will not patronize or hold business relations with those who deny to us our equal rights.

9th. *Resolved,* That we recommend that a Delegate Convention be held for the purpose of carrying out the foregoing objects and designs, and that, this meeting appoint a committee of seven to aid in getting up such Convention.

Meanwhile, in the month of May, President Johnson recognized the Alexandria Unionist government of Francis H. Pierpont as the official government of Virginia. Upon his inauguration, a call was issued for an election to the state assembly, to be held on May 25, with Negroes barred from the voting.

As a result, a proposal was immediately made in Norfolk, by a number of white men, for a "mass meeting of *all* loyal citizens without distinction of birth, or color, to be held at the City Hall, May the 23rd, 1865, to take such action as might be deemed desirable in view of the coming elections." The notice was extremely short, but so great was the political interest of the people, particularly the Negro people, that upon the appointed time about one hundred and fifty whites and two thousand Negroes gathered at Norfolk's City Hall.

The elected chairman was a radical white lawyer, Calvin Pepper.[10] The assembled Negro and white people unanimously adopted a series of resolutions recommended to them by a popularly chosen committee of two white and five Negro men. These resolutions demanded that the state government be reorganized on the basis of suffrage to all loyal citizens, "without distinction of birth, sect, creed, or color," urged Negroes to vote on May 25, regardless of the lily-white law and declared that, "in view of the exigencies of the times and the necessity that all men elected to state offices should be men of tried fidelity to the Union and of liberal sentiments, and that the candidates now before the public are in no way representative of the loyal citizens of Norfolk, but only of themselves," they urged the election of their own slate. This slate consisted of D. W. Todd, Sr., for the Senate, and Francis De Cordy and James H. Hall for the House—all white men.

These resolutions were forwarded to President Johnson and to radical Republican Congressmen, and appeared in the local paper as well as in the more progressive press of the nation generally. The next day another well-attended meeting was held at which the candidates were searchingly questioned as to their attitude toward enfranchising the Negro, and all but De Cordy pledged themselves to vote for universal manhood suffrage if elected.

On the morrow the election was held. The Negroes had agreed to meet at the Bute Street African Methodist Church and there collectively to decide as to the mechanics of their first attempt at voting. By eight in the morning of this May 25, over five hundred Negro men were present, and before nightfall the number was doubled. Again officers were elected, with the Rev. J. M. Brown as chairman and Dr. Thomas Bayne as secretary.

A committee of five was appointed at once which commenced preparations for voting by dividing the people present into four bodies in accordance with the wards in which they resided. Originally, the general feeling was that the Negroes so organized ought to proceed immediately, in a body, to the polls and attempt to vote, but, fearing "lest the obstruction to the polling, caused by the presence of such large bodies of men at the polling place, should afford a pretext for disturbance, it was decided to appoint four committees to proceed to the polling places in each ward, and ascertain, by tending their own individual votes, whether the votes of colored citizens would be received, either on the polling book, or, if not, on the separate list provided by law for contested or disputed votes."[11]

While the committees were on their errand, the Negroes prayed. Soon the men returned and it was learned that the officials of the first, third, and fourth wards had refused absolutely to receive the votes of Negroes, while those of the second ward said they might register their votes on the separate list only. The Negroes of the second ward then proceeded, ten at a time, to their polling place and so voted, while the ballots of the other Negroes were received, by name, by the committees themselves for each of the other three wards. This consumed the entire day, but the action was taken solemnly and "with the most perfect order and decorum." The results showed a solid vote of 1066 (712 at the Church and 354 at the polling place) for the ticket of Todd, De Cordy, and Hall.[12]

The Negroes adjourned for a late meal and returned that same evening. The result of the voting was then put into affidavit form and it was decided to present these to the Virginia legislature and contest the election. Funds were gathered making possible the publication of five thousand copies of a pamphlet detailing the foregoing facts.[13]

On June 5 these indefatigable Norfolk Negroes assembled again in a mass meeting, this one held in the Catherine Street Baptist Church. An elected committee, consisting of Dr. Thomas Bayne, Joseph T. Wilson, the Rev. Henry Highland Garnet, William Keeling, the Rev. J. M. Brown, the Rev. Thomas Henson, Thomas F. Paige, Jr., and George W. Cook, drafted an "Address from the Colored Citizens of Norfolk, Virginia, to the People of the United States." This document is of intense interest and of a most revealing nature.

The "Address" asserted as its purposes that of placing before the American people "the present position of the colored population of the Southern States generally" and of pressing "their claim for equal suffrage in particular." The Negro people demanded "the full enjoyment of those privileges of full citizenship," not only because these adhered to them as their "undoubted right," but also because they were "indispensable to that elevation and prosperity of our people which must be the desire of every patriot."

America was not a land belonging exclusively to its white inhabitants, the Address went on, for the Negro, too, had labored and fought here. The existing situation was intolerable. Recently, in Richmond, a secessionist, elected mayor, had thrown eight hundred Negroes into jail; in Portsmouth a mayor had just been elected on a white supremacy ticket; everywhere planters were organizing, offering a maximum of $60 per year as wages, and not paying even this; Negroes were being beaten and some killed for resisting such forced labor. Even in Norfolk, with a Union mayor, "some of our white friends who have nobly distinguished themselves by their efforts in our behalf, have been threatened with arrest."

We do not want the interminable military occupation of our Southland, said these Negroes, and if we have our rights, complete and unfettered, this will not be needed. But remember, the Address warned, if this is not done and the South is abandoned to the former slaveholders, not only the Negro but the entire nation suffers. For while the Negro will not vote, he will be counted towards the South's representation in Congress, and this will mean an even more numerous southern delegation than before the war. And leaving this canker of inequality in your midst means a lack of internal security for it creates four and a half million potential, if not actual, enemies.

Moreover, we are men, and by all the assertions you have made and all the doctrines you have ostensibly embraced you must treat us as men. We are not stupid, we are not lazy, and we do know what freedom means. Freedom means honest work at honest wages.

To their fellow Negroes, the Address said: Be not supine, be up and active. So very much depends upon ourselves. In addition to fighting for our political rights, we must battle for the land and for protection as workingmen. Specifically, said this remarkable document:

> Everywhere in Virginia, and doubtless in all other States, your late owners are forming Labor Associations, for the purpose of fixing and maintaining, without the least reference to your wishes or wants, the prices to be paid for your labor; and we say to you, "Go and do likewise." Let Labor Associations be at once formed among the colored people throughout the length and breadth of the United States, having

for their object the protection of the colored laborer, by regulating fairly the price of labor; by affording facilities for obtaining employment by a system of registration; and last, though by no means least, by undertaking, on behalf of the colored laborer, to enforce legally the fulfillment of all contracts made with him.

And as to the land, this Address declared:

The surest guarantee for the independence and ultimate elevation of the colored people will be found in their becoming the owners of the soil on which they live and labor. To this end, let them form Land Associations, in which, by the regular payment of small instalments, a fund may be created for the purchase, at all land sales, of land on behalf of any investing member, in the name of the Association, the Association holding a mortgage on the land until, by the continued payment of a regular subscription, the sum advanced by the Association and the interest upon it are paid off, when the occupier gets a clear title.[14]

While these events were occurring in Norfolk, southern Negroes in other areas were by no means inactive. In the spring, Georgia Negroes were circulating, signing, and forwarding to President Johnson a petition reading: "We, the undersigned, Colored Citizens of the State of Georgia, respectfully represent, that we are loyal, always have been loyal, and always will remain loyal; and, in order to make our loyalty most effective in the service of the Government, we humbly petition to be allowed to exercise the right of suffrage."[15] In June, a committee of five Savannah Negroes transmitted a petition, signed by three hundred and fifty of their fellows praying for the suffrage, to Senator Charles Sumner, with the request that he send it on to the President.[16]

In May, a petition to the President of similar purport, but greater length, was "being extensively circulated" in North Carolina. The Negroes addressed Andrew Johnson, himself a North Carolinian, with "great confidence" for they felt "that some of his [Lincoln's] great and good spirit lingers to bless his successor." While in many respects poor, still they felt themselves "rich in the possession of liberty" and proud to "have had the privilege of fighting for our country." They stood ready to offer their blood for her in the future and felt impelled "to say that such blood as that shed at Fort Wagner and Port Hudson is not altogether unworthy of such service." The petition prayed for "the privilege of voting." It seemed clear to these Negroes that men who were "willing on the field of danger to carry the Republic's muskets, in the days of Peace ought to be permitted to carry its ballots." They could see no justice in "denying the elective franchise to men who have been fighting for the country, while it is freely given to men who have just returned from 4 years fighting against it." The petition ended by reminding the President that free Negroes had voted in North Carolina as late as 1835, and repeating that what was wanted and needed now was the enfranchisement "of all loyal men without regard to color."[17] Accompanying this petition campaign, the Negroes of North Carolina held many meetings from May through September at which programs were formulated and delegates elected to a projected Negro State Convention, which met in Raleigh that fall.

On the last day of May, the Negroes of Petersburg, Virginia, held a mass meeting at the Union Street Methodist Church, discussed their needs and appointed a committee of nine to draft resolutions for presentation at a meeting to be held one week later. On June 6 the second gathering occurred, and resolutions were read and unanimously adopted as representing the views of the resident Negroes.[18]

In a preamble these men declared that since the slaveholders' rebellion had been crushed and "the supremacy of the United States Government has been maintained by the combined forces of the black and white soldiers on many bloody battlefields," therefore it was *"Resolved,* That we, the colored citizens of Petersburg, Virginia, and true and loyal citizens of the United States of America, claim, as an unqualified right, the privilege of setting forth respectfully our grievances and demanding an equality of rights under the law."

At Milliken's Bend, Port Hudson, Olustee, Fort Wagner, Petersburg and Richmond, "we have," said these Negroes, "vindicated our rights, and this was but a continuation of the services rendered the republic by our ancestors at Valley Forge and at New Orleans." On no proper ground could their disfranchisement because of color be sustained, and they demanded the "right to the ballot-box . . . the right of representation."

All and sundry were assured that "the allegation made against us that we understand Freedom to mean idleness and indolence" was worthy of but "scorn and contempt." No, freedom meant the "enjoyment of the legitimate fruits" of industry and upon that they would insist. Feelings of resentment were held against no man, and they would, concluded the resolutions, "treat all persons with kindness and respect who shall treat us likewise."[19]

Note has already been taken that all was not well with the Negroes of Richmond, and that a former ardent secessionist had been elected mayor of their city. Those Negroes by no means remained passive in the face of this; indeed, the fact is that they forced the mayor's removal from office.

The sequence of events was as follows: During the first week in June, the man who had been Mayor of Richmond throughout the course of the Civil War was returned to that office together with the entire old police force. The Army's Provost-Marshal for the area, General Patrick, ordered the institution of a pass system, and every Negro was required to have on his person, at all times, such a pass signed by his employer, or otherwise to be liable to seizure and forced labor. And to cap the series of indignities, the area commander, General Gregg, issued an order declaring that Negroes were to "have all the rights at present that free people of color have heretofore had in Virginia, and no more"; that is to say, this was an order reinstituting all the severe disabilities under which free Negroes had suffered during the slave era. One of the results of these actions was the closing of the recently established schools for Negroes.

On June 7 many Negroes of Richmond met, despite the police terror, and drew up "An Appeal from the Richmond Negroes for Protection" which was forwarded to Horace Greeley and printed by him in full in his New York *Tribune* five days later. This document reported many of the above-mentioned facts and demanded the end of police brutality.[20]

On June 8 several Negroes met at the home of one Peter Matthews "for the purpose of taking some action in relation to the persecutions of the colored people by the military and police authorities." A committee of four, consisting of Fields Cook, Peter Woolfolk, Nelson Hamilton, and Walter Snead, was appointed in order to investigate specific complaints. For two days these four men so occupied themselves, and on the evening of June 10, at another meeting, they presented a detailed report. Here another committee was appointed and charged by the assemblage with the responsibility of preparing a full statement of the facts and presenting this statement, in the form of an address, to the President of the United States.

That same evening this committee, consisting of the four Negroes last enumerated plus Richard Wells, William Williamson, and T. Morris Chester (Chester was a Negro visiting Richmond in his capacity as a correspondent for the Philadelphia *Press,* and had himself met rough handling from the police), drew up a statement as directed, and in the morning of June 16, they were received by President Johnson. By this time, and due to this pressure, the Governor of Virginia had already ordered the removal of the offensive Mayor.

The delegation informed the President that they represented "a population of more than 20,000 colored people, including Richmond and Manchester," and that while most of them were poor, there nevertheless were "at least 2,000 men who are worth from $200 to $500; 200 who have property valued at $1,000 to $5,000, and a number who are worth from $5,000 to $20,000." None was in the alms-house "and when we were slaves the aged and infirm who were turned away from the homes of hard masters, who had been enriched by their toil, our benevolent societies supported while they lived, and buried when they died." While during slavery education was legally forbidden us, nevertheless, "3,000 of us can read, and at least 2,000 can read and write, and a large number of us are engaged in useful and profitable employment on our own account."

During the slaveholders' rebellion we prayed for the Union and we gave "aid and comfort to the soldiers of Freedom (for which several of our people, of both sexes, have been severely punished by stripes and imprisonment). We have been their pilots and their scouts and have safely conducted them through many perilous adventures, while hard-fought battles and bloody fields have fully established the indomitable bravery, the loyalty and the heroic patriotism of our race." And what do we find? The old system of laws reinstituted, the Confederate mayor and the police force of Secessia back in office, a pass system initiated, political power in the hands of the former masters, violence, terror, peonage everywhere. We ask, Mr. President, said these

Negroes, "your protection, and upon the loyalty of our hearts and the power of our arms you may ever rely with unbounded confidence." In conclusion, they begged to be permitted to "respectfully remind your Excellency of that sublime motto once inscribed over the portals of an Egyptian temple: *Know all ye who exercise power, that God hates injustice!*"

In the course of the conference the President was able to announce the receipt of a dispatch stating that the odious pass system had been abolished and the Negro schools reopened, while he assured the delegation that an investigation, supervised by Major-General Oliver O. Howard, was then in progress.[21]

The fact is that on June 23 the newly-appointed commander of the Department of Virginia, Major-General Terry, issued a general order providing for the termination of all special laws applicable only to Negroes,[22] while on October 25, the Richmond City Council adopted "An Ordinance Repealing all Ordinances or parts of Ordinances Relating to Negroes or Negro Slaves."[23]

The Negroes of Vicksburg, Mississippi, held a mass meeting on June 19, with a soldier, Jacob Richardson of the 49th United States Colored Infantry, presiding "to discuss the question of civil rights of the colored citizens of Mississippi, and take measures to secure them." A committee of five was selected to draft appropriate resolutions, and while this was being done, the Reverend G. G. Edwards spoke on the needs of the Negro soldier and civilian. The resolutions were then reported, considered, and adopted with no dissenting voice. They protested President Johnson's actions in setting up a provisional government which ignored them, and in calling for a Constitutional Convention to be elected by that portion of the population which had had the vote prior to secession. They decided, too, to "earnestly appeal to Congress, that the State of Mississippi be not restored to Federal relations unless by her constitution she shall enfranchise her loyal colored citizens," and urged the "establishment of a paper within the State that will fearlessly and faithfully defend the rights of the colored citizens."[24]

The 1865 Constitutional Convention of Mississippi was composed of sympathizers with slavery and the instrument they produced envisaged the Negroes as a politically impotent and economically exploitable element of the population. Again the

Vicksburg Negroes convened, on September 18, to protest against this document and to issue this prophetic warning:

"That it is our firm conviction, and we hereby put it on record, that should Mississippi be restored to her status in the Union under her amended constitution as it now stands, that her Legislature, under pretext of guarding the interests of the State from the evils of sudden emancipation, will pass such proscriptive class laws against the freedmen as will result in their expatriation from the State or their practical reenslavement."[25]

Meanwhile, the month of August had seen at least two state-wide Negro conventions and several local ones. On the seventh, the Tennessee State Convention of Negroes that had been in preparation since April commenced its deliberations—which were to consume four days—at the Nashville African Methodist Episcopal Church. Present were one hundred and sixty-five delegates from all sections of the state, and the church "was filled to overflowing" throughout the proceedings by guests and visitors.

This convention condemned the state legislature for ignoring the repeated petitions of the Negro people for full citizenship rights and appealed to the people of Tennessee and of the nation to grant them justice. Resolutions were prepared for presentation, in petition form, before the United States Congress, and these were so presented by Senator Charles Sumner in December. Here "the colored people of Tennessee [did] respectfully and solemnly protest against the congressional delegation from this state being admitted to seats in your honorable bodies until the Legislature of this State enacts such laws as shall secure to us our rights as freemen." The document continued:

We cannot believe that the General Government will allow us to be left without such protection after knowing, as you do, what services we have rendered to the cause of the preservation of the Union and the maintenance of the laws. We have respectfully petitioned our Legislature upon the subject, and have failed to get them to do anything for us, saying that it was premature to legislate for the protection of our rights.

We think it premature to admit such delegation. It is true we have no vote, but we nevertheless desire and will do anything we can to support the government.

We deem it unnecessary to attempt to make an argument in favor of our protest, believing, as we do, the justice of our cause to be a far better argument than we could make; yet it may not be amiss to say that, inasmuch as the United States Constitution guarantees to every State in the Union a republican form of government, we are at a loss to understand that to be a republican government which does not protect the rights of all citizens, irrespective of color.

Being impressed with these convictions, we cannot refrain from appealing to your honorable and dignified assembly, entertaining the hope that we will be heard and our cause considered.

The Government did not forget to call for our help, and now we think that we have a right to call upon it.[26]

A statewide Virginia Negro convention assembled in Alexandria on August 2. Fifty delegates from seven cities and eleven counties were present. The spirit and purpose of this convention may be observed by citing brief and typical excerpts from the remarks of participants: Peter R. Jones of Petersburg: "We have had enough of war; but we will have our rights"; a Mr. Kneeland: "We ask only for what constitutes a man. If we cannot do it by words, we can do it by actions"; the Rev. Nicholas Richmond of Charlottesville: "We will contend to the last for our rights."[27]

At the same time regional meetings were being held elsewhere in Virginia in response to particular circumstances. In Richmond, for example, violent attacks upon Negro men and women, particularly by Federal troops, provoked the Negro community to petition General Terry to offer them protection, or, if he felt "unable to afford it," to permit them "the privilege of protecting ourselves."[28]

Around Hampton, Virginia, between four and five thousand Negroes had settled during the war on farm land abandoned by secessionists. By the summer of 1865, under Johnsonian restoration, many of the now pardoned owners were coming back and demanding the return of the land for their own use. On August 21, the Negroes of this area, in convention, appealed to the authorities to allow them to remain in occupation of the land which, they declared, had never been so productive. They pledged to one another resistance to the owners' claims. Shortly thereafter force was used against these Negroes, a detachment of Federal cavalry being employed in suppressing an alleged riot.

Twenty-one leaders said to have been "armed with revolvers, cutlasses, carbines, shotguns" were captured.[29]

Indicative of another method of attack upon the vital question of the land was the action taken by a group of Negroes of Lenoir County, North Carolina, in August. They formed themselves "into a society to purchase homes by joint stock" with the object of raising $10,000 by the close of 1867, the plan being for two hundred and fifty subscribers to pay, within the year, the sum of forty-eight dollars.[30]

Reference has already been made to the organizing activities of North Carolina Negroes during the spring and summer of 1865. Late in August these culminated in a call for "A Convention of the Colored Citizens of North Carolina." This was issued by a committee of three, A. H. Galloway, John Randolph, Jr., and George W. Price, appointed for this purpose by a mass meeting held in Wilmington.

> Let the leading men of each separate district issue a call for a meeting [said this document] that delegates may be chosen to express the sentiments of the Freedmen at Raleigh on the 29th of September, and let each county send as many delegates as it has representatives in the Legislature. Rally, old men, we want the counsel of your years and experience; rally, young men, we want your loyal presence, and need the ardor of youth to stimulate the timid; and may the spirit of our God come with the people to hallow all our sittings and wisely direct all our actions.[31]

Following this came local meetings held throughout the State. Typical of such preparatory meetings were those held in September in Raleigh and Wilmington. During the first week the Negroes of Raleigh met and elected a committee of three to prepare the physical facilities for the statewide convention. A hall sufficient to seat a minimum of five hundred people was obtained, housing arrangements for that number were made, and hundreds of circulars were issued for distribution in Wake County calling for attendance at a local mass meeting. The latter was held on the ninth and delegates to the State Convention were selected.[32]

Similar activities must have been occurring in Wilmington for on the 21st, to quote the headline in the local press, the Negroes held a "Large Mass Meeting at the City Hall." Accord ing to this paper, "The affair reflected great credit upon the freedmen, and the orderly, dignified, and attentive disposition shown among them was well worthy of emulation." Most attention was focused upon the address delivered by John P. Sampson, a native of Wilmington, who was then editing the weekly *Colored Citizen* of Cincinnati.

Mr. Sampson, reading from a carefully prepared paper, announced, "We ask for the immediate, unconditional, and universal enfranchisement of the black man in every state in this union. We claim that without this his liberty is a mockery. . . . The American people are now in tears," he went on. "The Shenandoah has run blood . . . we feel . . . a disposition to learn righteousness. . . . Now is the time to press this right." He concluded that "the charge of inferiority is an old dodge," used by all conquerors and exploiters to justify and rationalize their inhuman activities, and that the Negro people knew it to be a sham and a lie.[33]

There is evidence that violence was used to prevent the holding of such open meetings in some other parts of North Carolina. Thus, for example, a gathering of Negroes at Chapel Hill was attacked and forcibly disbanded.[34] Again, the Raleigh correspondent of the New York *Tribune,* in reporting the first day's meeting of the State Convention, said that about one hundred and fifty delegates "who were appointed by meetings and in formal bodies of the free people" were present, and that while some brought credentials establishing their representative character, "others had as much as they could do to bring themselves having to escape from their homes stealthily by night, and walk long distances, so as to avoid observation, such was the opposition manifested to the movement in some localities."[35]

There seems, also, to have been some opposition from conservative Negro elements in Raleigh to holding a convention there, particularly since its sitting was to coincide with that of the official State Constitutional Convention. Nevertheless, it was held, was well attended, widely reported, and attracted national attention. Its deliberations commenced on September 29 and concluded on October 3, and its essential character was expressed most clearly by the opening address of the chairman, the Reverend John W. Hood, of New Bern, and by the memorial presented to the Constitutional Convention.[36]

In both documents, and particularly in the memorial, a strain of conservatism and compromise was present that appears to have been quite unusual for the period. The chairman felt that "there has never been and never will be a more important assembly than this now convened here." Their slogan was "equal rights before the law," but "all harsh expressions toward anybody or about any line of policy" were to be avoided. The ideas of migration and colonization were nonsense so far as the mass of southern Negroes was concerned, and thus some mode of joint living—Negro and white—had to be contrived. In this connection, "if we respect ourselves we shall be respected," and, he concluded:

> I think the best way to prepare a people for the exercise of their rights is to put them in practice of those rights, and so I think the time has come when we should be given ours; but I am well aware that we shall not gain them all at once. Let us have faith, patience, and moderation, yet assert always that we want these things — first, the right to give evidence in the courts; second, the right to be represented in the jury box; and, third, the right to put votes in the ballot box. These rights we want, these rights we contend for, and these rights, under God, we must ultimately have.[37]

The demand for civil and political rights as urged in the above address does not appear in the memorial. The appeal is rather "for protection and sympathy" which it is hoped might be merited "by our industry, sobriety and respectful demeanor." Still certain specific enactments were requested. It was asked "that some suitable measures" might be adopted to forestall "unscrupulous and avaricious masters" from practicing physical cruelty, or from withholding wages. Education, of an unspecified nature, was desired, as well as protection of "the sanctity of our family relations." Public care of the helpless and infirm and state assistance for "the reunion of families which have been long broken up by war, or by the operations of Slavery" were advocated. And, "finally, praying for such encouragement to our industry as the proper regulation of the hours of labor, and the providing the means of protection of our property and of our persons against rapacious and cruel employers, and for the collection of just claims, we commit our cause into your hands."[38]

The conservative quality of this memorial evoked favorable comments from the local press.[39] It was submitted by Governor Holden to the Constitutional Convention, read to that body by its clerk, "and was listened to with respectful attention." It was referred to a special committee of five for consideration, the chairman of which, in reporting back, recommended no action. According to him, the Negroes were ignorant, legislation would accomplish nothing, and time alone was the healer. It was necessary to aim at "material and moral welfare, and to the general peace and prosperity of the State [rather] than to any theoretical schemes of social and political equality." Perhaps, concluded the report, it would be well to appoint another committee to further study the question.[40]

The month of September marks the appearance of another type of concerted activity among southern Negroes of great interest—namely, labor strikes.

On the morning of September 4, Negro stevedores and dock laborers at Savannah, Georgia, struck, demanding, according to the local press, wages of $2.00 per day instead of $1.50. Federal troops were used to crush the strike by arresting the leaders. "The arrests exerted a salutary influence on the balance of the strikers," the Savannah *Republican* reported the next day, "who speedily dispersed when they witnessed the fate of their foolish leaders."[41]

Two weeks later the owners of tobacco-processing plants in Richmond were presented with the following petition from their Negro workers:

Richmond, September 18, 1865

Dear Sirs: We the Tobacco mechanicks of this city and Manchester is worked to great disadvantage. In 1858 and 1859 our masters hiered us to the Tobacconist at a prices ranging from $150 to 180. The Tobacconist furnished us lodging food & clothing. They gave us tasks to performs. all we made over this task they payed us for. We worked faithful and they paid us faithful. They Then gave us $2 to 2.50 cts, and we made double the amount we now make. The Tobacconist held a meeting, and resolved not give more than $1.50 cts per hundred, which is about one days work—in a week we make 600 lbs apece with a stemer. The weeks work then at $1.50 amounts to $9—the stemers wages is from $4 to $4.50cts which leaves from $5 to 4.50cts per week about one half what we made when slaves. Now to Rent two small rooms we have to pay from $18 to 20. We see $4.50cts or $5 will not more then pay Rent say nothing about food Clothing medicin Doctor Bills Tax & co. They say we will starve through laziness that is not so. But it is true we will starve at our present wages. They say we will steal we can say for ourselves we had rather work for our living. give us a Chance. We are compeled to work for them at low wages and pay high Rents and make $5 per week and sometimes les. And paying $18 or 20 per month Rent. It is impossible to feed ourselves and family—starvation is cirten unless a change is brought about. Tobacco Factory Mechanicks of Richmond and Manchester.[42]

Somewhat later this year the Mayor of New Orleans told a visitor that he was delighted with the free-labor system. He went on to remark:

I thought it an indication of progress when the white laborers and negroes on the levees the other day made a strike for higher wages. They were receiving two dollars and a half and three dollars a day, and they struck for five and seven dollars. They marched up the levee in a long procession, white and black together. I gave orders that they should not be interfered with as long as they interfered with nobody else; but when they undertook by force to prevent other laborers from working, the police promptly put a stop to their proceedings.[43]

The greatest strike movement, however, of southern Negroes, beginning in the year of 1865, came from the great bulk of those whose lives had been, and were to continue to be, tied up with the cultivation of the land. This whole epic story merits a volume of its own, and here we must content ourselves with a few assertions.

Among these millions the following courses of action predominated in the first post-war year: (1) attempts to retain possession or, at least, occupation of lands abandoned by Secessionists; (2) wholesale flight to urban areas, particularly Washington, Richmond, Raleigh, Norfolk, Charleston, and New Orleans; (3) attempts to purchase or rent lands; (4) absolute refusal to enter into verbal agreements, and extreme hesitancy in signing contracts with members of the former master class, particularly where sharecropping was involved; (5) militant resistance, in a physical sense, to the introduction of peonage.[44]

Continuing the chronicle of the formal organizational activity of the southern Negro and returning to the month of September, we find ourselves turning to Louisiana. There, as the press reported, "The colored people . . . are taking an orderly and practical method of testing their claims to citizenship." They were conducting their own registration of all individuals they considered qualified voters with the idea of having this electorate select delegates to a State Convention which, in turn, was to designate candidates for Congress. The Negroes were said to feel "that if Louisiana is to be recognized the loyal citizens constitute the State, and are entitled to recognition." Since the alleged state authorities denied them the suffrage they proposed "to ask Congress whether it prefers that loyal blacks or disloyal whites should control Louisiana."[45]

The Negroes of Mississippi were active, too. Reference has already been made to the Vicksburg mass meeting of September 18. Shortly thereafter, finding open meetings no longer possible, a committee of Negroes was delegated to present a petition to the Congress of the United States, and this was done, through Senator Sumner, in January, 1866. In this document the men from Mississippi requested the basic right of suffrage because, "as we have fought in favor of liberty, justice and humanity, we wish to vote in favor of it . . . and also that we may be in a position in a legal and peaceable way to protect ourselves in the enjoyment of those sacred rights which were pledged to us by the emancipation proclamation."[46]

Since the Constitutional Convention of South Carolina was to assemble on September 13, there was a great deal of activity among the Negroes of that state who were intent upon getting their views before that body. Thus, the Columbia, S. C., *Daily Phoenix,* a paper certainly not friendly to the efforts of the Negro to complete and make real his freedom, reported the gathering, on September 4, of "a large meeting of freedmen, held on St. Helena Island." Here resolutions were adopted urging the members of the convention to grant the vote to the Negro as well as to the white. It was asserted that both justice and policy required this, and these Negroes assured everyone "that we will never cease our efforts to obtain, by all just and legal means, a full recognition of our rights as citizens of the United States and of this Commonwealth."[47]

Somewhat later the same month one hundred and three Negroes of Charleston assembled, drafted, signed, and forwarded to the same body a lengthy petition the essential prayer of which was that suffrage be extended to the Negro. The constitution-makers were informed "that nothing short of this, our respectful demand, will satisfy our people" and while the petitioners recognized "what prejudices and preconceived opinions must be overcome before our prayers can be granted" they hoped the recipients would be "capable of rising superior to the prejudices of habit and education." The hope was vain, however, for the Convention resolved, on September 27, "that the petition be laid on the table," and the clerk was careful to write on the back of the manuscript: "Note this Petition was not read in Convention."[48]

Having failed to move the convention, there remained the state legislature, the American Congress, and the people of the nation at large, to whom appeals might be made. For these purposes a "Colored People's Convention of the State of South Carolina" met at the Zion Church in Charleston from November 20-25. Delegates were present from the entire state including Columbia, Chester, Greenville, Kershaw, Beaufort, Richland, Sumter, Winyah, Orangeburg, and John's Island, and the sense of the convention was expressed in four public documents. These included a "Declaration of Rights and Wrongs," an "Address to the White Inhabitants of South Carolina," a "Petition to the State Legislature," and a "Memorial to Congress."

Summarizing one will give the spirit, and very largely the content, of all and for this purpose we choose the "Memorial." This paper begins by expressing joy and gratitude because of the destruction of chattel slavery and the efforts of the Freedmen's Bureau. It asserts a consciousness "of the difficulties that surround our condition" wherefore no right or privilege would be demanded except "such as rest upon the strong basis of justice and expediency, in view of the best interests of our entire country." These demands were, in the order of presentation, "that the strong arm of law and order be placed *alike* over the entire people of this State; that life and property be secure, and the laborer as free to sell his labor as the merchant his goods; that a fair and impartial construction be given to the pledges of government to *us* concerning the land question"; security for "the school, the pulpit, the press"; the right to vote; the right to be on juries; the right to bear arms; the end to Black Codes; the right of assembly; the "right to enter upon all avenues of trade, commerce, agriculture, to amass wealth by thrift and industry"; and finally, "the right to develop our *whole being,* by all the appliances that belong to civilized society. . . ."

In the address to the white people of South Carolina one additional note of considerable interest appears. This declares that:

> It is some consolation to know, and it inspires us with hope when we reflect, that our cause is not alone the cause of four millions of black men in this country, but we are intensely alive to the fact that it is also the cause of millions of oppressed men in other "parts of God's beautiful earth," who are now struggling to be free in the fullest sense of the word, and God and nature are pledged to their triumph.[49]

Some indication has already been given of the deep desire of the Southern Negro to possess land.[50] This appeared, once again, in organized form among Negro settlers on Edisto Island, South Carolina, towards the end of October. At that time they were visited by Major-General Oliver O. Howard who came as the President's personal representative to inform those Negroes that the former rebel land-owners had been pardoned and were claiming their property. Among other people present at this scene was a New England lady, serving as a teacher in the area. She recorded that "At first the people could not understand, but as the meaning struck them, that they must give up their little homes and gardens and work them again for others, there was a general murmur of dissatisfaction." The General proposed that a committee of three be selected to consult together and report to him.

During this interval the visitors asked for songs. The Negroes responded with, "Nobody knows the trouble I see" and "Wandering in the wilderness of sorrow and gloom." Two of the largest landholders had accompanied the general and spoke with some of the Negroes, but these asserted they would not work "for the Seces." The former slaveholders were told that they were forgiven for past evils but, said one Negro of himself, "he had lived all his life with a basket over his head, and now that it had been taken off and air and sunlight had come to him, he could not consent to have the basket over him."

Sometime later the committee of three appeared but informed the general that his news had distressed them so that "they were too much shaken to see things clearly" and requested more time. This was granted, and a few days thereafter they presented the general with the following petition for the President of the United States:

Dear President Johnson of the United States

Wee the freedmen of South Carolina wish to adress you with a few lines Conserning the sad feelings that is now resting upon our minds wee pray that god may guive you helth & good spirets that when you receive theas few notasis that you may receive them as the father did the prodical son wee have for the last four years ben studing with justis and the best of our ability what step wee should take to become a peple: we have lernt to respect all Just Causes that ever came from the union.

Mag genrl howard has paid the freedmen of South Carolinah a visit & caled a meating on Edisto Island South Carliner in the Centrel part of the island at the priskple Church thair hee beutifly addressed the freedmen of this island after his adress a grate many of the people understanding what was said they got aroused & awoke to perfect sense to stody for them Selves what part of this law would rest against us, we said in rafarence to what he said that nothing did apier at that time to bee very opressing upon us but the one thing that is wee freedmen should work for wages for our former oners or eny other man president Johnson of u st I do say . . . man that have stud upon the feal of battle & have shot their master & sons now Going to ask ether one for bread or for shelter or Comfortable for his wife & children sunch a thing the u st should not aught to Expect a man [to do] . . . the King of south Carolina [i.e., one of the former slaveholders] ask the Privalage to have the stage that he might a Dress the ordinance [audience] of the freedmen . . . [the] old master [claimed] such a fealing to Comply with the best order & also what was best for the freedmen. . . [We said to him] Here is Plenty Whidow & Fatherles that have serve you as slave now losen a home . . . give Each one of them a acres & a ½ to a family as you has the labers & the Profet of there Yearly [early] Youth . . . [when] the question was asked him by General Howard, what would it sell your lan for a acres his anser the I would not take a hundred $100 of a acres that is a part of his union fealing so then we therefore lose fate in this southern Gentleman . . . [They beseech] the wise presidon that sets on his seat [to give them] a Chance to Recover out of this trubble . . . these 3 Committee has Pleg the Trouth to you dis day. Oct. 25, 1865.[61]

Meanwhile on October 2, a mass meeting of Missouri Negroes

had assembled in St. Louis, denounced discrimination and Jim-Crowism, and appointed a State Executive Committee of eight to issue a public statement informing the country of their sentiments. Ten days later "An Address by the Colored People of Missouri to the Friends of Equal Rights" was written and appeared in pamphlet form later that year. This address reminded its readers that the Negro people were loyal fighters for freedom, and declared that they resented and repudiated any type of wardship. They demanded full equality: "We ask for a citizenship so broad and solid that upon it black men, white men and every American born can equally, safely and eternally stand."[52]

The closing weeks of 1865 witnessed no decline in the organized activities of southern Negroes. General Rufus Saxton, who had been in charge of the Freedmen's Bureau for the state of South Carolina from June, 1865, until January, 1866 (when he was removed, according to his own testimony, because of the pressure exerted upon the amenable Johnson administration by large plantation owners),[53] brought with him to Washington "a petition signed by several hundred freedmen [of South Carolina] asking that they may be allowed the rights of citizenship." The general was asked by a member of Congress whether or not he thought the Negro people would ever acquiesce in or "submit quietly" to a subordinate role. No, he did not. He based this upon "conversation with intelligent freedmen, men of thought and intelligence, who have told me so, and it is the result of all my experience of nearly four years with those people." Some, he said, were arming themselves. He, himself, had counseled patience and reliance upon the acts and good faith of the Federal government and this had, in his opinion, helped restrain them. But, he went on:

> I will tell you what the leader of the colored Union league and other colored men in Charleston said to me: they said that they feared they could not much longer control the freedmen if I left Charleston. I do not recollect their exact words, but the substance was, that they feared the freedmen would attempt to take their cause in their own hands.[54]

At least three state conventions of Negro people were held in December, one in Little Rock, Arkansas, another in Baltimore, Maryland, and the third in Florida. In all three the basic demand was for full citizenship rights. Of the Arkansas meeting, a judge of that state's Supreme Court testified in February, 1866, that he had been present and "was very much astonished listening to their proceedings . . . altogether they made a much better show than I supposed a body of negroes in that State could do."[55] The Maryland convention was held at the recently opened Frederick Douglass Institute in Baltimore and was attended by "155 regularly appointed delegates . . . from every part of the State. . . ."[56] One of the actions of this gathering was to appoint Lewis H. Douglass and William E. Matthews as representatives, or lobbyists, for Maryland Negroes in Washington. The Florida convention asked for land and education as well as the suffrage.[57]

Mass meetings held by Negroes in several cities of Virginia in December also resulted in electing and dispatching representatives, Negro and white, to urge their cause at the nation's capital. Typical of these meetings was that held in Norfolk, on the first. Here the Negroes denounced as slanders the rumors that they were planning an insurrection. These rumors, it was declared, were "vile falsehoods designed to provoke acts of unlawful violence against us," and a committee was appointed "to wait upon the military and civil authorities and co-operate with them in exposing those slanders and defeating the machination of still rebels and traitors and in allaying the fears of the timid and credulous."[58]

It was once again announced by the Negroes that they would "not cease to importune and to labor in all lawful and proper ways for equal rights as citizens" until these were granted. The committee of lobbyists for Washington—consisting of three Negroes, Dr. Thomas Bayne, the Rev. J. M. Brown, and E. W. Williams, and the white attorney, Calvin Pepper—were directed to work for the obtaining of full political and judicial rights, the power to elect local agents of the Freedmen's Bureau, the reduction of rents, the halting of the return of confiscated land, "and to attend to all other matters . . . pertaining to the interests of our people . . . and for this purpose they are to cooperate and act in harmony and unity with similar committees and delegations from this and other States." The delegation was urged particularly to oppose the recognition of the existing state government and the seating by Congress of those claiming admission who had been elected by a suffrage confined only to whites. In the following days similar meetings were held in Elizabeth City, Yorktown, Hampton, Old Point, Williamsburg and Portsmouth, and several more Negroes plus another white man joined Virginia's unofficial delegation to Washington.[59]

To recapitulate the salient features of the evidence: In 1865, southern Negroes rejected ideas of colonization or flight, welcomed the support of white allies, and protested vehemently against unfair labor practices, violence, peonage, and restrictions upon land ownership. They struggled to achieve the right to vote, to testify in courts, to serve on juries, to own land, to obtain a formal education, to bear arms, to better wages, and to eliminate all invidious distinctions based upon color.

# MISSISSIPPI RECONSTRUCTION AND THE NEGRO LEADER, CHARLES CALDWELL

Charles Caldwell's story deserves to be known. In telling it one must tell the story of the post-Civil War decade in Mississippi because his career is inextricably interwoven within the rich fabric of Reconstruction history. His name has appeared but rarely in books and then only in terms of execration: "a negro of desperate character"; "one of the most daring and desperate negroes of the day"; "a notorious and turbulent negro."[1]

Charles Caldwell lived all the days of his life—except his last ten years—as a slave and the anonymity that covered most such lives covered his, too. We know not even when or where he was born, but as an adult he lived in the village of Clinton, some dozen miles from Jackson, in Hinds County, Mississippi, worked as a blacksmith and had a son whom he called Charles, Jr.[2]

There is no direct evidence as to what this particular Negro did or thought or said in the years 1865 and 1866. But what years those were for Mississippi's half million Negroes![3] In May, 1865 the last of the disheartened and whipped troops of the defunct Confederacy had surrendered. In the big houses—those not abandoned and empty—were foreboding and deep despair; in the huts were rejoicing and ecstatic hope.

As a consequence of the war over two billions of dollars of capital—of constitutionally recognized private property—had been wiped out (some $300,000,000 in Mississippi alone) and with it went the traditional foundation of the Old South's social order. What was to replace it? Who was to determine and dominate the new order, and how new was it to be?

Those who had ruled were determined that the changes would be as few and as superficial as possible. One of the most astute among them—James Lusk Alcorn—who had owned some one hundred slaves and an estate worth $250,000, had been a state representative and senator for a decade and a Confederate brigadier-general, and was to be, in his role of vitiating radicalism by attaching himself to it, a Reconstruction governor and United States senator—wrote to his wife as early as May 16, 1865:

> We will now take the oath to support the Constitution and laws of the United States; elect our senators and representatives; claim that we have our slaves until slavery is abolished and upon the question of amending the constitution for its prohibition Mississippi has a vote.* [4]

And the President was with them. As Provisional Governor of Mississippi he appointed, on June 13, 1865, the former slaveholding anti-secessionist, William L. Sharkey, who from the start of his political career in 1828 had been one of the most important cogs in the apparatus of slavocratic rule, serving for nineteen years (1832-1851) as chief justice of the state's highest court.[5] This individual did the following: First, he provided for the election, early in August, of delegates to a Constitutional Convention, with the electorate restricted to those who had had the vote in January, 1861, and had taken the President's loyalty oath. Second, he reappointed all local officials who had been functioning under the Confederacy, requiring again only the taking of the same oath.[6] Third, he urged President Johnson to remove all Federal troops—the vast majority, Negroes—from the state.[7] And, lastly, he ordered—without even informing the Federal commander—the formation of a state militia to be made up of white men only and particularly, said Governor Sharkey, of those "young men of the State who have so distinguished

* Alcorn topped a devious career by serving as one of the two Republicans in the 1890 Bourbon constitutional convention and voting there to disfranchise the Negro people. He was typical of many wealthy Southern planters—mostly pre-Civil War Whigs—who joined the Reconstruction Republicans or advocated cooperation with the Negroes in order to prevent fundamental change. See D. H. Donald, "The Scalawag in Mississippi Reconstruction," in the *Journal of Southern History* (1944), X, pp. 447-60; and note the testimony of Josiah A. Campbell, a top Bourbon politician and one of the 49 signers of the Confederate constitution, in the *Boutwell Report,* p. 937, where he admitted his object in forming "an alliance with the negroes politically . . . [was to] acquire ascendancy over them, and become their teachers and controllers . . . ."

themselves for gallantry," *i.e.,* in the war against the United States, then but three months terminated!*

The election was held as scheduled and the political complexion of the approximately one hundred delegates was what one would expect: Seventy were old-line Whigs; eighteen were Democrats, that is, somewhat to the right of the majority; and nine were Conservatives—so much to the right of the majority as to tend to deny the termination of secession.[8] This constitutional convention, with the haste typical of the entire reactionary maneuver met August 14 and adjourned ten days later. In that time it accomplished this: After prolonged debate it was agreed that simply announcing Mississippi's ordinance of secession as null and void would cast the least aspersions upon those responsible for it. Following considerable argument it was decided to acknowledge the end of slavery in the State by merely asserting that "the institution . . . was destroyed" thus once again permitting no derogatory remarks (though even this found eleven members in opposition);[9] and, finally, provision was made for the election of local officers and a state legislature in October, the electorate being identical with that which had created the convention. Just in case anyone was so dull as not to have comprehended the essential function of this coming legislature that

* This militia order was too much even for the Federal commander, Major-General Slocum, politically sympathetic though he was to Johnson and to Sharkey. He therefore countermanded it, but told General Sherman: "I did not like to take this step; but Sharkey should have consulted me before issuing an order arming the rebels—and placing them on duty with the darkies in every county of the State. I hope the U. S. Military will soon be removed from the State, but until this is done it would certainly be bad policy to arm the militia."—dated Aug. 27, 1865—*In Memoriam Henry Warner Slocum* (Albany, 1904), p. 105. President Johnson ordered the General to rescind his own order and to allow Gov. Sharkey to proceed with the forming of the militia, an act Carl Schurz believed "the most unwarranted trick yet perpetrated at Washington."—letter to his wife, Sept. 2, 1865, in F. Bancroft, ed., *Speeches, Correspondence and Political Papers of Carl Schurz* (6 vols., N. Y., 1913) I, p. 267.

General Slocum resigned in September to head the Democratic ticket in the 1865 elections in New York. Before departing he was dined by the gentry of Vicksburg and there toasted Sharkey as "a sound statesman and true patriot. May he long be spared to the state he has served so well." An analysis of the class allegiance and political affiliations of Army administrators after the Civil War—indeed, throughout American history—has been almost completely ignored and with great damage to realistic historiography.

was spelled out for all the world to see: ". . . the Legislature at its next session . . . shall provide by law for the protection and security of the person and property of the freedmen of this State, and guard them and the State against any evils that may arise from their sudden emancipation."[10]

It has been observed that no direct evidence has been found as to Charles Caldwell's feelings and actions while all this was going on, but some record does exist concerning the Negro people as a whole. Thus, on June 19, 1865, a mass meeting of Negroes assembled in Vicksburg denounced Johnson's Provisional Government, protested against the meeting of a constitutional convention in the election of whose delegates they would have no voice and called upon Congress to refuse to restore Mississippi to the Union until she had enfranchised "her loyal colored citizens."[11] And following the constitutional convention but preceding the elections of October the Negro people gathered again in Vicksburg, reiterated their denunciation of Johnsonian Reconstruction, or, better, restoration, excoriated police brutality and peonage and warned the nation that real liberation was being thwarted. With perfect prescience they concluded:

> That is our firm conviction and we hereby put it on record, that should Mississippi be restored to her status in the Union under her amended constitution as it now stands, that her Legislature, under pretext of guarding the interests of the State from the evils of sudden emancipation, will pass such proscriptive class laws against the freedmen as will result in their expatriation from the State or their practical reenslavement.[12]

Under the gratuitous prodding of an over-eager press demanding "a well devised legislative system . . . so stringent in character as to compel the negroes to work as formerly, upon the plantations . . . willingly if possible, but forcibly if need be" and that the Negro "should remain a servant [and must not] have the right to hold real estate conferred upon him,"[13] the legislature of October-December 1865 met. With an ex-Confederate general as Speaker of the House and an ex-Confederate colonel as president of the Senate[14] the press's explicit directions were hardly needed, for the actions of these gentlemen were so blatantly reactionary as to be somewhat embarrassing to their more astute friends, including President Johnson.

The legislature refused to ratify the thirteenth amendment; it refused to even consider suffrage for the Negro no matter how circumscribed or limited, and among its acts were a memorial to the President begging him to free Jefferson Davis—"our blood . . . our treasure"—and a joint resolution calling upon the same official to remove all Federal troops from Mississippi.[15]

And for the majority of Mississippi's inhabitants, for the Negro people, came their "practical reenslavement" in a law entitled "An Act to Confer Civil Rights on Freedmen, and for other purposes"! The civil rights are quickly enumerated: Negroes might marry—among themselves; they might sue and be sued; they might possess personal property. But enumerating the "other purposes" takes a little longer. Negroes were forbidden to own land, nor might they even "rent or lease lands or tenements except in incorporated towns or cities." Negroes were required to carry written evidence of a lawful home and to have a contract for labor. From this labor they were not to leave "without good cause" under penalty of forfeiture of pay, a fine of $100 as a vagrant and the necessity of working out this fine in the employ of anyone who should pay it. No Negro might carry arms, and the militia as previously organized by Governor Sharkey was now provided for by law. Negro children, without means of support, were to be apprenticed to white employers (former masters being given priority) until reaching the age of eighteen.[16]

Once again the Negro people responded militantly. A delegation was appointed to go to Washington and to present a petition to Congress explaining precisely what was happening in Mississippi. In January Senator Sumner of Massachusetts presented their document, demanding immediate enfranchisement so that, said the Negroes, we might "protect ourselves in the enjoyment of those sacred rights which were pledged to us by the emancipation proclamation." Shortly thereafter Senator Wade of Ohio presented another petition, "very numerously signed," from Negro soldiers in Mississippi demanding the same right for themselves and all of their people.[17]

And the masses on the plantations responded too, for law or no law, the planters, though possessing the land and thus having the final word in terms of food—in terms of life and death—

found it very difficult to get the Negroes to sign contracts. They could not buy land, they could not rent land, yet many of them insisted that they would not work except for wages—stipulated regular monthly payments in cash.* Such a wage system made possible some degree of independence, some degree of effective struggle, and therefore many refused—let the planters do their worst—to acquiesce in a sharecropping regime of semi-slavery. This is the significant feature of the following passage from the report of the United States Commissioner of Agriculture for 1867:

> The payment of wages—a plan tried extensively in 1866— generally proved unprofitable, the freedmen being inclined to use too freely their newly-found liberty, and planters were generally quite as little at home in the management of free labor. Much of the labor was inefficient, and idleness became contagious, *of a more malignant type in proportion to increase of numbers working together,* crops were neglected, upbraiding and threats sometimes followed, and *the cotton-fields were in many cases left in the lurch at the critical season of picking.* [18]

Things had indeed come to a sorry state when Negro washerwomen in Mississippi's capital had the audacity, in June, 1866, of actually threatening to strike unless higher pay were forthcoming![19]

The planters, moreover, had moved too far, too fast, and too brazenly. The North, still burying its dead, with Republican supremacy by no means assured, with an economic *modus vivendi* still to be formulated vis-a-vis the South, with the prodding of the Negro people and their radical allies, called a halt. In November, 1865, the military disallowed those acts of the legislature forbidding Negroes to lease lands or bear arms. In March, 1866, Congress decided to seat no senator or representative from an insurrectionary state until it had declared the state entitled to representation, with the result that the individuals sent as

* In Mississippi, as throughout the South, the Negro's desire for the land was acute and his belief in an impending land distribution was widespread. Contemporary sources are filled with this. To cite one witness referring to this state in the summer of 1865, ". . . they ardently desire to become freeholders. In the independent possession of landed property they see the consummation of their deliverance . . . it must be admitted that this instinct is correct."—Carl Schurz's Report to the President, *Senate Ex. Doc. No. 2,* 39th Cong, 1st Sess., p. 31.

senators from Mississippi, William L. Sharkey and James L. Alcorn, were rejected. The next month the Civil Rights Law was passed, over Johnson's veto, and this declared the freedmen to be citizens and specifically endowed them with the civil rights adhering to citizens, including the right to possess all kinds of real and personal property.[20] In June Congress passed the Fourteenth Amendment and started it on its way through the state legislatures. That autumn the electorate presented the left wing of the Republican Party with an overwhelming majority for the ensuing Congress.*

Thus it came about that the new Congress enacted, in March, 1867, its Reconstruction legislation, the essential feature of which was that ten of the southern states were to hold constitutional conventions, the delegates to which were to be elected "by the male citizens . . . of whatever race, color, or previous condition." The registration of these voters and the conduct of the polling was to be administered and regulated under the supervision of the United States Army.[21]

In Mississippi registration continued for five months with a total of almost 140,000 potential voters as the final result, of whom 75,000 to 80,000 were Negro and 55,000 to 60,000 were white.[22] These figures, which dismayed the Bourbons, were reached despite some intimidation, and the enunciation of a

* There is, frequently, a profound distinction between the enunciation of policy from the top and its actual execution in practice, especially when the top levels themselves are split. Congress might legislate on Reconstruction policy, but the President appointed most of the administrators of that policy. Thus, for example, in Mississippi, the military commanders, Generals Ord and Gillem—Johnson's appointees—were not radical Reconstructionists, the latter in particular being a personal friend of the President. We find, then, that the 1865 legislature is allowed to reassemble late in 1866 and early in 1867. In accord with congressional legislation it repealed the anti-land-owning provisions of the Black Code and allowed Negroes to testify, but not to serve as jurors. Most of the apprenticeship law of 1865 was repealed, but a convict-leasing system was instituted. *Laws of the State of Mississippi at a Called Session . . . Oct., 1866, and Jan. and Feb. 1867* (Jackson, 1867), pp. 232, 443, 736. Perhaps the crowning act of these individuals was that in which they adopted the report of one of their joint committees recommending that the legislature decline to ratify the 14th amendment, while "an expression in the report that it was beneath the dignity of the State to hold any communication with Secretary of State Seward on the subject received special applause." J. L. Power, "The Black and Tan Convention" in *Proceedings of Mississippi Hist. Soc.* (1900), III, p. 76.

policy of boycott—"masterly inactivity"—on the part of most of the planters.[23] The vote itself, cast November 5, 1867, was overwhelmingly pro-radical and pro-convention; out of a total of about 76,000 voters, 69,739 favored a convention and 6,277 opposed.

We have already indicated that no direct evidence had been found as to the opinions and activities of Charles Caldwell whose career we proposed using as a spade with which to unearth something of Mississippi's—and the South's—history. But it is not possible to doubt what those opinions and activities were for he was among the sixteen Negro Republicans sent to the much maligned "Black and Tan" constitutional convention of 1868. Of the remaining eighty-four delegates—all of whom were white—twenty-nine were Conservatives and fifty-five were Republicans, of whom, incidentally, thirty-three were native-born Southerners.[24]

Ignoring provocations, the delegates assembled in Jackson on January 7, 1868, and upon their deliberations there promptly descended from the press a thick veil of silence which today is almost impenetrable.[25] Yet the convention's journal exists and while it is bare and formal it does record the proposals, amendments, votes, and results. And it does preserve the brief speech of greeting delivered at the convention's opening by its temporary president, a propertyless white man named Alson Mygatt of Warren County. He said, with an over-optimism born of fervent desire:

> This hour brings to a final end that system that enriches the few at the expense of the many—that system that hindered the growth of towns and cities, and built up large landed aristocracies—that system that discouraged agricultural improvements and mechanic[al] arts—that destroyed free schools, and demoralized church and State, has come to an end.

He concluded that in spite of opposition from the President, the planters, and the press they would continue to labor for justice and equality for all, and they would not fail.[26]

After a hundred and fourteen days of deliberation—prolonged in part by the obstructionist tactics of the reactionary minority—the delegates completed their constitution, an instrument aimed at creating a non-oligarchic bourgeois democracy. Property rights of women were recognized; imprisonment for debt was forbidden; a non-segregating public school system was provided for; local governmental organs were democratized; the judiciary was overhauled; the vote was given all men over twenty-one; and any and all discrimination by governmental units or private corporations, especially vested with public functions, on the basis of religion, color, or previous condition of servitude was illegalized. Included, too, after lengthy debate, were rather drastic disfranchising provisions aimed at all who had held office under the Confederacy or had voluntarily assisted her. As for Caldwell, during all this, the record makes it possible to assert only that he faithfully attended practically all meetings, was a member of one committee and generally voted with the radical majority.[27]

An event occurred involving Caldwell, however, in 1868, after the convention had adjourned, which vividly demonstrates that while Alson Mygatt was premature in hailing the end of "that system that enriches the few at the expense of the many," fundamental changes had indeed come to Mississippi. For in that year, in broad daylight and on a street of Jackson, Charles Caldwell shot and killed a white man, the son of a Judge Johnston, was tried and was acquitted, the verdict being based on the fact that the act had been committed in self-defense after the victim had attempted to shoot the defendant. It would appear safe to say that Caldwell was the first—perhaps the only—Negro to kill a white man in Mississippi, be tried for the act, win an acquittal and go unscathed.[28]

Caldwell was a leader in the bitter, and, at first, unsuccessful effort to obtain the constitution's ratification. Terror and intimidation and a Federal military command generally sympathetic to the planters largely account for the initial setback suffered in the voting late in June, 1868, when, by a majority of under 8,000 in a total of over 120,000, the constitution was rejected.[29]

Grant, however, finally removed General Gillem and replaced him with General Adelbert Ames. In April, 1869, Grant received authorization from Congress to order the submission of the constitution of Mississippi (and that of Virginia and Texas) without such provisions as he might deem it best to omit.[30]

When, therefore, the Mississippi constitution was voted upon in December, 1869, along with a slate of state officers, it was shorn of the disfranchisement clauses and was supported even by the Democrats. The latter, in an effort at deception equaling Hitler's National Socialist label, called themselves National Union Republicans, spoke up for the constitution and nominated President Grant's brother-in-law, Judge Lewis Dent, for the governor's seat (together with several Negroes for other positions). The maneuver had a sad denouement, for while it resulted in the almost unanimous adoption of the constitution (113,735 to 955), the Republican ticket scored a smashing victory with Alcorn, the gubernatorial candidate, beating Mrs. Grant's brother by almost 40,000 votes.[31]

The legislature that was then elected and which convened in January, 1870,[32] contained one hundred and seven representatives and thirty-three senators. In the House there were eighty-two Republicans, of whom thirty were Negroes, and in the Senate there were twenty-eight Republicans of whom five were Negroes. Among the five was Charles Caldwell who had had to resign his position as a member of the powerful Hinds County Board of Police to accept this new assignment.[33] And in this new position Caldwell remained until the counter-revolutionary *coup d'etat* of 1875.

Once again these men are known by their fruits alone, for little remains of their work, in terms of record, other than the legislative journals and the session laws. These may be summarized for the years from 1870 to 1874.

The fourteenth and fifteenth amendments were ratified; a uniform system of public education and many institutions of public welfare were established; the vagrancy laws were abolished; tax rates on the tools and implements of mechanics and artisans were lowered; and all acts having special and invidious reference to the Negro were repealed with this explanation appended:

> That it is hereby declared to be the true intent, meaning and purpose of this Act, to remove from the records of the laws of this State all laws of whatever character, which in any manner recognize any natural difference or distinction between citizens or inhabitants of this State, or which in any manner or in any degree, discriminate between citizens

or inhabitants of this State, founded on race, color or previous condition of servitude.

To put teeth behind this enactment another law provided a fine of $5,000 to be assessed against any officer or agent of any railroad or vessel guilty of Jim-Crowism.[34]

Two laws enhancing the rights of women were passed. One provided:

> That the wages and compensation of married women for service and labor done and performed by them, shall be free from the debt and control of their husbands, and their employers are allowed to pay such wages and compensation directly to such married women, and payment to them shall be a full discharge and acquittance of the employer.

The other declared:

> That it shall not be lawful for a married man to sell or otherwise dispose of his homestead without the consent of his wife, and no deed of conveyance from the husband for the homestead shall be valid unless the wife shall join in such conveyance. . . .[35]

Scores, perhaps hundreds, of incorporation charters were granted by the Reconstruction legislatures of Mississippi during their very short period of existence. Railroad, banking, public utility, mining and manufacturing concerns were established as the state officers consciously strove to break the stranglehold of an agrarian, one-crop, semi-feudal economy whose controllers were, of course, their political enemies. A most interesting law was passed to encourage industrialization providing a refund of all taxes for a period of ten years to manufacturing establishments earning a profit under four per cent.[36]

For the planters the situation was an impermissible one. With such laws and such legislators, with courts, juries, police, city and county governments, and schools falling more and more under the influence of the radicals and with the latter gaining experience, competence, and confidence with every passing month how long would their monopoly of the land remain decisive? How long before the political events and the economic developments they fostered and in turn mirrored and the developing class of Negro officials and entrepreneurs[37] would decisively challenge that monopoly itself?

More and more, too, the forms by which that monopoly expressed itself were being challenged. Thus, in 1869 and again in 1870 Negro mass meetings and organizations, particularly their Loyal Leagues, in Caldwell's county of Hinds and elsewhere, denounced sharecropping and even urged Negroes to refuse to work on plantations for wage pittances but to insist upon the status of renters and to pay, as rent, no more than $1.50 per acre. The planters were, of course, hysterical in their fury at such ideas and their press could hardly contain itself in hurling invectives at the "impudent and impertinent niggers," while even the leading Republican organ, edited and controlled by whites, thought these were the proposals of madmen.[38] Still, might not the insane propositions of today become the realities of tomorrow? Comparing 1860 with 1870 who was to say what 1880 might bring? There was no time to lose.

The ranks of the Democrats must be purged and closed; ruthless, co-ordinated and sustained terror must be employed upon the radical rank and file as well as the leadership; and splits in the Republican Party must be fostered and developed. Thus, the *Columbus Mississippi Democrat* was calling, in December, 1870, for a revitalized party whose "leading ideas [should be] that white men shall govern, that niggers are not rightly entitled to vote. . . . There are professed Democrats who do not understand Democratic principles, that want the party mongrelized . . . [such] unprincipled men . . . will sink lower in the social scale than the niggers themselves."

The knout, the rope, the club, the torch, the gun and the white hood are the instruments, the stuffed ballot boxes, the burned schoolhouses and churches, the heaped corpses are the results. And behind it all—wealth, corrupting, devastating wealth. Give up your dreams or starve; come over to us and prosper.

It is not possible to count the victims of this terror; it is very much easier to count the numbers punished for there is none. Reported the United States Attorney for the Northern District of Mississippi in April, 1872 on his execution of the Federal anti-KKK act passed the preceding year: two hundred arrests, no convictions except of twenty-eight men who had confessed their guilt, but even for these "the sentence was suspended." The report of the Attorney for the Southern District of the state was similar: one hundred and fifty-two indictments, twelve confessions, no convictions, no one punished.[39] Teachers, Negro and white, were the particular objects of this terror, and in Winston County, in 1871, *all* Negro schoolhouses and churches used as schools were burned.[40]

It was largely on the question of the suppression of this terror that the sought-for split in the Republican Party occurred,[41] for the conservative element in that party, notably the planter-governor himself, James L. Alcorn, helped frustrate all suggestions of vigorous counter-action. And even when, at the height of the terror, in March, 1871, President Grant informed Congress that neither life nor property was secure in much of the South and especially in Mississippi, and that body moved to the consideration of an anti-Klan law, Alcorn vehemently opposed such action. On April 2, he wired the Mississippi congressional delegation urging them to defeat the proposed legislation and declaring that doing nothing "will lead to absolute repose."

Learning of this several members of the state legislature wired to Mississippi's Senator Ames the next day that, "The auditor's books show 54 killed from March 1, 1869, to March 1, 1870, and 83 killed from March 1, 1870, to February 17, 1871. Report of inquests on many known to have been killed since January 1, 1871 not yet received by the auditor." On April 4th Ames was told by the same people: "Auditor's books show killed last three months: January, 11; February, 14; March, 23. Auditor states at least 15 more killed in March not officially reported."[42] In the ensuing months the division between the Alcorn, or moderate, Republicans, and the Ames, or radical, Republicans, grew.*

* Alcorn resigned his governorship in November, 1871, and took his seat in the Senate to which the legislature had earlier elected him. While there he opposed in December, 1871, Sumner's Civil Rights Bill, demanding: "Give us the removal of our disabilities [*i. e.*, disfranchisement of top Confederate figures and officials] and I will go with him who goes farthest to demand of the southern people obedience to the law. Down, then, with the Ku Klux, and I will go with you in all that is necessary to enforce that demand."—*Cong. Globe,* 42nd Cong., 2nd sess., p. 246. (In 1872 the disabilities were removed).

In a speech on the floor of the Senate Alcorn broke completely, and bitterly, with Ames. The latter, a native of Massachusetts, had risen to the rank of general in the Union Army (as an artillery lieutenant he had won the Congressional Medal of Honor) and was prominent in military affairs in Mississippi prior to aligning himself with the left-wing of the Republican Party. Benjamin F. Butler was his father-in-law. A biography of Ames is needed.

In 1873 this split reached the point worked for and dreamed of by the Bourbons for both Alcorn and Ames announced themselves as gubernatorial candidates. When the regular party nomination went to Ames, Alcorn bolted and ran as a so-called Independent Republican, whereupon the Democrats made no nomination and threw their support behind him. This tactic and the terrorism that had preceded it cut the radical majority, but to the intense chagrin of the planters Alcorn was beaten by almost 20,000 votes in a total of some 126,000.[43]

But one decision was possible for the Bourbons: the time for maneuvers and deals was passed. Nightly visits to annoying individuals, spies and stool-pigeons to reveal the names of leaders, remained useful. More important now, however, was to be the technique of mass assault and mass terrorization, the technique of the "riot" accompanied and followed by the slaughter of impertinent ones, in groups of five, ten, a score. And all this was to be in preparation for the supreme effort, the attempt at actually seizing the reins of government, to come during the elections of 1875.

This had worked elsewhere—Tennessee, Louisiana, Alabama—it must be made to work in Mississippi. There had been tentative stabs at it, as a matter of fact, in Mississippi. Thus, at Meridian, in March, 1871, about thirty Negroes were killed and the local Republican government was overthrown, but this had not resulted too happily for it had been the direct inspiration of a Presidential message to Congress calling for protective measures which in turn led to the anti-KKK act.[44]

But when a country distraught by the panic of 1873 and disgusted by the colossal corruption of the *nouveaux riches* industrial bourgeoisie and their political henchmen inflicted a resounding defeat upon the Republicans in the congressional elections of 1874, Southern Democrats, and particularly those in Mississippi, flung aside all restraint. In November and December, 1874, a systematic massacre of Negro leaders began with the killing of about half a dozen in Austin and anywhere from about 40 to 80 in Vicksburg. The latter event was so horrible that it resulted in the dispatching of some Federal troops in order to call a halt, after the legislature, meeting in special session, had appealed to the President.[45]

In the election year of 1875 the butchery went on with regularity—though not without resistance and occasional fatalities among the assassins—Water Valley, Louisville, Macon (here some dozen Negroes were killed by strong-arm squads coming in from Alabama), Vicksburg again, and, on September 1, Yazoo City where the radical white sheriff, A. T. Morgan, a former Union colonel, was driven out and the usurpers continued their reign of terror under the guise of a self-imposed martial law.[46]

The climax, however, came on September 4 near Caldwell's home village of Clinton at the so-called Moss Hill riot. The occasion was a Republican political celebration, parade, and barbecue, to be accompanied by speeches. At the suggestion of Caldwell, himself a candidate for re-election to the state senate and chairman of the Hinds County Executive Committee of the Republican Party, a Democrat was invited to debate the issues at this meeting.[47]

In the midst of the Republican's speech, loud cursing and heckling began. Caldwell himself, as he stated:

> proceeded to the spot indicated. When I got there I asked what is the matter. A policeman said this man Thompson has drawn a pistol on one of the colored men who was marching in the procession, using certain opprobrious epithets. I remarked, my young friend, for God's sake don't disturb the meeting. I soon saw that the feeling was so strong and so determined that I called upon some of the other white men to assist me in preserving the peace. No one responded. I saw Neil Wharton and Thompson (white) draw their pistols and I slipped up to Neil telling him that that would not do. I did the same with Thompson and they put their weapons back in their pockets. In a few minutes they had them drawn again; then the shooting began. I saw Thompson shoot the first shot that was fired, pouring some four or five shots into the crowd of which he had formed a part. At this time the firing had become general. The colored people soon concentrated at this point, when the white lines dispersed, and the firing ceased.[48]

The casualties at the scene were approximately two whites killed, four wounded; two Negroes killed, five wounded. There followed, in and around Clinton, four days of unbridled, systematic slaughter of Negro and white radical leaders, the total murdered coming to somewhere between thirty-five and fifty. This was accomplished by about two hundred local "citizen soldiery" as they were called, reinforced by a trainload of expertly trained and fully armed men, known as Modocs,[49] sent from Vicksburg at the request of Clinton's mayor. In the words of the Democratic leader of Hinds county, "Throughout the county for several days the negro leaders, some white and some black, were hunted down and killed. . . ."[50] but not all were captured for several hundred, including Caldwell, escaped to the capital.

The Modocs did not fail to visit Caldwell's home, where his wife was busy nursing two Negro victims of the riot. "About fifty came out to my house that night [Sept. 4]," Mrs. Caldwell tells us,[51] where they "plundered and robbed." They stayed until daybreak when, before leaving, their leader told her to inform the senator that they were "going to kill him if it is two years, or one year, or six; no difference; we are going to kill him anyhow. We have orders to kill him, and we are going to do it, because he belongs to this republican party, and sticks up for these negroes." Then, leaving her,

> they went to a house where there was an old black man, a feeble old man, named Bob Beasly, and they shot him all to pieces. And they went to Mr. Willis's and took out a man, named Gamaliel Brown, and shot him all to pieces . . . and they goes out to Sam Jackson's, president of the [Republican] club, and they shot him all to pieces . . . and they went out to Alfred Hastings . . and they shot Alfred Hastings all to pieces . . . every man they found they killed that morning. . . .

So it went for three more days, the Negroes meanwhile vainly beseeching the authorities for arms with which they might defend themselves.

In Clinton through all this a small detachment of Federal troops bestirred itself not at all, though on the fourth day, "An arrangement was made . . . that if they would stop the killing of the negroes, the United States officers would not assume command but leave matters in charge of the [self-imposed] civil authorities." At a dinner for these officers and gentlemen the guests all "arose, saluted and loudly cheered until the whole building resounded with their tokens of good will" when the genial guest of honor, Major Allen, the Federal commander, entered.[52]

On September 6 the leader of these usurpers, one S. M. Shelton, wired J. Z. George, head of the state Democratic Party:

> There can be no peace in Hinds County while the radical leaders are at large. We are fully prepared to meet the issue and accept no terms which do not assure their surrender or removal from the county. We do not recognize the Ames government but will have no conflict with the Federal authorities.[53]

The next day Governor Ames issued a proclamation taking note officially of the violence and terrorism and of the forceful overthrow of legal county governments in Yazoo and Hinds, and calling upon all extra-legal armed bodies, into which most of the Democratic clubs had by now transformed themselves, to disband.

This was greeted by defiance and ridicule. "Ha! Ha!! Ha!!!" said the *Mississippi Weekly Pilot* the next day, " 'Command.' 'Disband.' That's good." And the *Yazoo City Herald* snorted, on September 10:

> What impudence. Our dapper little Governor Ames comes to the front with a proclamation ordering the disbandment of all the military companies now organized in the State. If he had brains enough to know his right hand from his left, he ought to know that no more attention will be paid to his proclamation than the moon is popularly supposed to pay to the baying of a sheep-killing dog.

And behind it all, the bitterness, the derision, the terror, as the *Yazoo City Banner* admitted in a moment of frankness on September 23, was this: ". . . wenches wedded to carpet-baggers, and can't work out—young negroes ain't worth a damn. No cotton pickers to be found for the big crop. Ain't we in a hell of a fix?"

The day after his proclamation, Ames appealed to Grant for Federal assistance, but on September 11 George wired to the Attorney-General, Edwards Pierrepont, that "perfect peace prevails throughout the State, and there is no danger of disturbance unless invited by the State authorities, which I hope they will not do."[54] The two Mississippi Senators split on their advice to the President, the recently elected Negro, Blanche K. Bruce, urging Federal aid, while James L. Alcorn, true to his role, condemned such a course.[55] President Grant, through Pierrepont, informed Ames, on September 14, that "The whole public are tired out with these annual autumnal outbreaks in the South," that he, himself, was not convinced Federal aid was really needed, and that therefore he was sending none.[56] Meanwhile, Pierrepont secretly sent a personal agent to Mississippi to observe, report back, and to do his best to keep the disorder below the surface.*

With the handful of Federal troops in the state officered by men being dined and applauded by the planters, with legally elected county governments overthrown and the usurpers publicly asserting their defiance, with the press greeting appeals for the terror to cease as "impudence" and announcing that, "The people of this State are now fully armed, equipped, and drilled,"[57] with hundreds of refugees crowding Jackson, and with the Federal government announcing itself as "tired" of reports of disturbances, Ames turned to enrolling and activating a state militia.

State officers, both Negro and white, were appointed and the enlistment of companies begun. In September and early October seven companies were formed (five Negro, two white), and the first of these to be mustered and armed—being the first to offer itself—was Company A, 2nd Regiment of Mississippi Infantry, commanded by Captain Charles Caldwell and 1st Lieutenant Eugene B. Welborn.[58]

The first mission considered for Caldwell's company was that of spearheading a drive to overthrow the violently imposed reactionary regime in Yazoo county and to reinstate in the sheriff's office Colonel Morgan. When this proposition was put to the latter he rejected it on the ground that one or even two militia companies (*i.e.,* about two hundred men) would never succeed in such a task but would simply be wiped out, and so the attempt was not made. "It was certainly not the fault of the colored company that they did not try," Morgan wrote later, "My old

* This was a New York businessman, George K. Chase. It is clear that while Chase's own agents reported violence almost everywhere so that he himself told Pierrepont on October 27, 1875—rather late!—"It is impossible to have a fair election on November 2 without the aid of U. S. troops," his central function was to help maintain a semblance of order.—*Boutwell Report,* II, pp. 1801-19.

friend, Charles Caldwell, was its captain. They were at all times ready to go."[59] That Morgan's estimate of the situation was correct is apparent from a contemporary account of the preparations made to greet him in Yazoo when his coming was rumored—nine hundred mounted, armed men were waiting.[60]

But the governor did entrust Caldwell with a mission. It was possible to enroll men in the militia, but how to get arms to them? Some that had been sent from Jackson unprotected had been captured and appropriated by the "civilian army."[61] Now arms would be delivered under guard. There was a company formed at Edwards' Depot, some thirty miles due west of Jackson; it needed guns and Caldwell's company would see that it got them.

In the morning of October 9, 1875, Captain Caldwell and his one hundred and two Negro men, carrying four days' rations, and one hundred extra guns plus ammunition, set out—flags flying, drums beating, bayonets fixed—for a march of a day and a half via public road in the heart of Mississippi. They bivouacked overnight just outside Clinton—from which many of the men were refugees—sleeping lightly, it may be believed. Then, the next morning, on to Bolton and into Edwards' Depot before noon. Back they went, the same day, Caldwell leading two hundred men now. On the return trip they picked up another company—this from Brownsville, a town ten miles north of Bolton—and thus did Caldwell come marching into Jackson with three hundred Negro militiamen, two-thirds of them armed, completing a truly amazing feat of courage and, above all, leadership.[62]

While Caldwell and his men were marching, the Democratic managers were frantically telegraphing and visiting key personnel and begging them to offer no resistance to the Negro. For, as they pointed out, he would fight to the death, the battle could not be hidden from view, he was the Governor's official representative, and violence might lead to real Federal intervention, a supervised election and defeat.[63]

Desperately late as this action was—the election but three weeks away—had it been energetically pursued, throughout the state, the result might possibly have been different. But late in September the Democratic command filed suit for a warrant restraining the state auditor from issuing any funds for military purposes (since the state was not at war!) and this was granted by the Chief Justice, E. G. Peyton, another one of the wealthy old-line Whigs who, like Alcorn, had joined the Republican Party.[64] On October 12 Governor Ames, apparently deciding all was lost, ordered the disbanding of the militia companies and the disarming of their members, although the latter command does not appear to have been obeyed with alacrity or completeness.[65]

Three days later, at the prodding of the Democratic leaders and the agent of the attorney-general, the governor entered into a formal peace treaty with the former. This, while upon its face an armistice, actually represented Ames' capitulation. It pledged both parties to abstain from violence, fraud, and intimidation, while Ames agreed to maintain the demobilization of the militia, to complete its disarming, and to take no new step without first consulting George, leader of the forces engineering the coup d'etat.[66]

Meanwhile in the same month another "riot" occurred at Friar's Point resulting in the deaths of six Negroes and two whites, whereupon Senator Alcorn urged the attorney-general not to be unduly upset; ". . . there need be no alarm for the peace of this country. . . . A community of planters may be relied on for kind treatment of laborers." Thereupon the sheriff of Alcorn's own county of Coahoma was driven out two weeks before the voting to assure its result and to guarantee the "kind treatment."[67]

Newspapers bore upon their mastheads the slogan, "Carry the election peaceably if we can, forcibly if we must," bribery flourished, employers fired known radicals, physicians refused to treat them, and their names were published "for future reference" with the whites among them marked for special vituperation. And if, said the planters, it should by some miracle happen that we lose, "all landowners will resist payment of all taxes. Legal resistance will, when exhausted without giving results, be succeeded by such protection as that afforded by Winchester rifles and other peace-makers."[68]

On October 29, Caldwell wrote the governor that the peace treaty was a farce:

The intimidation and threatening of colored voters continues uninterrupted, and with as much system, determined purpose, and combination of effort as if it were a legitimate means of canvassing . . . the peace agreement is held in utter contempt, and only serves as a cover for perpetrating the very wrongs . . . it was intended to prevent. In behalf of the people whom I represent [he concluded] I appeal to your excellency for the protection which the laws of the State guarantee to every citizen regardless of party or race.[69]

The day before the election a Negro wrote the governor from Yazoo City:

I beg you most fulley to send the United soldiers here; they have hung six more men . . . now they are going to have war here to-morrow; send help; they told Mr. Richardson if he went to the telegraph office to-morrow they would hang him; help, help, help, help; soon as you can . . . fighting commence just as I were closing; 2 two killed; we would of carred this election, but you keep listen at the white people; pleas send troops and test the election; help; send troops and arms, pleas. . . .[70]

Meanwhile *The Nation* was informing its cultured and liberal clientele that "peace and harmony reign" throughout Mississippi where "arrangements have been made by which fairness and a spirit of concord will prevail in the future." This happy result eventuated because of the wise refusal to send troops into the area and despite the "large and ignorant black population, and among the whites a considerable number of lawless fellows fond of knifing and shooting. . . ."[71]

As for the voting the leader of the Democratic Party for Hinds county tells us what happened. First, the Republican registrar was bribed to stay away. And, as for the Negroes, there was "individual effort . . . persuasive, but if necessary, intimidation"; as for the ballots, "destruction of Republican tickets when they could be gotten," or "substitution of Democratic for Republican tickets." Precisely what was "intimidation"? Nine days after the election, the *Aberdeen Examiner*, published in the seat of Monroe county, explained that though a bridge had been torn down and pickets posted to prevent the appearance of Negro voters, still they came. As a result, "the man in charge of the Democratic war department" [!] surrounded them with cavalry imported from Alabama and with native infantry, kept the Negroes covered with an artillery piece "and then sent a strong arm squad into the crowd to beat the Negroes over the head."[72]

But, for *The Nation,* "The election passed off quietly," there had been "a fair vote" and Mississippi was "emancipated."*

Charles Caldwell voted. Eugene Welborne, who had been Caldwell's militia lieutenant, tells about it. On election day he said to Caldwell:

"Senator, I think we might just as well give up; I don't see any use trying to stay here any longer; we can't do anything here. Here these men are riding all about the country with their sixteen-shooters and cutting up in this manner."

Caldwell replied: "No; we are going to stay right here; you must just come right along, and keep your mouth shut. I don't care what they say to you, don't you say a word." And they voted.[73]

The Bourbons won the election. In Coahoma county while there had been 1,300 Republican votes in 1873, there were 230 in 1875; in Yazoo county where 2,500 Republican votes were cast in 1873 there were 7 in 1875. Yes, they won. But the remarkable thing is that there were tens of thousands of radicals who voted. In Caldwell's own county over 2,300 Republican votes were cast—true, over a thousand below that of two years before, but there were the votes. And in the state as a whole, while the Democrats won by over 30,000 nevertheless there were 67,171 Republican votes *counted.* And twenty-two out of seventy-four counties were won by the Republicans, a Negro Republican,

* Nov. 4, 1875, XXI, p. 285. Somewhat belatedly—on July 26, 1876—President Grant confessed to Governor Chamberlain of South Carolina, that, "Mississippi is governed today by officials chosen through fraud and violence such as would scarcely be credited to savages, much less to a civilized and Christian people." *The Nation,* Aug. 10, 1876, XXIII, p. 81. A Federal Grand Jury reported from Oxford, July 8, 1876, ". . . we must say that the fraud, intimidation and violence at the late election is without a parallel in the annals of history. . . ." *Boutwell Report,* II, Doc. Evid., pp. 150*f.* The findings of the Senate committee were the same, but. as *The Nation* declared: "Senator Boutwell's report seems to meet with universal condemnation from the Republican press. . . ."—Aug. 17, 1876, XXIII, p. 97. Reconstruction was old stuff, the Hayes-Tilden bargain was soon to be struck—let's get on with the Lord's work, getting rich. Was not Bishop William Lawrence of Massachusetts to usher in the twentieth century by remarking, "Godliness is in league with riches"?

John R. Lynch, was re-elected to Congress (with considerable white support) and sixteen Negroes were returned to the state House of Representatives, in spite of everything.*

Clearly, from the Bourbon's viewpoint, the victory of 1875 was much too uncertain to permit them to dispense with terror. No, the leaders whose names had been ostentatiously entered on "death lists" during the election and who still survived must be eliminated.[74] High on that list was such a one as Charles Caldwell, and his murder came quickly.

It happened on Christmas Day, 1875, and this is how it was:[75]

Living with the Caldwells was a nephew named David Washington. Early that Christmas David was in a Clinton blacksmith shop when several white men, whom he knew, entered. They wanted to know how many he, David, had killed on the day of the Moss Hill riot, and did he come to town now to kill some more, and if not what was he doing in town anyway? David hurried home and told his aunt about this, and she said, "Don't go out anymore. Probably they are trying to get up a fuss here."

Late in the afternoon Caldwell came home from work, learned of the conversation and went into town "to see about it." He returned shortly, had his dinner, and just before sundown went back to the village.

There a friend (white or Negro does not appear in the evidence—a Judas, in any case), named Buck Cabell, greeted him, and this was returned, for Caldwell "never knowed nothing against him." Cabell insisted that Caldwell go with him to Chilton's store and let himself be treated, on this holiday, to a drink. The two men went to the store's basement, poured their drinks, lifted their glasses, and then ". . . at the tap of the glasses . . . as

* Statistics from official figures in *Boutwell Report,* II, Doc. Evid., pp. 144-45. Mechanically comparing the Republican vote of 1875 with the Ames vote of 1873, as does Donald, *op. cit.,* p. 459, and concluding that the Republicans polled only 3,000 less in the former year than in the latter is completely unrealistic and ignores the fact that the 1873 election saw both candidates running, nominally, as Republicans, thus splitting the vote. The idea that Negro political activity and struggle simply and immediately ceased with the overthrow of Reconstruction, while very widespread, is quite erroneous. In Mississippi, for example, the pattern of 1875 was repeated at each election until 1890, when the illegal disfranchisement of the Negro was put into the constitution—a constitution, by the way, never ratified by the people. But that requires a separate study.

they struck their glasses, that was the signal to shoot." And he was shot in the back of the head by someone "from the outside of the gate window, and he fell to the ground."

In the street stood the assassins—many of them. But Caldwell was not yet dead. He called for Judge Cabaniss,[76] "a particular friend," but the judge did not come, and he called for the store-owner, but he did not come, and he called for "I don't know who else. They were all around, and nobody went to his relief; all of them men standing around with their guns." Finally one Preacher Nelson went to the cellar door and called in to Caldwell not to shoot him and he'd come to him. Caldwell said he would not harm him, just "take me out of the cellar" for he "wanted to die in the open air, and did not want to die like a dog closed up."

Preacher Nelson carried him to the street and Caldwell asked that they "take him home and let him see his wife before he died; that he could not live long." But they would not do it; instead "they all cried, 'We'll save him while we got him; dead men tell no tales.' " Caldwell "never begged them" and he stood up and then "taking both sides of his coat and bringing them up so, he said, 'Remember when you kill me you kill a gentleman and a brave man. Never say you killed a coward. I want you to remember it when I am gone." Then "they riddled him with thirty or forty of their loads" and he was dead. And Preacher Nelson told his widow that "a braver man never died than Charles Caldwell."

Just then up the streets of Clinton rode Caldwell's brother, Sam, a man quite unlike Charles, a mild man, "never known to shoot a gun or pistol in his life—never knew how," but they killed him, too, for fear he would spread the alarm.

Yet the alarm did reach the Negro community; it was still early—"the moon was quite young, and the chapel bell rang" and this was the signal of danger. "When the bell tolled [the Negro men] rushed right out; they went through the door and some slid down the window and over they sprang; some went over the fence. They all ran to the chapel and got their guns"—one hundred and fifty guns and then they stood guard over their homes.

Later that evening the bodies of Charles and Sam Caldwell—

Sam's wife now alone with three young ones—were brought home and laid out and the widows mourned. But not in peace did they mourn, for Caldwell's murder had so enraged the Negro people that the planters felt a need for reinforcements and in from Vicksburg once again came the Modocs.[77] And once again they called on Mrs. Caldwell. It was now one o'clock in the morning of the 26th.

"They all marched up to my house," said Mrs. Caldwell, "and went into where the two dead bodies laid, and they cursed them, those dead bodies, there, and they danced and threw open the window, and sung all their songs, and challenged the dead body to get up and meet them." "Get up and fight," they said to Charles Caldwell, and then they struck him, but this time, for the first and only time, Caldwell did not meet their challenge and did not answer blow for blow.

With such blood fertilizing its soil the *Commercial and Financial Chronicle* of New York could well tell its subscribers that the South "now presents a more hopeful condition than any other portion of the country. She is virtually out of debt; her people have learned to economize . . . labor is under control for the first time since the war, and next year will be more entirely so, permitting of further economies. . . ."[78]

So perished, as the chroniclers of Mississippi have asserted, "a notorious and turbulent negro." Those having different values may find other adjectives.

It is altogether likely that one day Mississippi school children, Negro and white, will be taught to revere the name and to hold precious the memory of Charles Caldwell.[79]

# APPENDIX

## Negro Members of Union Navy Killed in Action[1]

| *Name* | *Rating* | *Date* | *Scene* | *Ship* | *Source* |
|---|---|---|---|---|---|
| Stephen Jones | contraband[2] | 7/9/62 | off Plymouth N. C. | Commodore Perry | R-62, p. 147 |
| George B. Dewvent[3] | wdrm. steward | 6/28/62 | Shelling Vicksburg | Clifton | O-18, p, 643 |
| Daniel Moore | officer's steward | 12/31/62 | off Cape Hatteras | Monitor (sank, storm) | R-63,[4] p. 27 |
| Robert Howard | officer's cook | 12/31/62 | off Cape Hatteras | Monitor (sank, storm) | R-63,[4] p. 27 |
| Robert Cook | cabin boy | 12/31/62 | off Cape Hatteras | Monitor (sank, storm) | R-63,[4] p. 27 |
| James Lloyd | boy | 12/13/62 | off New-bern, N. C. | Ellis | O-8, p. 291 (compare R-63, p. 37) |
| William Ayler | pilot | 4/17/63 | Nansemond River | Coeur de Lion | R-63, p. 93 |
| Robert McKinsey | 2d cl. boy | 1/31/62 | off Charleston | Keystone State | R-63, p. 168-169 |
| Robert Willinger | 2d cl. boy | 1/31/62 | off Charleston | Keystone State | R-63, p. 168-169 |
| Joseph Mays | landsman | 1/30/63 | Stono R. | Isaac Smith | R-63, p. 184 |
| Henry Newton | 1st cl. boy | 1/1/63 | Galveston | Harriet Lane | R-63, p. 315-16 |
| Isaac Deer (missing, believed dead) | coalheaver | 2/23/63 | Berwick Bay | Col. Kinsman | R-63, p. 335 |
| William Parker | coalheaver | 2/23/63 | Berwick Bay | Col. Kinsman | R-63, p. 335 |
| George Jackson | contraband | 3/15/63 | Port Hudson | Mississippi | O-19, p. 683 |
| 3 unnamed | contraband | 3/15/63 | Port Hudson | Mississippi | O-19, p. 683 |
| James Haywood | contraband | 4/29/63 | Grand Gulf | Pittsburg | R-63, p. 480 |
| James Wilson | 1st cl. boy | 5/27/63 | Vicksburg | Cincinnati | O-25, p. 43 |
| Albert Williams | 1st cl. boy | 5/27/63 | Vicksburg | Cincinnati | O-25, p. 43 |
| Richard Howard | 1st cl. boy | 5/27/63 | Vicksburg | Cincinnati | O-25, p. 43 |
| Henry Freeman[5] | 1st cl. boy | 5/27/63 | Vicksburg | Cincinnati | O-25, p. 43 |
| Alfred Banks | boy | 2/2/64 | Newbern, N. C. | Underwriter | O-9, p. 446 |
| Lewis Liverman | ? | 2/2/64 | Newbern, N. C. | Underwriter | R-64, p. 172 |
| William Wilson | 1st cl. boy | 5/5/64 | Yorktown | Mystic | O-9, p. 726 |
| Jeremiah Sills | landsman | 6/4/64 | Ossabaw Sound | Water Witch | R-64, p. 344 |
| George Brimsmaid (murdered after capture) | landsman | 12/5/63 | Magnolia Beach, S. C. | Perry | O-15, p. 160 |
| Richard Ashley | boy | 8/5/64 | Mobile | Lackawanna | R-64, p. 465 |
| Many (less than 22) all unnamed; one stated as killed, others missing | | 9/7/63 | Sabine Pass | Clifton | O-20, p. 542 |
| Unnamed | | 6/24/64 | Clarendon | Queen City | R-64, p. 595 |
| Charles H. Thomas (missing) | seaman | 1/19/65 | Ft. Fisher | Minnesota | R-65, p. 103 |

| | | | | | |
|---|---|---|---|---|---|
| Johnson Smith | landsman | 4/1/65 | Blakely River, Ala. | Rodolph | O-22, p. 74 |
| Jule Baltour | boy | 4/1/65 | Blakely River, Ala. | Rodolph | O-22, p. 74 |
| Philip Williams | landsman | 4/1/65 | Blakely River, Ala. | Ida | R-65, p. 385 |
| G. D. Andrews | 1st cl. boy | 4/12/65 | Mobile Bay | Althea | R-65, p. 386 |
| J. Glen | landsman | 4/12/65 | Mobile Bay | Althea | R-65, p. 386 |
| Frank Davis | contraband | 10/3/62 | Franklin, N. C. | Hunchback | O-8, p. 111 |
| Unnamed | | 4/19/63 | Near Plymouth, N. C. | Smithfield | O-9, p. 422 |
| Unnamed pilot (wounded, murdered after capture) | | 4/?/62 | New Smyrna, Fla. | Henry Andrew | O-13, p. 83<br>O-12, p. 647 |
| William Moran | landsman | 5/23/64 | St. John's R., Fla. | Columbine | O-15, p. 449 |
| Stephen Downey | ? | 3/15/63 | Port Hudson | Mississippi | O-19, p. 683 |
| Scot Lewis | ? | 3/15/63 | Port Hudson | Mississippi | O-19, p. 683 |
| Moses Obenton (all 3 reported as missing) | ? | 3/15/63 | Port Hudson | Mississippi | O-19, p. 683 |
| 3 unnamed (one place, given as drowned; another, "badly scalded") | contraband | 3/25/63 | Vicksburg | Switzerland | O-20, pp. 18-20 |
| Chas. J. Pemberton | seaman | 8/5/64 | Mobile | Tecumseh | O-21, p. 492 |
| Nat. B. Delano | landsman | 8/5/64 | Mobile | Tecumseh | O-21, p. 492 |
| Charles Hannible | landsman | 8/5/64 | Mobile | Tecumseh | O-21, p. 492 |
| Charles C. Derris | landsman | 8/5/64 | Mobile | Tecumseh | O-21, p. 492 |
| John Jay | landsman | 8/5/64 | Mobile | Tecumseh | O-21, p. 492 |
| At least 37 (unnamed) | contraband | 7/15/62 | Yazoo R. | Lancaster | O-23, p. 244 |
| Robert Higgins | coal heaver | 4/26/64 | Junction Red and Cane R. | Juliet | O-26, p. 84 |
| Joseph Scott | ord. seaman | 4/26/64 | Junction Red and Cane R. | Ft. Hindman | O-26, p. 85 |
| George Matthews | ord. seaman | 8/11/64 | Rowdy Bend, Ark. (?) | Prairie | O-26, p. 505 |

[1] The key to the source column of this table is: R means *Report* of the Secretary of the Navy, and it is followed by the last two numbers of the pertinent year—thus, R-62 means Report of the Secretary for 1862; O means *Official Report of the Union and Confederate Navies* and this is followed by the appropriate volume. The volume, in every case, unless otherwise indicated, is of Series I.

[2] Where one found the term "contraband" for rating, this was generally equivalent to saying that the individual's rank was that of a first, second, or third-class boy, which carried a monthly pay of $10, $9, $8 respectively.

[3] In R-62, p. 411, this name is given as Derwent, but the above, from the muster-roll, seems to be correct.

[4] The source does *not* indicate that these men were Negro, but the muster-roll of the ship does.

[5] In R-63, p. 505, name given as Truman.

To complete the picture of casualties, as presented by the two basic sources used in compiling the above data, another table is herewith presented concerning Negro members of the Union Navy who were wounded or captured by the enemy.

## Engagements in which Negroes of Union Navy were Wounded or Captured

| *Number wounded* | *Date* | *Scene* | *Ship* | *Source* |
|---|---|---|---|---|
| 1 | 7/9/62 | Plymouth, N. C. | Shawsheen | R-62, p. 148 |
| 2 | 3/10/62 | Newport News | Minnesota | R-62, p. 96 |
| 1 | 7/15/62 | Vicksburg | Hartford | R-62, p. 417 |
| 1 | 1/31/63 | Charleston | Keystone State | R-63, p. 169 |
| 1 | 1/1/63 | Galveston | Owasco | R-63, p. 311 |
| 5 (captured) | 1/1/63 | Galveston | Harriet Lane | R-63, p. 318 |
| 22 (captured) | 1/23/63 | Galveston | Morning Light | R-63, p. 328-30 |
| 3 | 5/27/63 | Vicksburg | Cincinnati | R-63, p. 505 |
| 1 | 3/31/64 | Colleton R., S.C. | Chippewa | R-64, p. 308 |
| 2 | 8/5/64 | Mobile | Hartford | R-64, p. 464 |
| 2 | 8/5/64 | Mobile | Lackawanna | R-64, p. 465 |
| 1 | 8/5/64 | Mobile | Kennebec | R-64, p. 469 |
| several (number not stated; captured) | 9/?/63 | Sabine Pass | Clifton | R-64, p. 491 |
| several (number not stated; captured) | 4/22/64 | Yazoo City | Petrel | R-64, p. 581<br>O-26, p. 249 |
| several (number not stated; captured) | 6/24/64 | Clarendon | Queen City | R-64, p. 595 |
| 3 | 1/30/63 | Stono R., S. C. | Isaac Smith | O-13, p. 567 |
| 5 | 4/1/65 | Blakely R., Ala. | Rodolph | O-21, p. 132-33 |
| 1 | 4/1/65 | Blakely R. | Ida | O-21, p. 133 |
| 1 | 4/12/65 | Mobile Bay | Althea | R-65, p. 386 |
| 1 | 1/10/62 | Elizabeth City, N. C. | Valley City | O-6, p. 615 |
| 1 (captured) | 3/3/63 | Little River Inlet, N. C. | Matthew Vassar | O-8, p. 585 |
| 15 (captured aboard both vessels) | 5/6/64 | Sabine Pass | Granite City Wave | O-21, p. 264 |
| 1 | 6/17/62 | St. Charles, Ark. | Mound City | O-23, p. 181 |
| 1 | 8/30/62 | Between Paducah, Ky. & Hamburg, Tenn. | Terry | O-23, p. 333 |
| 1 | 4/12/64 | Pleasant Hill, La. (?) | Lexington | O-26, p. 50 |
| 9 (captured) | 6/24/64 | Clarendon (?) | Queen City | O-26, p. 419 |
| 1 | 3/17/65 | Mattox Creek, Va. | Don | O-5, p. 535 |

It will be observed that these tables specifically account for approximately two hundred battle casualties among Negro crew members of the Union fleet. The great limitations, however, of the sources used in compiling these tables are to be borne in mind. First, not every engagement involving casualties is reported. Second, in some cases, the fact that casualties were sustained is mentioned, but no indication is given of the numbers involved. Third, in many cases, where numbers are shown, and even, at times, where names are given, there is no way of discovering, from these sources alone, the color of the men involved.

That some of the men named in the *Official Records* as casualties, though not there identified as to color, actually were Negroes, is a demonstrable fact. For example, the names of four of the casualties aboard the U.S.S. *Stepping Stones* in engagements of April 13-14, 1863, on the Nansemond River, below Suffolk, Virginia, are given in the printed source, but their color is not indicated. When, however, one checks the muster-roll of the vessel he finds that three of those mentioned, Giles Scott, John Down, and Samuel Dent, were Negroes.[6]

Still another example is that of William H. Brown, whose name only is given as one of those wounded aboard the *Brooklyn* at Mobile Bay on August 5, 1864, but checking the muster-roll discloses that he was a Negro.[7]

[6] ORN, ser. I, vol. VIII, p. 725; muster-roll, *Stepping Stones*, June 30, 1863, Navy Department Records, National Archives, Washington, D. C.

[7] ORN, ser. L, vol. XXI, p. 409; muster-roll dated June 30, 1864, NDR. A truly definitive study of the Negro in the Union Navy and the casualties he suffered would require the checking of the muster-rolls of the over one thousand vessels composing that force, and comparing all casualty reports with those rolls, a task probably outside the capabilities of a single individual. Note should be taken, too, of the fact that Negroes were in the crews of commercial ships and privateers during the War. For note of the legal problems arising from the capture of some of these by the Confederacy, see W. M. Johnson, Jr., *The Confederate Privateers* (New Haven, 1928), pp. 40, 95.

# REFERENCE NOTES

## SLAVE GUERRILLA WARFARE

1 Similarly, in the *Encyclopedia of the Negro—Preparatory Volume* (rev. edit., N. Y. 1946), p. 119, edited by W. E. B. Du Bois and G. B. Johnson, the entry under maroons describes them as outlying belligerent fugitive Negroes of the West Indies and Central and South America, but not within the United States. Some contemporary writers and a few later historians have noticed, in a general and meager way, the existence of this feature of American slavery. See Charles W. Janson, *The Stranger in America* (London, 1807), pp. 328-30; William H. Russell, *My Diary, North and South* (Boston, 1863), pp. 88-89; Frederick L. Olmsted, *Journey in Seaboard Slave States* (2 vols., London, 1904), II, pp. 177-78, Olmsted, *Journey in the Back Country* (London, 1860), pp. 30, 55; T. W. Higginson, *Army Life in a Black Regiment* (Boston, 1870), p. 248; James Parton, *Life of Andrew Jackson* (2 vols., Boston, 1860), II, pp. 397-98; W. H. Siebert, *The Underground Railroad* (N. Y., 1899), p. 25; S. M. Ellis, *The Solitary Horseman* (Kensington, 1927), p. 169; V. A. Moody, in *Louisiana Historical Quarterly* (1924), VII, pp. 224-25; R. H. Taylor, in *North Carolina Historical Review* (1928), V, pp. 23-24; U. B. Phillips, in *The South in the Building of the Nation* (Richmond, 1909), IV, p. 229.

2 See an article by Edmund Jackson in *The Pennsylvania Freeman*, January 1, 1852; Harriet Beecher Stowe, *Dred* (2 vols., Boston, 1856); Margaret Davis in *South Atlantic Quarterly* (1934), XXXIII, pp. 171-84; and references in footnote 1 above.

3 W. Hening, *Statutes At Large of Virginia*, II, p. 299; P. A. Bruce *Economic History of Virginia in 17th Century* (2 vols., N. Y., 1896), II, p. 115; MS. Order Book, Middlesex County, 1680-1694, pp. 526-27, in Archives, Virginia State Library, Richmond.

4 E. C. Holland, *A Refutation of the Calumnies . . .* (Charleston, 1823), p. 63; D. D. Wallace, *The History of South Carolina* (4 vols., N. Y., 1934), I, p. 372.

5 Virginia Manuscripts from British Record Office—Sainsbury, IX, p. 462 in Va. State Library.

6 MS. Council Journal, V, pp. 487, 494, XI, pp. 187, 383, in South Carolina Historical Commission, Columbia, S. C.

7 D. D. Wallace, *op. cit.*, I, p. 373; *The Boston Chronicle*, Oct. 3-10, 1768; A. D. Candler, ed., *The Colonial Records of Georgia* (Atlanta, 1907), XIV, pp. 292-93.

8 A. D. Candler, ed., *op. cit.*, XII, pp. 146-47, 325-26.

[9] M. D. Conway, *Omitted Chapters in History Disclosed in the Life and Papers of Edmund Randolph* (N. Y., 1888), pp. 50-51.

[10] W. B. Stevens, *A History of Georgia* (2 vols., Phila., 1859), II, pp. 376-78; *Historical Manuscripts Commission, Report on American Manuscripts* (London, 1904), II, p. 544; Carter G. Woodson, *The Negro in Our History* (Washington, 1928), p. 123. A wealthy Charlestonian, William Reynolds, Sr., in a letter of December 12, 1783, declared that thirty of his slaves had fled, followed the British General Provost's army "from this state to Savannah," and that thereafter most of them had fled again and joined Creek Indians. Slavery File, S. C. Hist. Comm.

[11] All cited MSS. in S. C. Hist. Comm.

[12] Letter dated Richmond, Nov. 19, 1792, in Boston *Gazette,* Dec. 17, 1792.

[13] Wilmington *Chronicle,* July 3, 10, 17, 1795 (photostats, Lib. of Cong.); Charleston *City Gazette,* July 18, 23, 1795; R. H. Taylor in *North Carolina Historical Review* (1928), V, pp. 23-24.

[14] MSS., S. C. Hist. Comm.

[15] Raleigh *Register,* June 1, 1802 (State Library, Raleigh); N. Y. *Herald,* June 2, 1802; Edenton *Gazette,* March 22, 1811; G. G. Johnson, *Ante-Bellum North Carolina* (Chapel Hill, 1937), p. 514.

[16] J. W. Pratt, *Expansionists of 1812* (N. Y., 1925), pp. 92, 116, 192-95, 212.

[17] T. F. Davis in *Florida Historical Quarterly* (1930), IX, pp. 106-07, 111, 138; *Niles' Weekly Register* (Baltimore), Dec. 12, 1812, III, pp. 235-37.

[18] See, for example, Richmond *Enquirer,* July 10, 1816.

[19] Hartford *Connecticut Courant,* Sept. 10, 24, 1816; *State Papers,* 2d sess., 15th Cong., Vol. IV; J. B. McMaster, *History of the People of the U. S.,* IV, p.431; McMaster's account is practically copied by H. B. Fuller, *The Purchase of Florida* (Cleveland, 1906), p. 228.

[20] H. T. Cook, *Life and Legacy of David R. Williams* (N. Y., 1916), p. 130.

[21] Raleigh *Register,* Nov. 13, 27, 1818.

[22] G. G. Johnson, *op. cit.,* p. 514.

[23] U. B. Phillips, ed., *Plantation and Frontier Documents* (2 vols., Cleveland, 1909), II, p. 91; Edenton *Gazette,* May 12, 1820, quoted by N. Y. *Evening Post,* May 17, 1820.

[24] N. Y. *Evening Post,* June 11, 1821.

[25] See petition of John H. Hill, colonel of the Carteret Militia, dated December, 1825, and accompanying memoranda in Legislative Papers, 1824-25 (No. 366), North Carolina Historical Commission, Raleigh; R. H. Taylor, *op. cit.,* V, p. 24; G. G. Johnson, *op. cit.,* p. 514.

[26] N. Y. *Evening Post,* May 11, 1824.

[27] Washington *National Intelligencer,* July 23, Aug. 24, 1822.

[28] See N. Y. *Evening Post,* May 15, 29, June 5, 30, 1823.

[29] Charleston *City Gazette,* quoted in N. Y. *Evening Post,* Oct. 24, 1823; *Niles' Weekly Register,* Oct. 18, 1823, XXV, p. 112; T. J. Kirkland and R. M. Kennedy, *Historic Camden* (Columbia, 1926) pt. two, p. 190.

[30] MSS, S. C. Hist. Comm.

[31] Mobile *Register,* quoted in N. Y. *Evening Post,* July 11, 12, 1827; U. B. Phillips in *The South in the Building of the Nation,* IV, p. 229.

[32] N. Y. *Evening Post,* Dec. 4, 1827.

[33] N. Y. *Evening Post,* Aug. 10, 1829.

[34] MS., S. C. Hist. Comm.

[35] G. G. Johnson, *op. cit.*, pp. 515, 517; R. H. Taylor, *op. cit.*, V, p. 31.

[36] See letter Nov. 15, 1830, Newbern, from J. Turgwyn to Gov. John Owen in Governor's Letter Book, XXVIII, pp. 247-49, and letter from J. I. Pasteur to Gov. Owen same date and place, in Governor's Papers, No. 60.—N. C. Hist. Comm., Raleigh.

[37] See, *The Liberator,* Jan. 8, Mar. 19, 1831; Richmond *Enquirer,* Aug. 30, 1831.

[38] *Louisiana Advertiser,* June 8, quoted by *Liberator,* July 2, 1836; New Orleans *Picayune,* July 19, 1837.

[39] *The Liberator,* Mar. 18, 1837; John T. Sprague, *The Origin, Progress, and Conclusion of the Florida War* (N. Y., 1848), p. 309; J. R. Giddings, *The Exiles of Florida* (Columbus, 1858), pp. 121, 139; Grant Foreman, *Indian Removal* (Norman, 1932), pp. 336, 383.

[40] Wilmington *Chronicle,* Jan. 6, 1841, in *The Liberator,* Jan. 22, 1841.

[41] New Orleans *Bee,* Oct. 4, 1841; Lafourche (La.) *Patriot,* in *Liberator,* Nov. 12, 1841.

[42] St. Louis *Argus,* July 23, 1841, quoted in *Niles' National Register,* Aug. 7, 1841, LX, p. 360; John D. Lang and Samuel Taylor, Jr., *Report of a Visit to Some of the Tribes of Indians Located West of the Mississippi* (Providence, 1843), p. 41. Compare with Joseph B. Thoburn, *A Standard History of Oklahoma* (4 vols., Chicago, 1916), I, pp. 254-55.

[43] Hanesville *Free Press,* Mar. 1, 1844, quoted by *Liberator,* Apr. 5, 1844; New Orleans *Picayune,* quoted by *Liberator,* Dec. 4, 1846.

[44] J. R. Giddings, *op. cit.*, pp. 316, 334, 337; F. L. Olmstead, *Seaboard . . .*, Vol. I, p. 177; *Back Country,* pp. 30, 55.

[45] Governor's Letter Book, No. 43, pp. 514-15, N. C. Hist. Comm.

[46] Vicksburg *Whig,* quoted by *The Liberator,* Apr. 3, 1857; Norfolk *Day Book,* Oct. 13, 1859; Laura White, in *Journal of Southern History,* (1935), I, p. 47.

[47] N. Y. *Tribune,* March 11, 1861; H. M. Henry, *Police Control of the Slave in South Carolina* (Emory, 1914), p. 121.

[48] *Official Records of the Union and Confederate Armies* (hereafter cited as ORA), ser. I, Vol. IX, p. 199.—Burnside to Stanton, Mar. 14, 1862.

[49] ORA, ser. I, Vol. LIII, p. 233.

[50] *Calendar of Virginia State Papers,* XI, pp. 233-36.

[51] ORA, ser. I, Vol. XV, p. 947; G. L. Tatum, *Disloyalty in the Confederacy* (Chapel Hill, 1934), p. 63.

[52] Tatum, *op. cit.*, p. 88; ORA, ser. I, Vol. XXV, pt. 2, p. 607.

[53] Richmond *Daily Examiner,* Jan. 14, 1864.

[54] See, for example, Stuart Jamieson, "Labor Unionism in American Agriculture," in *Monthly Labor Review* (1946), LXII, p. 26.

## BUYING FREEDOM

[1] Helen T. Catterall, ed., *Judicial Cases concerning American Slavery and the Negro* (5 vols., Washington, 1926-1937), I, pp. 157, 302; IV, pp. 172, 177,

180; V, p. 213. See also Kate E. Pickard, *The Kidnapped and the Ransomed* (Syracuse, 1856), p. 47.

[2] Lorenzo J. Greene, *The Negro in Colonial New England* (N. Y., 1942), pp. 184, 291.

[3] Catterall, ed., *op. cit.*, I, p. 81. See, Marion J. Russell, "American Slave Discontent in Records of the High Courts," in *Journal of Negro History* (1946), XXXI, p. 425.

[4] *Logan v. Commonwealth*, 1845, in Catterall, I, p. 208. Later a lower court ruled a contract between master and slave, calling for the payment of $350 for freedom and providing that the Negro be at liberty while earning this sum, invalid as being contrary to public policy, but this was reversed, in 1859, it being held "this contract is not void as being against public policy." —*Shue v. Turk, ibid.*, I, pp. 248-50; see also pp. 134, 152, 158.

[5] *Craig v. Mullen*, 1840, *ibid.*, I, pp. 348-49; see also pp. 302, 412.

[6] *Ford v. Ford*, 1846, Catterall, II, p. 530; see also pp. 479, 514, 534, 585. For the Tennessee law see R. L. Caruthers and A. Nicholson, *Compilation of the Statutes of Tennessee* (Nashville, 1836), p. 279. The text of this act makes clear the fact that contracts for self-purchase had been recognized prior to its enactment.

[7] Articles 174 and 177. See Catterall, III, p. 631, and 670. Under Spanish rule slaves in Louisiana had had the right to demand their assessment if they could produce anyone willing to pay for their emancipation, and they might, also, challenge the price thus fixed.—*Ibid.*, III, pp. 427, 440, 444. See, however, the case of *Suriray v. Jenkins*, 1776 (*Louisiana Hist. Quart.* 1928, XI, pp. 338-52) where the Attorney of the Royal Audiences at Havana advised freedom at the price of the slave's acquisition, but the Royal Governor of Louisiana, de Galvez, refused to heed this as he felt that while it might be proper for Cuba, it did not cover "the rest of His Majesty's Dominions."

[8] *Guardian of Sally* (*a Negro*) *v. Beaty*, 1792, in Catterall, II, p. 275; in 1846, however, this court found it necessary to rule that "all the acquisitions of the slave are the property of the master."—*Gist v. Toohey, Ibid.*, II, p.398.

[9] *Ibid.*, IV, pp. 87, 170, 172, 180.

[10] John H. Franklin, *The Free Negro in North Carolina 1790-1860* (Chapel Hill, 1943), pp. 27-29. The quoted provision was part of a general anti-manumission law, but its enforcement was not rigid.

[11] These practices existed despite repeated laws illegalizing them. For an example of such a law note that of Tennessee, enacted 1823, providing a fine of from one to two dollars per day for every day that a master "shall hire to any slave or slaves, the time of such slave. . . ," in Caruthers and Nicholson, eds., *op cit.*, p. 679. In the city of Richmond there were, in 1860, eighteen hiring agents, that is, men whose profession it was to serve as employment bureaus for the approximately five thousand slaves who were hired workers in or near that town. In 1852 the Petersburg *Daily Express* professed alarm at this practice in its town, and said the Negroes were approaching "the condition of the whites."—L. Jackson, *Free Negro. . .*, pp. 176, 181. See also, Wright, *op cit.*, p. 75; Turner, *op cit.*, p. 60; J. H. Easterby, ed., *The South Carolina Rice Plantation. . .* (Chicago, 1945), p. 34; H. Aptheker, *American Negro Slave Revolts* (N. Y., 1943), p. 64; W. R. Hogan, *The Texas*

*Republic* (Norman, 1946), p. 22. A slave blacksmith, John Dogan, of Knoxville, Tenn., agreed with his master to turn over all money earned during the first ten hours of each day's labor, while he was permitted to retain everything made thereafter. Two years after this agreement the slave had accumulated enough money to purchase his wife-to-be, and in another two years he paid his master $600 for his own freedom—Charles W. Cansler, *Three Generations: The Story of a Colored Family of Eastern Tennessee* (n.p., 1939), p. 23; and J. M. England, "The Free Negro in Ante-Bellum Tennessee," in *The Journal of Southern History* (1943), IX, p. 40.

[12] Slaves, for example, participated in lotteries and, as winners, were allowed to retain the prize. In this way Newport Gardner of Providence, Rhode Island, and Denmark Vesey of Charleston were able to buy their freedom.—L. Greene, *op. cit.*, p. 294; H. Aptheker, *op. cit.*, p. 268.

[13] Wright, *op. cit.*, p. 79.

[14] U. B. Phillips, *American Negro Slavery* (N. Y., 1918), p. 427.

[15] Carter G. Woodson, *The Negro in Our History* (Washington, 1929), p. 293.

[16] L. P. Jackson, *Free Negroes. . .*, pp. 184-85, 188-89. Virginia, in 1806, required that manumitted slaves leave the state within one year from the date of emancipation. Permission, however, could be granted by the legislature to remain permanently. In the state archives at Richmond there are such petitions from at least ninety-one Negroes who had purchased their freedom. Most of these were urban, skilled workers. See J. H. Johnston, "Race Relations in Virginia and Miscegenation in the South, 1776-1860," unpub. doctorate, University of Chicago, 1937, pp. 4-6. For similar data for Norfolk see L. P. Jackson, "Negro Enterprise in Norfolk during the Days of Slavery," in *The Quarterly Journal of the Florida A.&M. College* (April, 1939), VIII, pp. 5-12. See also J. P. Guild, *Black Laws of Virginia* (Richmond, 1936), p. 72.

[17] A. Mott, *Biographical Sketches of People of Color* (N. Y., 1839), p. 240.

[18] Letter dated Cincinnati, March 18, 1834, in G. H. Barnes and D. L. Dumond, eds., *Weld-Grimke Letters* (2 vols., N. Y., 1934), I, p. 134. An investigation of Cincinnati at about the same time found that of the approximately 2,500 Negroes then in the city, 1,129 had been in slavery of whom 476 had purchased their freedom at a total cost of over $215,000. Moreover, it was stated: "There are a large number in the city who are now working out their own freedom—their free papers being retained as security . . . others are buying their husbands and wives, and others again their parents or children." *Report on the Condition of the People of Color in the State of Ohio, From the Proceedings of the Ohio Anti-Slavery Convention, held at Putnam, on the 22nd, 23rd, and 24th of April, 1835* (n.d., n.p.). Similarly, a careful census of the Negro population of Philadelphia, made in 1847, found that of 1,077 residents who had been born slaves, 275 had purchased their own freedom at a cost of over $60,000.—*A Statistical Inquiry into the Condition of the People of Colour, of the City and Districts of Philadelphia,* (Phila., 1849), p. 10.

[19] See *The Journal of Negro History,* III (1918), p. 91; XIII (1928), p. 534

[20] E. M. Boykin, "Enterprise and Accumulation of Negroes prior to 1860," unpublished master's thesis, Columbia University, 1933, p. 26.

[21] L. P. Jackson, *op. cit.*, p. 191.

[22] J. H. Franklin, *op. cit.*, p. 31.

[23] L. P. Jackson, *op. cit.*, p. 186.

[24] Guion G. Johnson, *Ante-Bellum North Carolina* (Chapel Hill), p. 587; W. W. Hening, *Statutes at Large of Virginia* (Phila., 1823), XIII, p. 619; L. P. Jackson, *op. cit.*, pp. 178, 187; J. H. Johnston, *op. cit.*, p. 6; Booker T. Washington, *The Story of the Negro* (2 vols., N. Y., 1909), I, p. 195. See also *Transcriptions of Parish Records of Louisiana prepared by the Historical Records Survey Division . . .* WPA. *Jefferson Parish* (*Gretna*) Series I, *Police Jury Minutes,* Vol. I, 1834-1843 (New Orleans, 1939, mimeographed), pp. 137, 139, 169, 173, 177, 185, 239, 290; *Ibid., Iberville Parish* (*Plaquemine*), I, (1850-1862), pp. 8, 47; *The Journal of Mississippi History* (1941), III, pp. 44-45.

[25] *Narrative of the Life of Rev. Noah Davis* (Baltimore, 1859), preface. Davis here appeals for more money with which to free his last two children; K. Pickard, *op. cit., passim.;* W. G. Hawkins, *Lunsford Lane* (Boston, 1863), *passim.*

[26] *Annals of Cleveland 1818-1935. A Digest and Index of the Newspaper Record of Events and Opinions in 200 volumes, written, edited and multigraphed by the workers of the Works Progress Administration of Ohio* (Cleveland, 1937-38), XXXVIII, pt. I, pp. 278, 564, 571, 572; XXXIX, pt. 1, p. 456; XXXIX, pt. 2, pp. 323, 325. The Newbern, N. C. *Journal* of Sept. 19, 1855, reported that a free Negro of its town, the Rev. Robert Green, was then in New York trying to raise $2,500 with which to free his five children —Franklin, *op. cit.*, p. 31.

[27] See, as examples, the five volumes of Mrs. Catterall's work, using the index under "manumission by self-purchase"; D. Beasley, *The Negro Trail Blazers of California* (Los Angeles, 1919), p. 70; F. Bremer, *The Homes of the New World* (2 vols., London, 1853), I, p. 371; K. Bruce, *Virginia Iron Manufacture in the Slave Era* (N. Y., 1931), p. 241; B. Drew, *A North-Side View of Slavery* (Boston, 1856), pp. 149, 250, 252, 270; D. L. Dumond, ed., *Letters of James G. Birney* (2 vols., N. Y., 1938), I, p. 487; J. H. Russell, *The Free Negro in Virginia* (Baltimore, 1913), pp. 170 ff; A. Debo, *The Road to Disappearance* (Norman, 1941), p. 115; of twenty Negro leaders of Savannah, Georgia, questioned by Gen. Sherman in 1865, two had bought their own freedom, one had bought his own and his wife's freedom, and the mother of a fourth had thus liberated herself.—N. Y. *Tribune,* Feb. 13, 1865, p. 5.

[28] See B. Brawley, *Negro Heroes and Builders* (Chapel Hill, 1937), pp. 200, 273; C. Wesley, *Richard Allen* (Washington, 1935), pp. 16, 59; E. F. Frazier, *The Negro Family in the United States* (Chicago, 1939), p. 209; K. E. Pickard, *op. cit.*, appendix; D. B. Porter, "Afro-American Writings," unpublished master's thesis, Columbia, 1932, p. 19; W. Still, *Underground Railroad Records* (Phila., 1886), pp. 175, 187; B. T. Washington, *op. cit.*, I, p. 290; C. B. Roussève, *The Negro in Louisiana* (New Orleans, 1937), pp. 51, 107; L. P. Jackson, *Negro Office-Holders in Virginia, 1865-1895* (Norfolk, 1945), pp. 4, 14, 28. The above is by no means an exhaustive list. One might add, for example, Lott Cary, Venture Smith, and Gustavus Vasa. Note, too, that both James W. C. Pennington and Frederick Douglass, having escaped from slavery, still found it advisable to buy their legal freedom, and both made effective use, in their agitational work, of the bills of sale.

[29] Examples are: Georgia, 1801; Virginia, 1805; South Carolina, 1820. Catterall, I, p. 72; II, pp. 4, 268; III, p. 1.

[30] J. Russell, *op. cit.*, p. 92; Wright, *op. cit.*, p. 79; *Journal of Negro History*, IX (1924), p. 41.

[31] *Reminiscences of Levi Coffin* (Cincinnati, 1876), p. 577.

[32] Letter dated Feb. 26, 1849, in C. E. Norton, *Letters of James Russell Lowell* (2 vols., N. Y., 1894), I, p. 151. Henry Ward Beecher and Harriet Beecher Stowe, among others, bore similar testimony. The latter, in 1852, organized a tour for a Mrs. Milly Edmundson embracing churches in Portland, Boston, Brooklyn, New York, and New Haven and resulting in funds sufficient to free her two children. Among those contributing was the world-famous Jenny Lind.— See C. E. Stowe, *Life of Harriet Beecher Stowe* (Boston, 1891), pp. 178 ff.

## MILITANT ABOLITIONISM

[1] A pacifistic and non-political Abolitionist, Lydia Maria Child, in a letter to Ellis Gray Loring, dated New York, Jan. 25, 1842, asserted that a belief in the propriety of political action would lead, inevitably, to the justification of militant action. According to Mrs. Child: "Then politics and military force not only *seem* allied together, when looked at through non-resistance spectacles, but they really *are* allied together. . . . Both are founded in want of faith in spiritual weapons; both seek to shape the inward by the outward; both aim at controlling and coercing, rather than regenerating. . . . The time will come when you and Wendell Phillips . . . will confess that I looked at this subject with candid discrimination, and not through the 'peeping-stone' of non-resistance merely."—Lydia Maria Child MSS, New York Public Library.

[2] Herbert Aptheker, "The Quakers and Negro Slavery," in *The Journal of Negro History* (1940), XXV, pp. 336, 338. Observe Jefferson's note to Governor James Monroe of Virginia after the great Gabriel slave plot, urging mercy in the punishment of the rebels: "The other states & the world at large will forever condemn us if we indulge a principle of revenge, or go one step beyond absolute necessity. They cannot lose sight of the rights of the two parties, & the object of the unsuccessful one."—Letter dated Monticello, Sept. 20, 1800, in P. L. Ford, ed., *The Writings of Thomas Jefferson* (10 vols., N. Y., 1903), VII, pp. 457-58.

[3] MS Council Journal, VIII, p. 13, South Carolina Historical Commission, Memorial Building, Columbia, S. C.

[4] L. Hartz, "Otis and Anti-Slavery Doctrine," in *The New England Quarterly* (1939), XII, pp. 745-47.

[5] John Adams to William Tudor, dated Quincy, June 1, 1818, in C. F. Adams, ed., *The Works of John Adams* (10 vols., N. Y., 1850-56), X, p. 315; incorrectly quoted by Hartz, *op. cit.* Observe the remark of Mrs. John Adams in a letter to her husband, dated Boston, Sept. 22, 1774, telling of the discovery of a slave plot: "I wish most sincerely there was not a slave in the province; it always appeared a most iniquitous scheme to me to fight ourselves for what we are daily robbing and plundering from those who have as good a right to freedom as we have."—C. F. Adams, ed., *Letters of Mrs. Adams, the Wife of John Adams* (2 vols., 3rd edit., Boston, 1841), I. p. 24.

[6] Quoted by A. M. Baldwin, *The New England Clergy and the American Revolution* (Durham, 1928), p. 119.

[7] Reprinted often, as Samuel Hopkins, *Timely Articles on Slavery* (Boston, 1854).

[8] *The American Museum* (Philadelphia, 1789), VI, p. 80. Note the statement of James Madison, made in 1783, in connection with the capture of a runaway slave belonging to him: "[I] cannot think of punishing him by transportation merely for coveting that liberty for which we have paid the price of so much blood, and have proclaimed so often to be the right, & worthy the pursuit of every human being."—Quoted by Abbot E. Smith, *James Madison* (N. Y., 1937), p. 221.

[9] Philip S. Foner, ed., *The Complete Writings of Thomas Paine* (2 vols., N. Y., 1945), II, p. 1286.

[10] W. F. Poole, *Anti-Slavery Opinions Before the Year 1800* (Cincinnati, 1873), p. 17.

[11] *The American Museum,* 1791, XII, pp. 299-300.

[12] David Rice, *Slavery Inconsistent with Justice and Good Policy* (London, 1793), p. 9. This pamphlet was originally issued in Philadelphia in 1792.

[13] Theodore Dwight, *An Oration Spoken before the Connecticut Society for the Promotion of Freedom and the Relief of Persons Unlawfully Holden in Bondage, Convened in Hartford on the 8th Day of May, A. D. 1794,* pp. 20, 23. See M. S. Locke, *Anti-Slavery in America from the Introduction of African Slaves to the Prohibition of the Slave Trade (1619-1808)* (Boston, 1901), pp. 169-71.

[14] Locke, *op. cit.,* points out items of this nature in issues of Dec. 12, 1796, and Aug. 28, 1797; see also, issues of Aug. 21, and Sept. 4, 1797.

[15] *A Charge, Delivered to the African Lodge, June 24, 1797, at Menotomy,* by the Right Worshipful Master, Prince Hall (*n.p.,* 1797), pp. 11-12; B. Brawley, *The Negro Genius* (N. Y., 1937), pp. 30-31. An earlier charge, however, is in large part devoted to advising against plots or rebellions. See *A Charge Delivered to the Brethren of the African Lodge on the 25th of June, 1792, at the Hall of Brother William Smith, in Charlestown, by the Right Wor shipful Master, Prince Hall* (Boston, 1792), *passim.*

[16] Letters from Savannah dated Apr. 28, 1804, and two not dated, but same approximate days, in the N. Y. *Evening Post,* May 8, 9, June 2, July 3, 1804. U. B. Phillips mentions fears of rebellion in Georgia in 1804—*American Negro Slavery* (N. Y., 1918), p. 476. A work published in Washington in 1804, by W. T. Washington, contains this sentence: "It is a melancholy reflection that while the energies of white men directed to shake off impositions, merely on trade, in every part of the world, meet with applause, the struggles of the blacks for liberty should meet with death if unsuccessful."—*Political Economy Founded in Justice and Humanity,* pp. 3-4.

[17] St. Louis *Enquirer,* Oct. 20, 1819, in H. A. Trexler, *Slavery in Missouri* (Baltimore, 1914), p. 114. New England Federalist opposition to the War of 1812 provoked considerable denunciation of the slavery existing in the predominantly Democratic South. At times this led to expressions tending to favor slave revolt. Thus, the Reverend Elijah Parish of Massachusetts, in July, 1812, urged his congregation to "let the southern *Heroes* fight their own battles, and guard . . . against the just vengeance of their lacerated

slaves. . . ."—Quoted by Joseph Dorfman, *The Economic Mind in American Civilization* (2 vols., N. Y., 1946), I, p. 345.

[18] Lionel H. Kennedy and Thomas Parker, *An Official Report of the Trials of Sundry Negroes Charged with an Attempt to Raise an Insurrection in the State of South Carolina. . .* (Charlestown, 1822), appendix. The editor of the Portland, Maine, *Christian Mirror,* John L. Parkhurst, demanded in the issue of Sept. 2, 1825, the immediate abolition of slavery. He raised the question of insurrection and, in regard thereto, said: "Calamitous as such a struggle must be to our citizens, dreadful as must be the horrors of *servile war,* we should regard even these as less to be deplored than the perpetual existence of slavery in our land."—C. M. Clark, *American Slavery and Maine Congregationalists* (Bangor, 1940), p. 28.

[19] As originally issued this was called *The Hope of Liberty Containing a Number of Poetical Pieces* (Raleigh, 1829, Gales & Seaton). It is mentioned by G. G. Johnson, *Ante-Bellum North Carolina* (Chapel Hill, 1937), p. 826, but this writer has not seen the original. He has seen a copy published in Philadelphia in 1837, called *Poems by a Slave* which owed its existence to the fact that an Abolitionist, Joshua Coffin, came across the original and reprinted it. The work was published in the hope of raising money to purchase Horton's freedom, but this failed. The publisher, Gales, said he was an "honest and industrious slave," but Collier Cobb (*An American Man of Letters,* reprint from *University of North Carolina Magazine,* 1909), has Horton merely loafing away his time, and feels that his anti-slavery poems were "playing to the grand-stand." This was based on the recollections of white people in 1909! How a slave "played to the grand-stand" by denouncing slavery in a slave state is not clear.

[20] [Robert Alexander Young] *The Ethiopian Manifesto issued in defence of the black man's rights, in the scale of universal freedom* (N. Y., 1829). Compare with Gilberto Freyre, *The Masters and the Slaves* (trans., by S. Putnam, N. Y., 1946), p. 100*n.*

[21] *Freedom's Journal,* Dec. 18, 20, 1828; B. Gross, "Freedom's Journal," in *The Journal of Negro History* (1932), XVII, p. 259*n.*; N. S. Chase, "The attitude of the Negro toward slavery: a study in opinion, 1828-1850," unpublished master's thesis, Howard University, 1936, pp. 14-16. David Walker's son, Edwin G. Walker, was elected to the Massachusetts State Legislature in 1866, one of the first Negroes so honored.

[22] [*David*] *Walker's Appeal, in Four Articles together with a preamble to the Coloured Citizens of the World, but in particular, and very expressly to those of the United States of America, written in Boston, State of Massachusetts, September 28, 1829* (3rd ed., Boston, 1830). The three editions are in the Boston Public Library.

[23] "A Colored Bostonian" reported in *The Liberator,* Jan. 22, 1831, that it was believed Walker had been murdered. A rumor was current that some person or persons in the South offered a large reward to the individual who would kill him. Recently it has been asserted that Walker's death was due to "natural causes," but this was not documented—R. A. Warner, *New Haven Negroes* (New Haven, 1940), p. 100.

[24] *Journal of the House of Representatives of the State of Georgia, at an annual session of the General Assembly begun and held in the Town of Milledgeville, on Monday the second day of November, 1829* (Milledge-

ville, 1830), p. 353. See C. Eaton, "A dangerous pamphlet in the old South," in *The Journal of Southern History* (1936), II, pp. 327-28.

[25] J. H. Johnston, "Race relations in Virginia and Miscegenation in the South, 1776-1860," unpublished doctorate, University of Chicago, 1937, p. 108; L. P. Jackson, *Free Negro Labor and Property Holding in Virginia, 1830-1860* (N. Y., 1942), p. 19*n*.

[26] U. B. Phillips, "The public archives of Georgia," in *The Annual Report of the American Historical Association for the Year 1903* (2 vols., Washington, 1904), I, p. 469.

[27] The quoted words are those of Merle Curti, from *The Learned Blacksmith, the Life and Journals of Elihu Burritt* (N. Y., 1937), p. 118*n*. Professor Curti does not mention, however, the Walker pamphlet. That Elijah safely reached the north appears in a letter from S. S. Jocelyn to W. L. Garrison, dated New Haven, July 12, 1832, asking that *The Liberator* be sent to Burritt at Berlin, Connecticut, "the gentleman who suffers so much on acct of Walker's pamphlet. I had an interview with him yesterday—he is a noble soul—lived 20 years in Geo.—has facts on the subject of slavery most horrible."—MS Letters to Garrison, II, Boston Public Library.

[28] *Niles' Weekly Register* (Baltimore), Apr. 24, 1830, June 19, 1830, XXXVIII, pp. 157, 304.

[29] James F. McRae, Magistrate of Police, to Governor John Owen, dated Wilmington, Aug. 7, 1830, in Governor's Letter Book, Historical Commission, Raleigh.

[30] L. D. Henry to Gov. Owen, in Governor's Papers, vol. 60, N. C. Hist. Commission. See Eaton, *op. cit.*, pp. 330-31. A prominent North Carolinian, Calvin Jones of Wake Forest, drawn from his "secluded retreat" by "the great excitement and alarm that exists in several portions of the state as to an apprehended insurrection of the slaves," urged the Governor, in a letter of Dec. 28, 1830, among other things, to be sure to get hold of Walker (in case, he added, he still was alive).—*Ibid.*

[31] Walker's *Appeal, op. cit.*, pp. 5-6, 9, 29. William Lloyd Garrison who did not agree with Walker's call for violence affirmed that he personally knew that Walker himself wrote the *Appeal.*—*The Liberator,* Jan. 29, 1831. See C. G. Woodson, *The Mind of the Negro as Reflected in Letters Written during the Crisis, 1800-1860* (Washington, 1926), p. 224. According to the Negro Abolitionist, the Rev. Amos G. Beman, the Walker pamphlet was read to gatherings of Negroes in Connecticut—R. A. Warner. *op. cit.*, p. 100.

[32] Original letter as well as a printed clipping are in MS Letters by Garrison, I, Boston Public Library.

[33] *The Liberator,* July 23, 1831. See also letter signed "Consistency" on "The Non-Resistance Doctrine," *Ibid,* July 9, 1831.

[34] *Ibid.*, Sept 3, 1831. For a striking instance of what Garrison was lambasting see "The Call of Poland" by Thomas Campbell, on the editorial page of the *Richmond Enquirer,* Aug. 23, 1831 (two days after the start of Nat Turner's slave rebellion), containing lines asking whether "the hell-mark of slave must still blacken their name," and asserting:

The call of each sword upon Liberty's aid
Shall be written in gore on the steel of its blade!

[35] Robert Dale Owen in the *Free Enquirer* (N. Y.), Sept. 23, 1831; the account in *The Liberator* of the same day is also very full. A. B. Hart in *Slavery*

*and Abolition, 1831-41* (N. Y., 1906), p. 236, incorrectly gives the date of this incident as 1832.

[36] James Forten to Garrison, dated Philadelphia, Oct. 21, 1831, MS Letters to Garrison, I, Boston Pub. Lib.

[37] This, all of which was printed except the month, day, signature, and the word "great," which were written, was enclosed in a letter to Governor Monfort Stokes of North Carolina by James Somervell, dated Warrenton, Oct. 2, 1831. Mr. Somervell was postmaster of Warrenton, and stated that he believed the same circular had been sent to every postmaster in the state. Governor's Papers, vol. 62, Hist. Comm., Raleigh.

[38] Executive Papers, Virginia State Archives, State Library, Richmond; quoted by J. H. Johnston, *op. cit.*, pp. 260-67. Johnston thinks this may have been the work of David Walker, but since it was written subsequent to Sept. 1, 1831, and since Walker's death occurred several months earlier, he could not have been its author.

[39] Garrison's pacifism greatly influenced Tolstoy, to whom, in turn, Gandhi is indebted. See Leo Tolstoy, "Garrison and Non-Resistance," in *The Independent* (1905), LIX, pp. 881-83; H. R. Mussey, "Gandhi the Non-Resistant," in *The Nation* (1930), CXXX, p. 608.

[40] *The Liberator,* Apr. 11, 18, 1835. See also George Thompson, *Letters and Addresses . . . 1834-35* (Boston, 1837), pp. 58-60, 95. Certain remarks by Mr. Thompson make him out to be, at this time, rather a conservative than a radical anti-slavery man. Thus, at the 1835 New York Anti-Slavery Society meeting he declared he opposed the immediate liberation of the slaves without outside control. "All we ask is, that the control of the masters over their slaves may be subjected to supervision, and to legal responsibility." *op. cit.*, p. 72. According to Claude G. Bowers, George Thompson "proposed that the slaves should arise and cut their masters' throats."—*The Party Battles of the Jackson Period* (Boston, 1928), p. 434. Arthur Y. Lloyd says the same thing, *The Slavery Controversy* (Chapel Hill, 1940), p. 115, and cites James Schouler. That historian, however, merely stated that Thompson used "imprudent language."—*History of the United States under the Constitution* (rev. edit., 6 vols., N. Y., 1894), IV, pp. 217-18. The fact is that George Thompson did not advocate servile rebellion, and did not say what Bowers and Lloyd claim he did.

[41] Dated Ipswich, Aug. 20, 1835, in Letters to Garrison, V.

[42] *Fifth Annual Report of the Board of Managers of the Massachusetts Anti-Slavery Society, with some account of the annual meeting, January 25, 1837* (Boston, 1837), pp. xxvii, xxxv, xxxix. Yet Vernon Loggins, *op. cit.*, p. 90, citing Easton's work, *A Treatise on the Intellectual Character . . . Condition . . . of the Coloured People of the United States* (Boston, 1837), says it is, as compared with Walker's *Appeal,* "equally radical." A comparison of the works does not substantiate this characterization.

[43] Dated Brookline, Nov. 30, 1837, in G. H. Barnes and D. L. Dumond, *Letters of Theodore Dwight Weld, Angelina Weld and Sarah Grimke 1822-1844* (2 vols., N. Y., 1934), I, p. 486.

[44] Dated Hudson, N. Y., 12 mo 21st 1837, emphases in original, Letters to Garrison, VI. The same complaint came from Samuel J. May to Garrison in a letter dated South Scituate, Dec. 26, 1837, and from the Buckingham Female

Anti-Slavery Society in a letter to Garrison from J. P. Magill, dated Bucks County, Pa., Jan. 13, 1838.—Letters to Garrison, VI, VII.

[45] George Helmick to Garrison, dated Putnam, Feb. 3, 1838. Letters to Garrison, VII.

[46] Quoted by V. Loggins, *op. cit.*, p. 70. It is pertinent to observe that William Lloyd Garrison, himself, was writing, privately, at this time: "I have relinquished the expectation that they [the slaveholders] will ever by mere moral suasion, consent to emancipation of their victims."—Garrison to the English abolitionist, Elizabeth Pease, Nov. 6, 1837, in Garrison MSS, II, Boston Pub. Lib.

[47] Hammond to Smith, Cherry Valley, May 18, 1839, in R. V. Harlow, *Gerrit Smith Philanthropist and Reformer* (N. Y., 1939), p. 260.

[48] N. Y. *Daily Tribune,* Jan. 29, 1841; W. S. Savage, *The Controversy over the Distribution of Abolition Literature 1830-1860* (Washington, 1938), p. 109.

[49] *The Liberator,* Aug. 13, 1841; Loggins, *op. cit.*, p. 79*n.*; Woodson, *Mind, op. cit.*, p. 252. In a letter from the Pennsylvania Abolitionist, Edward M. Davis, written while on a visit to England and dated London 9 mo. 19, 1840, and addressed to Elizabeth Pease, a leading British Abolitionist, there is enclosed a printed tribute, including a portrait, to Joseph Cinque, leader of the slaves who rebelled aboard the *Amistad* in 1839, as one deserving honor, since he "prefers death to slavery."— Letters to Garrison, IX.

[50] Barnes and Dumond, eds., *op. cit.*, II, pp. 911-12. See also D. L. Dumond, *Antislavery Origins of the Civil War in the United States* (Ann Arbor, 1939), p. 111.

[51] G. W. Julian, *The Life of Joshua R. Giddings* (Chicago, 1892), pp. 118-19; J. R. Giddings, *Speeches in Congress* (Boston, 1853), pp. 19, 22, 24; D. L. Dumond, *op. cit.*, p. 99. An interesting eulogy of Madison Washington, leader of the slave rebels aboard the *Creole,* written by Frederick Douglass and entitled "The Heroic Slave," appeared in Julia Griffiths, ed., *Autographs for Freedom* (Boston, 1853), I, pp. 174- 239.

[52] James McCune Smith, "Sketch of the life of Rev. Henry Highland Garnet," in *A Memorial Discourse; by Rev. Henry Highland Garnet, delivered in the hall of the House of Representatives, Washington, D. C., on Sabbath, February 12, 1865* (Phila., 1865), pp. 17-68; W. M. Brewer, in *The Journal of Negro History* (1928), XIII, pp. 36-52; C. G. Woodson, *Negro Orators and their Orations* (Washington, 1925), pp. 149-156; V. Loggins, *op. cit.*, p. 192; B. Brawley, *op. cit.*, p. 49. Walker's *Appeal* and Garnet's *Address* were issued in one volume in 1848. Brewer, Loggins, and Woodson state that John Brown paid for its publication. In 1849 a convention of Ohio Negroes resolved "that five hundred copies of Walker's Appeal and Henry H. Garnet's Address to the Slaves be obtained in the name of the Convention, and gratuitously circulated."—*State Convention of the Colored Citizens of Ohio, Convened at Columbus, Jan. 10-13, 1849* (Oberlin, 1849) p. 18.

[53] D. L. Dumond, ed., *Letters of James Gillespie Birney 1831-1857* (2 vols., N. Y., 1938), II, p. 742.

[54] This information is given in B. T. Washington, *The Story of the Negro* (2 vols., N. Y., 1909), II, p. 158; and H. Whittaker, "The Negro in the Abolitionist Movement 1830-1850," unpublished master's thesis, Howard University, 1935, p. 63, but neither cites sources. Washington, who seems to have

known Dickson, states he served in the Union Army, and, following the Civil War, was active in establishing Lincoln Institute in Jefferson City, Missouri.

[55] J. G. Birney to W. E. Austen, *et. al.*, dated Lower Saginaw, Michigan, Feb. 23, 1844, in Dumond, ed., *op. cit.*, II, p. 790.

[56] Francis Jackson to Governor George N. Briggs, Boston, July 4, 1844, in *The Anti-Slavery Examiner* (N. Y., 1845), XI, p. 123. Mr. Jackson was reiterating the resolution adopted in 1841 by the American Anti-Slavery Society. He was not, and it did not, however, advocate slave rebellion. It did denounce the obligation to suppress such rebellion. According to Thomas Wentworth Higginson, his friend, Dr. Samuel Gridley Howe, who had been active in Greek and Polish revolutions, had asserted in 1844, "that in his opinion some movement of actual force would yet have to be made against slavery, and that but for the new duties he had assumed by his marriage (1843) he should very likely undertake some such enterprise himself."—*Contemporaries,* (Boston, 1899), pp. 294-95.

[57] Herman Schlüter, *Lincoln, Labor and Slavery* (N. Y., 1913), pp. 58-59; C. H. Wesley, *Negro Labor in the United States 1850-1925* (N. Y., 1927), p. 73. A Boston workingmen's paper, *The New Era of Industry,* July 27, 1848, declared, "Slavery must be extinguished. We go for direct and internecine war with the monster."—Quoted by N. Ware, *The Industrial Worker 1840-1860* (Boston, 1924), p. 226.

[58] Such activity on the part of Indians and fugitive slaves had recently required the United States Army seven years (1836-43) to overcome. As has been shown guerrilla warfare waged by outlying runaway Negroes was everywhere a regular part of the slave institution.

[59] *Life and Times of Frederick Douglass* (Hartford, 1882), p. 217.

[60] Julian, *op. cit.*, p. 243.

[61] Woodson, *Orators,* p. 191.

[62] O. B. Frothingham, *Gerrit Smith* (N. Y., 1879), p. 190.

[63] Reported by William C. Nell in *The Liberator,* Dec. 10, 1852. Earlier "A Colored American" (Henry Bibb?) published a pamphlet the title of which referred to the Vesey martyrs as "patriots."—*The Late Contemplated Insurrection in Charleston, S. C., with the Execution of Thirty-Six of the Patriots* (N. Y., 1850).

[64] Dated Philadelphia May 14, 1852, in *The Liberator,* May 21, 1852, and in Woodson, *Mind,* p. 293. Martin Robison Delany studied medicine at Harvard, served as a newspaper editor for several years in Pittsburg, and was a Major in the Union Army. See Frank A. Rollin (Frances E. R. Whipper), *Life and Public Service of Martin R. Delany* (Boston, 1868).

[65] Jabez D. Hammond, to Smith, Feb. 28, 1852, in Harlow, *op. cit.,* p. 304.

[66] Julia Griffiths, ed., *op. cit.,* I, p. 34, italics in original.

[67] Loguen to Garrison, April 28, 1854, in Woodson, *Mind,* p. 267. This individual act of defiance of slavocratic law by Loguen was *typical* of the statements and behavior of the Negro people north of the Mason-Dixon line, *i.e.,* of those who, in a physical sense, were able to act in this manner. It is typical, too, of the expressions emanating from collective bodies of Negroes. For example, a meeting of Cleveland Negroes resolved, in Sept., 1850: "We will exert our influence to induce slaves

to escape from their masters, and will protect them from recapture against all attempts, whether lawful or not, to return them to slavery." Cleveland *Daily True Democrat,* Sept. 30, 1850. By the 1850's outstanding Negroes like Dr. Charles H. Langston of Ohio publicly declared that "circumstances being favorable" he would be happy to see the slaves assert their freedom "and cut their masters' throats if they attempt again to reduce them to slavery." *Minutes of the State Convention of the Colored Citizens of Ohio...1851* (Columbus, 1851), p. 11. Similar sentiments were expressed thereafter by men like William Howard Day and John Mercer Langston—See *Proceedings of a Convention of the Colored Men of Ohio* . . . 1858 (Cincinnati, 1858), p. 17.

[68] Julia Griffiths, ed., *op. cit.,* II (Auburn, 1854), p. 132. The same volume contains a long eulogistic poem on the Haitian rebel, Vincent Ogé, by a Negro, George B. Vashon.

[69] N. Y. semi-weekly *Tribune,* June 16, 1854, quoted by C. Wesley, *op. cit.,* p. 58.

[70] Benjamin Drew, *A North-Side View of Slavery,* p. 1.

[71] Letter in Syracuse *Journal,* May 31, 1856, in Harlow, *op. cit.,* p. 350.

[72] Douglass' Rochester paper of Nov. 28, 1856, quoted in William Chambers, *American Slavery and Colour* (London, 1857), p. 174. Chambers, in introducing Douglass' remarks asserts that very few Abolitionists held this viewpoint, but the evidence herewith presented refutes that idea.

[73] Dated Hamilton, Canada, Jan. 5, 1857, in William Still, *Underground Railroad Records* (rev. edit., Phila., 1886), pp. 191, 200.

[74] A printed copy of this circular will be found on page 73 of the collection of Lysander Spooner manuscripts in the Boston Public Library. Several handwritten drafts are also there. There is a brief sketch of Spooner in the *Dictionary of American Biography,* but the manuscripts in the Boston Library are not mentioned, nor is this very interesting episode in his life, with which those papers very largely deal.

[75] The Boston *Courier,* Jan. 28, 1859, reporting the contents of the circular, stated it had received copies from a friend in Georgia, and from an unnamed Congressman. It was noticed, too, in the N. Y. *Tribune,* Jan. 28, 1859, and the Boston *Post* of the next day. The latter paper and the Boston *Courier* of Jan. 31, 1859, thought the circular to be a joke, or, in the language of the day, a "quiz." The Boston *Atlas and Bee* of Jan. 31, 1859, decided it was "too absurd to be treated seriously and too silly to be laughed at."—Clippings in the Spooner MSS; that of the *Tribune* enclosed in a letter to Spooner from Hinton R. Helper, dated New York, Jan. 31, 1859.

[76] So declared Spooner in a letter to Governor Henry A. Wise of Virginia, signed "The Author of the Circular," dated Nov. 2, 1859. He wrote in order to clear Brown of any suspicion of being the author for, "I apprehend that the Circular may be considered more disrespectful, and insulting to slaveholders personally, than Brown's enterprise itself. . . ."—Spooner MSS.

[77] Dated Dec. 25, 1858. This was probably the printed circular, for Francis Jackson, in a letter of December 3, already referred to it as printed. French had formerly been associated with the New Hampshire leader, Nathaniel P. Rogers, in the publication of the *Herald of Freedom.*

[78] Dated New York City, Oct. 7, 1858.

[79] Dated Boston, Dec. 3, 1858.

[80] Dated New York, Dec. 18, 1858.

[81] This reference is to Professor Benjamin S. Hedrick, once of the University of North Carolina, who was forced to leave the South in 1856 because of his free-soil views and his expressed preference for John C. Frémont in the Presidential election of that year. A good brief account of this is in Clement Eaton, *Freedom of Thought in the Old South* (Durham, 1940), pp. 202-04. As appears in a letter from Helper to Spooner of Jan. 31, 1859, requesting another copy of the circular, Professor Hedrick kept the one Spooner originally sent him. On Oct. 28, 1859, Helper asked Spooner to send a copy of his letter of Dec. 18, 1858, opposing the circular, in order to help convince those who suspected him of complicity with John Brown of his non-involvement.

[82] Dated Nov. 30, 1858.

[83] Dated Jan. 8, 1859.

[84] Dated Jan. 16, 1859. The information concerning Mann is in J. R. French's letter to Spooner from Painesville, Dec. 25, 1858. Mann wrote in pencil at the end of his letter, "Use, as you choose."

[85] *The Roving Editor: or, Talks with Slaves in the Southern States* (N. Y., 1859).

[86] *Ibid.*, pp. 10, 129. In view of later historical writing, it is interesting to note these words in this work: "The second American Revolution has begun. Kansas was its Lexington...," p. 300. Redpath wrote the first biography of John Brown, and later published other volumes including a collection of the speeches of Wendell Phillips. For his relations with Lincoln, see Carl Sandburg, *Abraham Lincoln, The War Years* (4 vols., N. Y., 1939) I, p. 578.

[87] Redpath, *op. cit.*, p. 306; see also pp. 84, 299.

[88] W. S. Heywood, ed., *Autobiography of Adin Ballou* (Lowell, 1896), pp. 417-22. Ballou was particularly shocked at the fact that the Massachusetts Anti-Slavery Society adopted a resolution praising Brown, and that William Lloyd Garrison specifically associated himself with that act.

[89] Carlos Martyn, *Wendell Phillips: The Agitator* (N. Y., 1890), p. 299; R. V. Harlow, *op. cit.*, pp. 410*ff.*; O. G. Villard, *John Brown* (N. Y., 1909), p. 323.

[90] L. T. Jones, *The Quakers of Iowa* (Iowa City, 1914), p. 197.

[91] H. S. Canby, *Thoreau* (Boston, 1939), chap. XXIV. Mr. Canby aptly states (p. 391): "Subtly, slowly, as is happening with many idealists in the twentieth century, the belief in justified violence had been capturing Thoreau's mind. Passive resistance was not enough in a state that had ceased to recognize human rights and was over-riding personal integrity."

[92] Martyn, *op. cit.*, pp. 295-96.

[93] *The Liberator*, Jan. 10, 1851.

[94] Henry C. Wright, *The Natick Resolution; or, Resistance to Slaveholders the Right and Duty of Southern Slaves and Northern Freemen* (Boston,

1859), *passim*. On the day of Brown's execution, Wright, in a letter, pointed out to Governor Wise that the state seal of Virginia itself attested Brown's righteousness. Senator Henry Wilson of Massachusetts was present at the Natick meeting but denied, on the floor of the Senate, Dec. 6, 1859, that he favored rebellion.

95 Letter dated Jan. 22, 1860, in A. Nevins, *Hamilton Fish, The Inner History of the Grant Administration* (N. Y., 1936), p. 77.

96 W. E. Smith, ed., *The American Civil War, An Interpretation,* by Carl Russell Fish (London, N. Y., 1937), pp. 53-54.

97 Garrison to Redpath, Dec. 1, 1860, in MS letters by Garrison, V.

98 Reported in the N. Y. *Evening Post,* Sept. 27, 1860.

99 See, Bayard Tuckerman, *William Jay and the Constitutional Movement for the Abolition of Slavery* (N. Y., 1894); T. W. Higginson, *Contemporaries* (Boston, 1899), p. 264.

100 *Speech of John Quincy Adams in the Joint Resolution for Distributions to the Distressed Fugitives from Indian Hostilities in the States of Alabama and Georgia* delivered in the House of Representatives, May 25, 1836 (Washington, 1836), pp. 5, 7.

101 Letter dated Oct. 15, 1860, in *Principia* (N. Y.), Nov. 3, 1860. Note an editorial in the N. Y. *Weekly Tribune,* Dec. 13, 1856, in which are these words: "They ask for more territory to be subject to the taskmaster and his cruelties, to the slave and his insurrections...What claim will the South have on the North when insurrections do come?"

102 *The Liberator,* May 24, 1861. In Jan., 1861, Gerrit Smith went to Canada to protest the attempt by Missouri to extradite a fugitive slave, John Anderson, on a charge of murder, the Negro having killed his master who tracked him to Ohio. Smith based the defense on, as he saw it, man's right to be free. In killing the person who attempted to enslave him, the Negro had done, said Smith, "a manly, heroic deed, entitling the man to praise and not to punishment." The extradition request was denied—Harlow, *op. cit.,* p. 425; Frothingham, *op. cit.,* p. 116. Similar ideas recur even in non-Abolitionist papers. For example, the Cleveland *Leader* (Jan. 25, 1858), in reporting the case of a Kentucky slave who had recently killed his master while the latter was whipping the Negro's wife, commented: "We cannot blame this negro for obeying one of the first laws of nature, self-defense. . . ."

103 N. Y. *Daily Tribune,* May 11, 1861.

104 *Ibid.,* June 16, 1861.

105 Letter from T. Bourne, *Ibid.,* July 27; from M. T. V., Aug. 3; editorial, Sept. 19, 1861.

106 MS in collection labeled "The Negro in the the Military Service of the United States," eight volumes of manuscripts, II, p. 827, located in the National Archives, War Records Branch, Washington. So far as has yet been discovered, the first suggestion to arm the Negroes, specifying they be free, came from one Major Burr Porter, of the "Ottoman Army, 3 campaigns," in a letter to Secretary of War Cameron, dated Washington, Apr. 16, 1861. On Apr. 23, 1861, the Negroes of Boston held a mass meeting, requested that they be armed, and pledged that 50,000 Negroes

would come forth at once to help suppress the slaveholders' assault. On the same day a Negro employed by the U. S. Senate, Jacob Dodson, wrote to Cameron that he knew "of some three hundred" Negroes in Washington anxious to get into uniform; but this offer was rejected by the Secretary six days later. Thereafter a veritable flood of similar demands descended upon the Lincoln Administration. See the Boston *Journal,* Apr. 24, 1861, and letters in MS Collection as cited above in this note, II, pp. 803, 806.

[107] See, as examples, N. Y. *Daily Tribune,* Jan. 15, 20, 1862; P. G. and E. Q. Wright, *Elizur Wright* (Chicago, 1937), p. 217.

[108] N. Y. *Daily Tribune,* Jan. 1, 1863. During the war years an occasional pacifistic Abolitionist raised his voice in protest. See, for example, the letter from A. Brooke, dated Marlboro', Ohio, Feb. 20, 1864, in *The Liberator,* Mar. 11, 1864, and the reply thereto by W. S. Flanders of Cornville, Maine, dated Mar. 16, 1864; *Ibid.,* Apr. 8, 1864.

[109] Many who entered the South did so in order to help slaves flee. The existence of the possibility of gaining liberty via flight acted as a safety valve and may well have served to cut down the number of mass uprisings.

[110] For information on this see A. M. Ross, *Memoirs of a Reformer* (Toronto, 1893), *passim.*; Annie Abel and F. Klingberg, *A Side-Light on Anglo-American Relations* (N. Y., 1927), p. 258; D. L. Dumond, ed., *op. cit.,* I, pp. 388*n.,* 527; Harlow, *op. cit.,* p. 275; J. W. Coleman, Jr., *Slavery Times in Kentucky* (Chapel Hill, 1940), pp. 142*ff.;* Eliza Wigham, *The Anti-Slavery Cause in America and its Martyrs* (London, 1863), pp. 63, 64, 81. Torrey's work led to his being sentenced to six years' imprisonment in Baltimore in 1844, but he died in jail in 1846. See his letter to J. M. McKim, dated Baltimore Jail, Nov. 29, 1844, asking that McKim thank several Philadelphia Negroes who had sent money for his defense. MS Letters to Garrison, XIV. Calvin Fairbank aided Lewis Hayden to escape and for this was jailed in Lexington, Ky., in 1848. Hayden learned that his owner would sign, for $650, a petition to pardon Fairbank, and so within sixty days Hayden raised the money, by public and private appeals. In August, 1849, Fairbank was freed. In 1851 he was sentenced to fifteen years' imprisonment, again for aiding in the liberation of Negroes. For thirteen years he rotted in a Kentucky prison, until pardoned in 1864. See an undated manuscript signed by Francis Jackson and Ellis G. Loring in MS Letters to Garrison, XVIII; and *The Liberator,* May 13, 1864, p. 80. In 1879 Garrison and Phillips were attempting to raise money for Fairbank who was absolutely destitute. N. Y. *Daily Tribune,* Jan. 2, 1879, p. 2.

[111] *Reminiscences of Levi Coffin* (London, Cincinnati, 1876), pp. 428-46.

[112] See Earl Conrad, *Harriet Tubman* (Washington, 1943).

[113] W. H. Siebert, *The Underground Railroad* (N. Y., 1899), pp. 28, 152. Not a few residents of the South, Negro and white, aided in this work. See, J. H. Russell, *The Free Negro in Virginia* (Baltimore, 1913), p. 165*n.*; Helen T. Catterall, *Judicial Cases Concerning the Negro and American Slavery* (5 vols., Washington, 1926-35), I, pp. 188, 216-21, 247, 441; II, pp. 67, 511; III, pp. 187, 200; IV, pp. 222, 232.

[114] Dated Charleston, S. C., Feb. 1, 1844, in MS Letters to Garrison, XIV.

[115] This refers to the Abolitionist and author, Lydia Maria Child, whose *Appeal for that Class of Americans Called Africans,* published in Boston in 1833, was particularly popular and influential. A good brief sketch of this lady will be found in Higginson, *op. cit.,* pp. 108-41.

[116] Aug. 1, 1834 was the day upon which the act emancipating the slaves of the British West Indies took effect.

[117] Above the word "plantation" in another hand is written "country seat."

## NEGRO CASUALTIES IN THE CIVIL WAR

[1] *The War of the Rebellion. Official Records of the Union and Confederate Armies* (128 serial volumes, Washington, 1880-1901), Ser. III, vol. V, p. 665*n.*—hereafter cited as ORA. The Provost Marshal General's full report appears in House Executive Document No. 1, 39th Cong. 1st Sess. (Washington, 1866), Vol. IV, parts 1 and 2.

[2] William F. Fox, *Regimental Losses in the American Civil War 1861-1865* (Albany, 1889), p. 574.

[3] *Ibid.*

[4] Joseph T. Wilson, *The Black Phalanx* (Hartford, 1888), p. 123. Wilson was a member of the 2nd Regiment of Louisiana Native Guards, and, later, of the 54th Regiment of Massachusetts Volunteer Infantry. He makes clear his belief that the numbers involved in this behavior ran into the thousands, and asserts: "An order was issued [in the Department of the Gulf] which aimed to correct the habit and to prevent the drawing, by collusion, of the dead man's pay."

[5] Conveniently presented in Frederick H. Dyer, *A Compendium of the War of the Rebellion* (Des Moines, 1908), p. 18. These revised figures represent an increase of about 5,000 over the casualty total embodied in the *Report of the Secretary of War for 1866* (Washington, 1866), p. 89.

[6] Actually the latter figure should be increased considerably for there were 3,306 deaths from causes not stated upon the service records, and the vast majority of these were due, in all probability, to disease. See W. F. Fox, *op. cit.,* p. 529.

[7] *A History of the Negro Troops in the War of the Rebellion 1861-1865* (N. Y., 1888, Harper), p. 324.

[8] When Negro regiments were first formed it was customary to have white men in the higher non-commissioned posts, particularly on the regimental staffs. These men were generally, in time, replaced by Negroes, but what their casualties may have been, or how those casualties were reported—whether as white troops or as part of the Colored units' totals—is not clear. On July 11, 1863, General Lorenzo Thomas, the Adjutant General of the Army, had instructed a Lieutenant K. Knox, on recruiting duty, that "...the Non-commissioned Staff of Regiments and 1st Sergeants of Companies of Colored Troops, are to be in all cases white men...," but in his report to Secretary Stanton, March 25, 1864, he indicated that Negroes were steadily replacing white non-commissioned officers. Thomas' report is in House Executive Document No. 83, 38th Cong., 2d Sess., p. 29. The letter to Lieutenant Knox is on page 1407 of the massive collection

of manuscripts and transcripts of printed and unprinted material compiled by Elon A. Woodward, Chief of the Colored Troops Division, for Brigadier General Richard C. Drum, Adjutant General, U.S.A., in 1888. This is entitled *The Negro in the Military Service of the United States: a compilation of official records, state papers, historical extracts, etc., relating to his military status and service from the date of his introduction into the British North American Colonies,* and is located in the War Records Office, National Archives, Washington. While there are some disappointing features to this collection (for example, at times the source of extracts is not given, or given in so fragmentary a manner that even the very efficient staff of workers at the War Records Office are unable to locate the original items) it contains about five thousand pages of handwritten, typed, and printed source material—about ninety per cent of it on the Negro in the Civil War—and forms a veritable mine—hitherto unused to this writer's knowledge, which will repay study by all interested in the history of the Negro or of the United States. On April 25, 1888, Secretary of War W. C. Endicott recommended to the Speaker of the House that Congress print 2,000 copies of this collection (in three volumes) at a cost of about $7,000, but Congress decided it could not spare this sum of money for such a purpose. See House Ex. Doc. No. 284, 50th Cong., 1st Sess. This collection will be cited hereafter simply as Woodward.

Another error of a contrary nature repeatedly made in handling data on the Negro troops of the Civil War is the assumption that all the officers of Negro regiments who suffered casualties were white men (see, for example, W. Fox, *op. cit.*, pp. 53, 523), but this is false. There were, of course, Negro commissioned officers during the Civil War, and the death of at least one, Capt. Andrew Cailloux, while heroically leading Company E of the 73rd U. S. Colored Infantry (formerly the 1st Louisiana Native Guards) at Port Hudson, La., on May 27, 1863, is well known. See *Official Army Register of the Volunteer Force of the U. S. Army . . . 1861-65* (Washington, 1867, 8 vols.) VIII, p. 247; Williams, *op. cit.*, p. 215; Wilson, *op. cit.*, p. 214*f*. Pertinent, too, is the fact that the father of the famous William Monroe Trotter of Boston, James Monroe Trotter, was wounded at Honey Hill, S. C., on Nov. 30, 1864, when a commissioned (though not yet mustered) 2d lieutenant in the 55th Regiment of Massachusetts Volunteer Infantry. See [Charles B. Fox] *Record of the Service of the 55th Regiment . . .* (Cambridge, 1868), p. 108.

[9] Thomas L. Livermore, *Numbers and Losses in the Civil War in America* (Boston, 1901), p. 9.

[10] A study of individual Negro regimental losses, as shown, for example, in monthly accounts of activities (occurring frequently in Woodward) will show this ratio of 2.75:1 to be conservative. To cite a few instances of better known engagements: the 49th U. S. Colored Infantry lost, at Milliken's Bend, June 7, 1863, 28 officers and men killed, 66 wounded; in storming Fort Wagner, July 18, 1863, the 54th Massachusetts lost 34 killed and 146 wounded, and 92 captured or missing; at Honey Hill, S. C., the same regiment lost three killed and 38 wounded and four missing; in the Battle of the Mine, Petersburg, of July 30, 1864, General Ferrero, commanding the 4th Division, made up of nine Negro regiments, reported

the next day 173 killed and 676 wounded, as well as a large number still unaccounted for.

[11] House Exec. Doc. No. 1, 39th Cong., 1st Sess., vol. IV, p. 83 (serial number 1251). Later revisions, while considerable as already shown, would not seriously affect these figures in a relative sense. A point to be noted here is the fact that many of the so-called "white" Volunteer regiments actually contained a goodly number of Negro soldiers. This will be developed in detail later.

[12] W. Fox, *op. cit.,* p. 49. A few Negro troops were organized, semi-officially, in the summer and fall of 1862 in South Carolina, Louisiana and Kansas, but they were not enrolled, on a mass scale, until the latter months of 1863 and early in 1864.

[13] *Report of the Secretary of War, with accompanying papers* (Washington, 1866) p, 130.

[14] Facts obtained by checking all regimental losses as detailed in W. Fox, *op. cit., passim.* The white regiments suffering very heavy losses were the 1st Maine Heavy Artillery with 683, the 2d Pennsylvania Heavy Artillery with 616, and the 1st Vermont Heavy Artillery with 576. A heavy artillery regiment, frequently used as infantry, and always in the thick of the fighting, had 12 companies rather than the 10 of an infantry regiment, so that, with some 250 more men, its numerical casualty rate was normally greater than that of infantry units of comparable service. It is important to note that the *earliest* organization date for the above-mentioned Negro units was August, 1863, while the *latest* date for the white units listed was September, 1862.

[15] House Exec. Doc. No. 1, 39th Cong., 1st Sess., Serial No. 1249, p. 73.

[16] To Major C. T. Christensen, Asst. Adj. Gen., dated New Orleans, July 18, 1864, in Woodward, pp. 2640-41.

[17] See also, House Exec. Doc. No. 83, (1865), 38th Cong., 2d Sess., p. 29.

[18] The six serving in hospitals in the capital were Charles B. Purvis, Alpheus Tucker, John Rapier, William Ellis, Anderson R. Abbott, and William Powell. John V. De Grassee served briefly as an assistant surgeon with the 35th U. S. Colored Infantry, while Alexander T. Augusta was originally assigned to the 7th USCI. See text for further data on Augusta (breveted a Lieutenant Colonel on March 13, 1865); and G. W. Williams, *op. cit.,* p. 143.

[19] Woodward, p. 1171.

[20] Woodward, pp. 2377-78. This letter is signed by J. B. McPherson, E. M. Pease, C. C. Topliff, M. O. Carter, J. O'Dounde, J. Morse, and H. Grange.

[21] Letter from Col. James A. Hardie, Inspector General of the Army, to Senator Wilson, Apr. 15, 1864, in Woodward, p. 2483.

[22] Sec. 12, Public Act No. 166, in *ORA,* Ser. III, vol. 2, p. 218. Actually, of course, Negroes were already so employed by various agencies of the government, and were regularly enlisted personnel of the Navy.

[23] Halleck to Grant, dated Washington, Mar. 31, 1863, in full in Woodward, pp. 1148-50, in part in G. Williams, *op. cit.,* p. 106. Grant, in reply (dated Milliken's Bend, April 19, 1863), assured Halleck that he would make use of the Negroes. In General Order No. 25, issued three days later, he

called this to the attention of all officers, and asserted that the employment of Negroes as soldiers would aid in "removing prejudice." (Woodward, pp. 1190, 1194.) From Vicksburg, July 24, 1863, Grant informed Halleck that he intended using Negro troops for labor on that city's works. He added: "The negro troops are easier to preserve discipline among than our white troops, and I doubt not will prove equally good for garrison duty. All that have been tried have fought bravely." (Woodward, p.1429).

[24] Woodward, p. 1586.

[25] Major G. L. Stearns to Stanton, *ORA,* Ser. IV, vol. 3, p. 840.

[26] Woodward, p. 1607. The items from Tennessee probably refer, in particular, to Negro workers rather than soldiers, but the evidence as to sentiment and conduct is clear.

[27] Woodward, p. 1766.

[28] Capt. R. T. Auchmuty to Col. Townsend, Dec. 20, 1863, in Woodward, 1854.

[29] Brig. Gen. J. S. Wadsworth to Brig. Gen. L. Thomas, Dec. (?), 1863, in Woodward, p. 1816.

[30] Colonel Morgan, letter dated Gallatin, Tenn., Dec. 6, 1863, in G. Williams, *op. cit.,* p. 162.

[31] Letter dated Port Hudson, La., Mar. 7, 1864, in Woodward, p. 2412.

[32] Maj. G. L. Stearns to Wilson, Nashville, Mar. 4, 1864, in Woodward, pp. 2404-05.

[33] In Woodward, pp. 3525-28.

[34] An enlisted man of another Negro regiment (the 54th Mass.) engaged in this labor, wrote: "For four months we have been steadily working night and day under fire. And such work! Up to our knees in mud half the time . . . ." Letter to Theodore Tilton, sent by him from New York on Dec. 12, 1863, to the Boston *Journal.* See Luis F. Emilio, *History of the Fifty-Fourth Regiment . . .* (Boston, 1891), p. 136.

[35] Order No. 21, dated Louisville, Ky., June 14, 1864. Woodward, p. 2621.

[36] Italics mine.—H. A. It is not likely that a junior officer would complain to his own senior officer of the unjust act of the latter with the expectation that this complaint would go to higher headquarters.

[37] Adjutant General L. Thomas to Stanton, Nov. 7, 1864, in House Exec Doc. No. 83, 38th Cong., 2d Sess., p. 29.

[38] General Order No. 39, Department of the Cumberland, Maj. Gen. T. Chattan, Mar. 2, 1864, in Woodward, p. 2403; for another example, dated Feb. 19, 1864, see *Ibid.,* p. 2385.

[39] Dyer, *op. cit.,* pp. 1733, 1734, 1738; Woodward, p. 3619. These "fatigue" regiments are not to be confused with the so-called "invalid" or "veteran reserve" units composed of meritorious men somewhat incapacitated in service but able to perform non-combat duties, as those required of guards and attendants. The total number of men and officers so serving numbered about 31,000 and some of these were Negroes. Gen. Thomas authorized John Eaton, Jr., to organize the first Negro invalid regiment on Sept. 26, 1863. See Woodward, p. 1606; House Exec. Doc. No. 83, 38 Cong., 2d Sess., p. 57; Exec. Papers, 1st Sess., 39th Cong. (ser. no. 1252), p. 110.

[40] Thus, an enlisted man of the 54th Mass. in his letter of late 1863 (already cited, see note 34) complained that his work schedule was "causing the wearing and tearing out of more than the volunteer's yearly allowance of clothing" and that they were "denied time to repair and wash (what we might by that means have saved)."

[41] W. Fox, *op. cit.*, p. 524.

[42] Woodward, p. 2475. Five regiments are enumerated as suffering particularly from this condition.

[43] Gen. Thomas to Col. Townsend, Apr. 8, 1864, Woodward, p. 2477. Thomas added that he desired this impressed upon the Commanding General, because the Negroes "on every occasion of conflict have shown themselves most worthy of confidence, and I think the time has fully arrived for placing in their hands the best arms."

[44] Gen. Ullman to Senator Wilson, Port Hudson, Dec. 4, 1863. Woodward, p. 1784. Ullman's troops had played an important part, a few months before in the assault, siege, and capture of Port Hudson, and had suffered heavily. Note also Col. Montgomery's report that his men (34th U. S. Colored Infantry) who saw heavy fighting in South Carolina possessed "no opportunity of seeing [*i.e.*, caring for] their guns except by candle light" because of their constant assignment on fatigue details. *Ibid.*, p. 2528.

[45] Hawkins to Sec. of War, Feb. 7, 1864; Asst. Sec. of War A. A. Davis to Hawkins, Mar. 2, 1864, in Woodward, p. 2401.

[46] Col. Shaw to Gov. Andrew of Mass., dated St. Helena Island, S. C., July 2, 1863, Woodward, p. 2416.

[47] Testimony before American Freedmen's Commission, May, 1864, Woodward, p. 2576.

[48] Dana to Stanton, dated "below Vicksburg," June 7, 8, 1863, in ORA, Ser. I, vol. XXIV, pt. 1, p. 95, and pt. 2, p. 446. According to the annual return of one of the regiments in this battle, "...very few of its men had ever before that day fired a gun—they having received their arms but the night before."—1st Miss. Vols., A. D., later the 51st U. S. C. T. This regiment had but 150 men at this battle, of whom 24 were killed and wounded—Woodward, p. 2143. See also ORA, Ser. I, vol. XXIV, pt. 2, pp. 455-56, where it appears that a request for more weapons and artillery made just before the battle was refused.

[49] Lt. Col. J. C. Chadwick, letter dated June 13, 1864, Woodward, p. 3129. The regiment sustained 12 casualties in this brief encounter.

[50] Brig. Gen. Ullman, commanding 1st Div. Corps d'Afrique, Port Hudson, La., Dec. 4, 1863, to Senator Wilson, Woodward, p. 1784.

[51] This, by the way, was important in explaining the chronic shortage of junior officers for Negro units. See, for example, Gen. Banks to Sec. Stanton, Oct. 26, 1863, in ORA, Ser. I, vol. XXVI, pt. 1, p. 776.

[52] Brig. Gen. J. Wadsworth to the Adj. Gen., Dec., 1863, Woodward, p. 1816.

[53] Brig. Gen. D. Ullman to Senator H. Wilson, Dec. 4, 1863, Woodward, p. 1786.

[54] Letter dated Norfolk, Feb. 18, 1863, in Woodward, pp. 1100-01. Several resignations of officers followed the enlistment of Negroes, and the freeing of slaves. Gen. Banks of the Department of the Gulf, in General Order

No. 18, Feb. 14, 1863, finally ordered the dishonorable discharge of one such officer, and threatened similar treatment for others. Upon learning of the issuance of the Emancipation Proclamation one Army officer said "he would like to cut the damned black heart out of the President" for having written it. See Woodward, pp. 854, 1068, 1105, 1106, 1318.

[55] Fred A. Shannon, *The Organization and Administration of the Union Army* (2 vols., Cleveland, 1928), I, p. 226.

[56] As was done by Lt. Col. A. W. Benedict of the 4th Regt. Corps d'Afrique whose men finally mutinied in Dec., 1863.—ORA, Ser. I, Vol. XXVI, pt. 1, pp. 456*ff*.; B. I. Wiley, *Southern Negroes, 1861-1865* (New Haven, 1938), p. 317.

[57] Woodward, pp. 1658-59.

[58] Woodward, p. 2674.

[59] Circular, dated Nashville, Feb. 15, 1864, signed by Capt. R. D. Mussey, Woodward, p. 2383.

[60] Paragraph II, General Order No. 26, Feb. 18, 1864, Woodward, p. 2384.

[61] Another motive behind changing the plans was perfectly legitimate—many of the Negro troops had seen but little, and some no, actual fighting prior to this major attack upon veteran soldiers.

[62] See Battle Report 457, Col. Hallowell to Gen. Seymour, Nov. 7, 1863, in Woodward, pp. 2221-23; Emilio, *op. cit.*, pp. 75-88. Gen. Seymour, in over-all command of this operation, was further criticized for the piece-meal fashion in which he committed the other forces at his disposal, thus losing that without which an assault ever fails—massed concentrated power.

[63] Gov. S. I. Kirkwood to Halleck, Aug. 5, 1862, in Woodward, p. 933. A current "joke" of the period had the mythical Irishman declaring: "The right to be killed I'll divide with the nayger, and give him the largest half." J. Wilson, *op. cit.*, p. 290.

[64] Given before the American Freedmen's Inquiry Commission in May, 1864. Quoted in full in Woodward, p. 2548.

[65] This has already been noticed for Milliken's Bend. It is true, also, of such engagements as that at Paducah, Ky., Mar. 1864; Simmsport, La., May, 1864; Saltville, Va., October, 1864 (where about 600 men of the 5th U. S. Colored Cavalry, as yet "unassigned and unorganized recruits," fought, and suffered over 100 casualties); Nashville, Tenn., December, 1864.—Woodward, pp. 3062-65, 3129, 3366, 3484-85.

[66] See the very long letter from Gov. Andrew to Col. R. G. Shaw, July 11, 1863, in Woodward, pp. 1384-1406; and letter from Stanton to Brig. Gen. R. Saxton, Aug. 25, 1863 (*after* the Congressional act allowing enlistment of Negroes), where this occurs: "The [Negro] persons so received into the service and their officers, to be entitled to and receive the same pay and rations as are allowed, by law, to volunteers in the service . . . ." *Ibid.*, pp. 958-60.

[67] This subject requires, and merits, a paper of its own.

[68] Woodward, pp. 2480, 2484-85; G. Williams, *op. cit.*, p. 157. Another item of importance in terms of morale, though not to be compared with that

of pay, was the extreme difficulty Negroes faced in their efforts to obtain commissions. This whole subject of Negro commissioned officers in the Civil War needs extended treatment.

[69] B. Dyer, "The treatment of colored Union troops by the Confederates," *Journal of Negro History* (1935), XX, pp. 273-86.

[70] Letter dated Richmond, Aug. 12, 1863, in Woodward, p. 4573.

[71] The wounded officer was Lt. G. W. Fitch of the 12th U. S. Colored Infantry. The two murdered men were Lt. D. C. Cooke of the 17th USCI and Capt. C. G. Penfield, 44th USCI. See, statement of Lt. Fitch dated Nashville, Jan. 3, 1865, in Woodward, p. 4381. The service records of Cooke and Penfield, read, respectively, as follows: "Captured & Shot by De Forest's [sic] men"; "Murdered by . . . Forest's Cavalry near Columbia, Tenn., Dec. 22/64." Service records may be found in the Old Records Section, A. G. O. division, National Archives. Compare this with B. Dyer, *op. cit.*, p. 282.

[72] One such "indignity" was the burial, in a common grave, of Negro soldiers and their white officers, as in the well-known case of Col. R. G. Shaw and his men of the 54th Mass. Another episode of more serious consequences is described by one F. J. D'Avignon, Surgeon of the 96th New York Volunteers, in a letter to Gen. B. F. Butler, dated Oct. 13, 1864 (in Woodward, p. 4371). Dr. D'Avignon was a prisoner at Petersburg, Virginia, and was placed in charge of many of the wounded Federal soldiers captured at the Battle of the Mine, a large proportion of whom were Negroes. In August, 1864 ". . . about one hundred and thirty wounded of our soldiers were brought to me for treatment. This lot of wounded were looked upon by the Rebels with a great deal of hatred and with an earnest desire to degrade them. For this object General Henry A. Wise, commanding the first military district, issued an order to mix the negroes with the white soldiers. A non-commissioned officer read to me the order, to place one white man, especially an officer, between two negroes. The order was strictly followed and the wounded were crowded. I objected to this crowding and also to place the men promiscuously against the good judgment of physicians and surgeons to separate those affected with Erysipelas from the others; but to no effect. And I can safely say that this arrangement was a cause of destroying the life of our soldiers." Thomas S. Gholson, Virginia member of the Confederate House stated there on Feb. 1, 1865, that, "White and black prisoners, captured by us at the 'explosion' at Petersburg, were placed in the same hospital, and occupied cots adjoining each other."—Woodward, p. 3859.

[73] ORA, Ser. II, vol. V, pp. 455, 469, 484, and vol. VIII, pp. 640, 703. Also, B. Dyer, *op. cit.*, p. 283.

[74] Sec. of War Seddon, CSA, to Gov. Bonham of S. C., Aug. 31, 1864, in ORA Ser. II, vol. VI, p. 703.

[75] The Woodward collection is particularly rich in material concerning Negro prisoners. See, as examples, pp. 4298-99, 4604, 4609, 4614, 4647, 4653*a*. Negroes, both slave and free, were, in many cases, confined in ordinary prison camps. See *Ibid*, p. 4653.

[76] In addition to the material mentioned by B. Dyer (*op. cit.*, pp. 283-84),

establishing this point by citing relevant statements from Lt. Gen. E. Kirby Smith, Col. Shingler, and the Confederate Sec. of War, note these facts: Maj. Gen. R. Taylor, reporting from Richmond, Louisiana, June 8, 1863, said of a recent battle that "unfortunately" some Negroes were captured (ORA, Ser. I, vol. XXIV, pt. 2, p. 459); while Maj. Gen J. G. Walker reporting July 10, 1863, from Delhi, Louisiana, referred to the taking of a few Negro prisoners, and added: "I consider it an unfortunate circumstance that any armed negroes were captured . . . ."—Woodward, p. 2175.

77 Woodward, p. 4606. Gen. Buford was with Gen. Forrest at Fort Pillow.

78 Woodward, p. 4367.

79 That mass slaughter of helpless and even wounded Negro and Southern white Federal troops occurred at Fort Pillow is clear from an investigation of the available evidence. See Senate Reports No. 63, pt. 1, 38th Cong., 1st Sess., and Woodward, pp. 3069-89. This is the conclusion of a recent writer not at all friendly to the radicals responsible for the Congressional investigation.—See Harry Williams, "Benjamin F. Wade and the atrocity propaganda of the Civil War," in *Ohio State Archaelogical and Hist. Quarterly* (1939), XLVIII, p. 40*n*. Williams misses the fact that one of the features of the defense of Fort Pillow that particularly infuriated Forrest was that the Negroes were fighting alongside Tennessee white men.

80 F. Dyer, *op. cit.*, p. 18.

81 Ned Warren to Col. Griffith, dated near Crystal Springs, Mississippi, Sept. 2, 1863, Woodward, p. 4579.

82 Woodward, pp. 4580-82; ORA, Ser. II, vol. VI, pp. 258, 924. B. Dyer (*op. cit.*, p. 284), barely mentions this incident, but does not present these facts. There was a Federal investigation of these murders by Brig. Gen. G. L. Andrews, who reported to Maj. Gen. Hitchcock from Port Hudson, La., Feb. 7, 1864, that he had made a careful survey and was convinced several Negro prisoners of war had been killed by the Confederates. Woodward, p. 4301.

83 Woodward, pp. 3018, 3067.

84 Major R. G. Shaw to Major C. T. Christenson, Plaquemine, La., Aug. 9, 1864, in Woodward, p. 4337. The three men were Anthony King, Samuel Mason, and Samuel O. Jefferson. Their service records bear the notation: "Captured while on Picket Plaquemine La & shot by the Rebels in cold blood Aug. 6, '64." Old Records Section, A. G. O., National Archives.

85 Report of Capt. E. A. Barker, dated Fort Gibson, C[herokee] N[ation], Sept. 20, 1864. The attack occurred fifteen miles west of Fort Gibson.—Woodward, p. 3306.

86 Report dated Chattanooga, Oct. 17, 1864.—Woodward, pp. 3383-90; see letter from Col. Johnson to Brig. Gen. W. Whipple, same date, giving additional circumstantial evidence, and accounts of other mistreatment, *Ibid.*, pp. 4373-75.

87 See Col. Williams to Major Livingston, CSA, dated May 26, 1863, and the reply of May 27, 1863, in Woodward, pp. 4181-82; and service record of Pvt. Samuel Jordan, Co. D, 5th USCI, together with letters from

Generals Wild and Butler, and Col. Spear filed therein.—Old Records, A. G. O., Nat'l. Arch.

[88] Letter to Sec. Stanton, New Orleans, June 6, 1863. Woodward, p. 1298. It is the factors named here, plus considerable familiarity with terrain, that enabled the Negro soldier to overcome the difficulties placed before him and to emerge as an efficient and courageous fighter during the Civil War.

[89] Report dated March 5, 1864—Woodward, pp. 3042-43. The Negro regiment involved was the 7th USCI, and its losses in this engagement were severe—eighty-six officers and men killed and wounded. See extract from its muster-out roll in Woodward, p. 3040.

[90] Figures from F. Dyer, *op. cit.*, pp. 1016, 1240, 1266, 1267. The statement in ORA, Ser. III, vol. V, p. 661 (apparently by the editor) that, "With the exception of the two Massachusetts regiments mentioned above [54th and 55th], the military organization composed of colored men were mustered directly into the service of the United States, and were organized and officered by officers acting under the authority of the US and not of any particular State" is false insofar as it omits the other two regiments. W. Fox in printing the official report of total deaths among colored troops states (*op. cit.*, p. 527*n.*) that this does not include "loss in the three Massachusetts colored regiments . . . their enrollment and loss is included with that of the white troops from Massachusetts," but he omits the Connecticut regiment. In a letter from Maj. C. W. Foster, in charge of the Bureau of Colored Troops, to Brig. Gen. T. M. Vincent, dated Aug. 17, 1866, there is a table which clearly distinguishes these four regiments from the U. S. Colored Troops—Woodward, p. 3791.

[91] Woodward, p. 2776. The Negro people of Philadelphia, at a mass meeting, pledged the Governor their support, denounced discrimination, demanded more Negro officers and urged wide attendance at a forthcoming Negro National Convention in New York.—*The Liberator,* Aug. 5, 1864, p. 123.

[92] Woodward, p. 2801.

[93] The Negro officers were neither commissioned nor mustered by the War Department. For the original General Order No. 154, see Woodward, p. 2810. In Special Order 48, Feb. 20, 1865, Gen. Hurlbut announced revocation of that General Order, and transferred those enlisted under it to other Negro units.—*Ibid.*, p. 3575.

[94] The officers were, Capt. H. Ford Douglass, 1st Lt. Wm. Mathews, and 2nd Lt. Patrick H. Minor.—see Woodward, pp. 3569, 3687, and G. Williams, *op. cit.*, p. 141. There were, also, two Negro army bands not included in the totals of U. S. Colored Troops.—F. Dyer, *op cit.*, p. 18; and see Woodward, p. 3791, Maj. Foster to Gen. Vincent, Aug. 17, 1866.

[95] Gov. Andrew to Col. R. G. Shaw, July 11, 1863, Woodward, p. 1394.

[96] Woodward, p. 2564. In May, 1864 one John E. Revels of Des Moines, attempted to enlist in the 44th Iowa Infantry but, in this case, the effort failed for he was rejected as of "African descent."—*Report of the Adjutant General . . . State of Iowa, 1864-65* (Des Moines, 1865), p. 84.

[97] J. T. Wilson, *op cit.*, pp. 94*n.*, 179.

[98] Henry Wilson, *History of the Rise and Fall of the Slave Power in*

*America* (3 vols., Boston, 1877), III, pp. 287-88. This is referred to, not quite correctly, by Wiley, *op. cit.*, p. 311.

99 G. Williams, *op. cit.*, pp. 76-77. Williams says (p. 141) that Lt. Col. W. N. Reed of the 1st North Carolina Infantry "was supposed by the officers of his regiment and other persons" to be Negro. He was mortally wounded at Olustee, Florida.

100 We do not refer to the *hire* of Negroes as laborers *attached* to quartermaster, commissary, engineer, and medical departments, nor to those *hired* in a similar manner by individual units. The non-enlisted Negroes will be considered separately. This distinction, important for a discussion of casualties, is missed in the very rare cases where the subject has been even broached. See, for example, Wiley, *op. cit.*, p. 341.

101 General Order No. 67 issued at Memphis, in ORA, Ser. I, vol. XVII, pt. 2, pp. 158-60.

102 General Order No. 6, Murfreesborough, Tenn., Jan. 27, 1863, in ORA, Ser. I, vol. XXXIII, pt. 2, pp. 17-18.

103 Public Act No. 57, section 10, approved Mar. 3, 1863 in ORA, Ser. III, vol. III, p. 94.

104 General Order No. 172, Winchester, Tenn., July 23, 1863, in Woodward, p. 1940.

105 General Order No. 53, dated Vicksburg, Miss., Aug. 23, 1863, *Ibid.*, p. 1950. In this case it is not clear that the Negroes were to be enlisted.

106 ORA, Ser. III, vol. 3, p. 843, italics in original.

107 *Report of the Adjutant General of the State of Kansas, 1861-65*, I (Topeka, 1896), pp. 25, 27, 32, 36, 45, 48, 53, 57, 60, 62. In this total duplications, resulting from transfers of individuals, are eliminated.

108 Ms in Old Records Office, A. G. O., Nat'l. Arch. Nevertheless, in the *Official Roster of the Soldiers of the State of Ohio in the War of the Rebellion*, V (Akron, 1887), p. 695, James Woods is listed as having entered the service on Aug. 11, 1863.

109 Whether or not their pay was equalized in 1864 with that of other Negro soldiers is a moot point, though presumably it was. In Jan. 1863, the Dept. of the Cumberland ordered that Negro cooks be paid by the Quartermaster. But in October that service pointed out that the cooks were regularly enlisted soldiers, and so on Oct. 10, 1863 Gen. Rosecrans ordered them to be paid in the same manner as other enlisted men. See Woodward, p. 1664.

110 This may help clear up occasional contemporary references to Negro soldiers serving in "white" regiments. See the story about William Sawyer and his five sons in the service, including one in the 5th Indiana Cavalry in *The Liberator*, Aug. 12, 1864, p. 131; and diary entry, dated June 23, 1863, of Isaac L. Taylor, of the First Minnesota Infantry: "In the 18th Pa. I observed several *colored* troopers fully armed and equipped," in Hayd C. Wolf, "Campaigning with the First Minnesota," *Minnesota History* (1944), XXV, p. 357. Italics in original.

111 These remarks are based on a small sampling of service records—totaling some thirty individuals of various regiments—and conclusions based thereon are to be considered, therefore, as tentative.

[112] The final statement of Pvt. Charles Danna shows that he had been issued clothing to the value of $29.27, but that he had never been paid. Old Rec'ds Sect., AGO, Nat'l Arch. Danna will be found listed in the *Official Roster of the Soldiers of the State of Ohio in the War of the Rebellion,* II (Cincinnati, 1886) p. 546, where his date of enrollment is inaccurately given.

[113] There were 2 teamsters, 4 wagoners (a position ranking above that of private) and 600 under-cooks. These figures were compiled on the basis only of those clearly listed as Negro in the *Report of the Adjutant General of the State of Illinois* (vols. IV-VIII, Springfield, 1867). Some may have been missed, so the above figures represent a minimum. Spot-checking available records shows that the other states had similar conditions. Note of the condition in one Kansas regiment has already been taken, and the data for one Ohio regiment will be presented subsequently. See also *Report of the Adjutant General of State of Iowa, 1864-65* (Des Moines, 1865), pp. 409, 412, 414, 416, 425, 430, 488, 601, *et. seq.;* and *Report of the Adj. Gen. of the State of Indiana,* VIII (Indianapolis, 1868), pp. 80, 201, 213, 281, 285, 301, 309.

[114] Source as note 113. The mortality rate alone would be a little over 6 per cent. The mortality rate for Illinois troops as a whole, from all causes, was 16.5 per cent—W. Fox, *op. cit.,* p. 526.

[115] Ms in Old Records Section, A. G. O., Nat'l Arch. *Official Roster of the Soldiers of the State of Ohio. . .* V, p. 695. Normally this work carries a notation of wounds received in action.

[116] For reference to use of Negro women as workers see, for example, ORA, Ser. I, vol. XVII, pt. 2, p. 369.

[117] These are the figures generally cited; see, for example, Wiley, *op. cit.,* p. 341. Until a serious study is undertaken of the subject, however, these remain little more than educated guesses.

[118] Major E. Waring, Jr., in a letter to Gen. Asboth, dated Rolla, Mo., Dec. 19, 1861, mentions this use, as well as that of hired teamsters and hospital attendants.—Woodward, p. 454. The Provost Marshal of St. Louis informed the police that they would, hereafter, arrest fugitive slaves only if claimed "in a legal manner by [their] owner," for the practice of arresting Negroes on slight pretext was most annoying to army officers whose orderlies frequently were among those jailed.—ORA, Ser. I, vol. VIII, p. 584. General Orders occasionally referred to this practice, Gen. Rosecrans sanctioning it (Jan. 27, 1863, in ORA, Ser. I, vol. XXXIII, pt. 2, pp. 17-18), and Gen. Sherman forbidding it (Aug. 8, 1862, ORA, Ser. I, vol. XVII, pt. 2, pp. 158-60). Sherman's prohibition was based upon the fact that officers authorized servants received the latter's salaries (equivalent to that of a private) in their own monthly wage, while such a sum was not generally paid Negro servants—indeed, by law, should not have been paid them. See also Report of the Secretary of War, House Exec. Doc. 83, 38th Cong., 2 Sess. (1865), p. 29.

[119] This appeared most clearly on the question of what payment was to be made to these Negroes. Gen. Rosecrans, commanding the Department of the Cumberland, had ordered, July 23, 1863, that officers' servants be paid by the Quartermaster Department. On Aug. 11, 1863, Gen. Meigs, the

Quartermaster General of the Army, asked J. M. Brodhead, 2nd Comptroller, U. S. Treasury, whether that was legal. The latter, on Aug. 15 said it was not legal, that they were to be paid as regular soldiers (just as whites acting as officers' servants were); that is, they were to be paid from money appropriated to the officers for their servants' pay. The Secretary of War directed Gen. Rosecrans, on Aug. 27, 1863, to so modify his order. Ms in box marked "Negroes," among Quartermaster Records, War Records Office, Nat'l. Arch.

[120] Woodward, p. 4148; ORA, Ser. II, vol. III, p. 804.

[121] Woodward, p. 4149; Letters Sent, (MS.) Department of Virginia, vol. III, p. 134, War Records Office. Entry dated Feb. 23, 1862. Note that these Negroes were exchanged as prisoners of war, *i. e.,* since they were used as servants the Confederacy apparently did not object. Servants of Confederate officers were also returned, but the Confederate Commissioner for Exchange of Prisoners, Robert Ould, denied, in a letter to Sec. of War Seddon, June 24, 1863, that they were accepted "as prisoners of war. They were not," he wrote, "counted in exchange."—Woodward, p. 4549.

[122] *Official Records of the Union and Confederate Navies in the War of the Rebellion* (30 vols., Washington, 1894-1922), Ser. I, vol. XIX, p. 462. (It was these two free Negroes of Massachusetts who were sold into slavery, as noted before.) Hereafter to be cited as ORN.

[123] *The Liberator,* Dec. 16, 1864, p. 203 (where Small's first name is given as Thomas); *ibid.,* Dec. 30, 1864, p. 210.

[124] Earl Conrad, *Harriet Tubman* (Washington, 1943), pp. 149-89.

[125] Col. Charles P. Stone in report dated Camp near Pooleville [Md.], June 28, 1861, in ORA, Ser. I, vol. II, p. 118.

[126] Gen. Hamilton to Gen. Halleck, near Madrid, Mo., Mar. 20, 1862, in Woodward, pp. 484-85.

[127] Woodward, pp. 491-92.

[128] The Secretary of War ordered Heath "detained in custody and placed at hard labor in a secure place and for other attention." The meaning of the last three words is obscure.—ORA, ser. II, vol. VI, p. 1053. See also, ORA, ser. IV, vol. II, pp. 36-38; and Herbert Aptheker, *Essays in the History of the American Negro* (N. Y., 1945), pp. 193-94.

[129] Vincent Colyer, *Report of the Services rendered by the Freed People to the United States Army in North Carolina* (N. Y., 1864) pp. 9-10. Colyer was Superintendent of the Poor under Gen. Burnside from March through June, 1862. He makes clear that these Negroes were armed. Two in particular, William Kinnegy and Samuel Williams, are praised by him. In May, 1862, Williams acted as a guide in an expedition composed of three regiments. *Ibid.,* pp. 16-25.

[130] Gen. T. Williams to Capt. R. Davis, July 4, 1863.—Woodward, p. 554.

[131] Maj. Gen. W. S. Rosecrans, "The Battle of Corinth," in Robert U. Johnson and C. Buel, eds., *Battles and Leaders of the Civil War* (4 vols., N. Y., 1887), II, p. 741.

[132] Capts. F. E. Prime and C. B. Comstock, Nov. 29, 1863, in ORA, ser. I, vol. 24, pt. 2, p, 177; see also, p. 203. Capt. Prime had reported on Feb. 9,

1863, that 550 contrabands were laboring for the engineer department before Vicksburg.—*ibid.*, pt. 1, p. 119.

[133] Report of Col. F. M. Cockrell, dated Demopolis, Ala., Aug. 1, 1863, in ORA, ser. I, vol. XXIV, pt. 2, p. 416.

[134] Telegram, Gen Sherman to Gen Thomas, June 26, 1864, in Woodward, p. 2819a.

[135] Dated Kingston, Ga., Nov. 9, 1864, in Woodward, p. 2821. Note this passage from the 1865 report of Major General M. C. Meigs, the Quartermaster General of the Army to the Sec. of War: "Colored men continued to the close of the war to be employed in connexion with the trains of the Quartermaster's department as laborers at depots, as pioneer with the marching columns. In all these positions they have done good service and materially contributed to that final victory which confirmed their freedom and saved our place among nations."—Exec. Doc. No. 1, vol. 3, 39th Cong., 1 Sess. (ser. no. 1249), p. 117.

[136] ORA, ser. III, vol. III, pp. 1077, 1085, 1104-05.

[137] Woodward, pp. 1906, 1930, 1950. See petition of Simon Douglas and seven other Negroes requesting payment for work as teamsters from June through August, 1863, in Virginia with a Pennsylvania artillery unit, in box marked "Negroes," Quartermaster records, War Records Office, Nat'l. Arch., and many other manuscripts of similar content in the same collection, and in an envelope marked "Contrabands." Pay of $25 and even $30 a month, plus rations (high wages indeed for the period) was not unusual for these Negroes. This was true particularly in 1864 when, because of the draft, states were forbidding whites to accept jobs as teamsters or in other public service.

[138] Letter from Brig. Gen. R. Ingalls to Gen. Meigs, Aug. 15, 1863. This and subsequent letters to Meigs are from Ms. in Quartermaster records file on "Negroes," Nat'l. Arch. In a telegram of Aug. 4, Gen. Ingalls had estimated 11,000 Negroes as attached to his Army.

[139] Lt. Col. J. W. Taylor to Meigs, Aug. 6, 1863. Capt. F. Winslow thought 11,000 was a correct figure for the Department of the Cumberland—telegram to Meigs, Aug. 5, 1863.

[140] Capt. A. R. Eddy to Gen. Meigs, Aug. 8, 1863. Capt. W. Dickerson (to Meigs, Aug. 5, 1863), estimated there were 250 Negroes employed by the quartermaster alone in the Department of the Ohio.

[141] Brig. Gen. D. Rucker to Meigs, Aug. 5, 1863.

[142] Letters of Jan. and March 1865, in New Orleans *Daily True Delta*, Jan. 30 and Mar. 19, 1865, quoted by Wiley, *op. cit.*, p. 211.

[143] Report of Maj. Gen. Meigs to Secretary Stanton, Nov. 8, 1865, in Exec. Doc. No. 1, vol. 3, 39th Cong., 1st Sess. (ser. no. 1249) p. 110.

[144] *Ibid.*, p. 257. How incomplete even these figures are may be seen from the fact that the total burials of contrabands in Virginia are given as 59!

[145] Woodward, p. 825. A Negro physician, G. P. Miller, of Battle Creek, Michigan, wrote to Secretary Cameron on October 30, 1861 that he had learned Gen. Sherman was authorized to enroll Negroes. He, therefore, wished "to solicit the privilege of raising from five to ten thousand free men to report in sixty days to take any position that may be assigned us

(sharpshooters preferred)," or, he went on, "If this proposition is not accepted we will, if armed and equipped by the government, fight as guerrillas." This offer was rejected by the War Department, but Mr. Scott's reply contained these words: ". . . you are respectfully informed that the orders to Genl. Sherman and other officers of the United States service, authorize the arming of colored persons only in cases of great emergency and not under regular enrolment for military purposes."—Woodward, pp. 827, 828.

[146] Saxton to Stanton, in ORA, Ser. I, vol. XIV, p. 375. See also the report of Major R. Jeffords, C. S. A., dated June 14, 1862, telling of his leading 105 men in a reconnaissance of Hutchinson Island, S. C., during which "Some 10 [Negroes] were killed and 10 or 15 wounded."—*ibid.*, p. 38.

[147] *Ibid.*, p. 189.

[148] Col. Clayton, in his report of this battle, declared: "The negroes also did me excellent service, (see Captain Talbot's report, which I fully endorse), and deserve much therefor."—Woodward, pp. 2245-47.

[149] Maj. Gen. O. O. Howard, *Autobiography* (2 vols., N. Y., 1907), II, p. 163. Casualties suffered are not stated.

[150] Col. R. D. Mussey to Major Foster, Louisville, June 12, 1864.—Woodward, p. 3160. Many employees of the Quartermaster department took part in the defense of Nashville, but how many were Negroes is not known.

[151] On this see the following by the present writer: *The Negro in the Civil War* (N. Y., 1938), pp. 18-25; *American Negro Slave Revolts* (N. Y., 1943), pp. 359-67; "Notes on slave conspiracies in Confederate Mississippi," in *The Journal of Negro History* (1944), XXIX, pp. 75-79. In addition, see ORA, ser. I, vol. XXVI, pt. 2, pp. 187-88, letter from Lt. Col. S. A. Roberts, C. S. A., to Capt. E. P. Turner, dated Bonham, Texas, Aug. 29, 1863, telling of the discovery of a plot to rebel among Negroes and whites in Dallas, Cooke, Grayson and Denton counties, "and perhaps others." In Denton, eighteen Negroes and six whites were arrested. Other details are lacking, but the Colonel said it was "certain that a deplorable condition of affairs exists in the counties named and probably in some adjoining ones."

[152] For Tennessee, see ORA, ser. IV, vol. I, p. 409; Alabama—Woodward, p. 1044. The Louisiana Native Guard Regiment of the Confederacy had but 120 muskets for 906 men and officers, was in no engagement, and did not leave New Orleans as did the other Confederate units when Union forces entered. See, Woodward, p. 1027, and Charles Wesley, "The employment of Negroes as soldiers in the Confederate Army," in *The Journal of Negro History* (1919), IV, pp. 239-53. Professor Wesley writes that "there is no evidence that" Negro troops participated "in any important battles." He presents no evidence, however, that they participated in *any* battles, and the present writer has seen no such evidence.

[153] Woodward, pp. 1037, 1038.

[154] This is said notwithstanding the following: N. W. Stephenson, "The question of arming the slaves," in *American Historical Review* (1913), XVIII, pp. 295-308; T. R. Hay, "The South and the arming of the slaves," *Mississippi Valley Hist. Rev* (1919), VI, pp. 34-73; and J. B. Ranck, *Albert Gallatin Brown* (N. Y., 1937), pp. 242-51. There is much

material on this scattered throughout the Woodward Ms. The whole subject of the Negro in the Confederate service needs thorough study.

[185] Moses Dallas, a Negro pilot in the Confederate Navy, was killed when, with a party of rebels, he stormed the U. S. S. *Water Witch,* in June, 1864.—ORN, ser. I, vol. XV, p. 495. Nineteen Negroes, serving as teamsters for the Confederacy, and taken in battle, insisted, successfully, upon being returned when prisoners of war were exchanged.—Report of Lt. Col. W. H. Ludlow to Gen. L. Thomas, Fort Monroe, Va., Oct. 8. 1862.—Woodward, p. 4151. The Secretary of War directed that Negroes who served as servants of Confederate officers and were captured, were in no case to be returned, even if they desired this. See letter from Brig. Gen. E. R. S. Canby to Brig. Gen. W. W. Morris, Washington, Dec. 18, 1863, *Ibid.,* p. 4263.

## THE NEGRO IN THE UNION NAVY

[1] Thus Richard S. West, Jr., mentions that many fugitive slaves flocked to Federal vessels, and adds: "A number of able blacks were enlisted on the ships as powder monkeys and coal passers."—*Gideon Welles Lincoln's Navy Department* (Indianapolis, 1943), p. 184.—In the three volume *The Navy in the Civil War,* issued by Scribners in 1883, volume one (*The Blockade and the Cruisers* by J. R. Soley), and volume three (*The Gulf and Inland Waters* by A. T. Mahan), do not mention the Negro, while the second volume (*The Atlantic Coast* by D. Ammen), notes (p. 34) the slaves' joy at the approach of Federal forces, and the exploit of Robert Smalls in delivering a Confederate vessel to the Union blockading fleet (p. 65). John W. Cromwell mentions Negro sailors who won Medals of Honor in the Civil War, though his account is marred by several errors (*The Negro in American History,* Washington, 1914, pp. 252-53). The subject is not discussed in C. G. Woodson's various editions of *The Negro in Our History,* while my own *The Negro in the Civil War* (N. Y., 1938), did little more than Daniel Ammen, as cited above.

[2] *Official Records of the Union and Confederate Navies in the War of the Rebellion* (30 vols., Washington, 1894-1922). Hereafter cited as ORN, with volume references for series I, unless otherwise indicated.

[3] *Massachusetts Soldiers, Sailors, and Marines in the Civil War* (8 vols., Norwood, 1931-35). See vols. VII, VIII.

[4] See endorsement, dated May 25, 1903, to request for information from the Adjutant General of Ohio, dated May 13, 1903, in Navy Department Records, National Archives, Washington.—hereafter cited as NDR.

[5] See E. R. Turner, *The Negro in Pennsylvania* (Washington, 1911), p. 41; L. Greene, *The Negro in Colonial New England* (N. Y., 1942), pp. 114-16.

[6] Among others may be mentioned Crispus Attucks, Paul Cuffee, Prince Hall, Denmark Vesey, James Forten, and Henry Highland Garnet.

[7] Herbert Aptheker, *Essays in the History of the American Negro* (N. Y., 1945), pp. 95-96; L. P. Jackson, *Virginia Negro Soldiers and Seamen in the Revolutionary War* (Norfolk, 1944). Professor Jackson has been able to establish the names of 179 Negroes who served revolutionary Virginia as regular soldiers and sailors, the total for the latter equaling 75.

[8] See A. S. Mackenzie, *The Life of Commodore Oliver Hazard Perry* (2 vols., N. Y., 1840), I, pp. 165-66, 186-87; *Niles' Weekly Register* (Baltimore), Feb. 26, 1814, V, pp. 429-30.

[9] Usher Parsons to George Livermore, letter dated Providence, Oct. 18, 1862, in G. Livermore, *An Historical Research respecting the Opinions of the Founders of the Republic on Negroes as Slaves, as Citizens, and as Soldiers* (3rd. edit., Boston, 1863) pp. 159-60. Parsons, one of the most noteworthy of American physicians, served as a Naval Surgeon throughout the War of 1812 and until 1821 under Perry and Macdonough. For a sketch of his life see *Dictionary of American Biography*, XIV, pp. 275-76.

[10] See Table 14, *Negro Population* 1790-1915 (Bureau of the Census, 1918), p. 511; E. Turner, *op. cit.*, pp. 124-25; R. A. Austin, *New Haven Negroes* (New Haven, 1940), p. 21; L. P. Jackson, *Free Negro Labor and Property Holding in Virginia 1830-1860* (N. Y., 1942) pp. 77-79; J. H. Franklin *The Free Negro in North Carolina 1790-1860* (Chapel Hill, 1943), p. 141

[11] Outstanding examples are the 1822 act of South Carolina and its national and international repercussions, and a similar law passed by North Carolina in 1830 and repealed, the next year, because of the "great howl [that] went up from employers in the seaport towns" of that state—Franklin, *op. cit.*, p. 141. See Herbert Aptheker, *American Negro Slave Revolts* (N. Y., 1943) p. 275, and sources therein cited; protest petition of Negro seamen presented to the House of Representatives by John Q. Adams, Feb. 7, 1842 in *Journal of the House . . . 2d sess, 27th Cong . . .* Washington, 1842), p. 325; *Exec. Doc. No. 119*, 27th Cong., 2d sess., Vol. 2; "Memorial of sundry masters of American vessels lying in the port of Charleston, S. C.," dated Feb. 7, 1823, in *Niles' Register* (Baltimore), Mar. 15, 1823, XXIV, pp. 31-32; and another petition from Negro seamen presented to the House of Representatives on Feb. 27, 1843, in Journal of the House . . . 3rd. sess., 27th. Cong . . . (Washington, 1843), p. 475.

[12] Opinion dated Nov. 7, 1821, in H. D. Gilpin, ed., *Opinions of the Attorneys General of the United States . . .* (Washington, 1841), I, pp. 382-84; note that a free Negro of Petersburg, Va., John Updike, was the owner of four commercial vessels from 1824-62.—L. Jackson, *op. cit.*, p. 141.

[13] Opinion dated Nov. 29, 1862, in J. H. Ashton, ed., *Official Opinions of the Attorneys General of the United States . . .* (Washington, 1868), X, pp. 382-413.

[14] R. Peters, ed., *The Public Statutes at Large of the United States . . .* (Boston, 1845), II, p. 809.

[15] Letter dated Navy Yard, Boston, Sept. 13, 1839, in file marked "Circulars from Secretary Apr. 19, 1836, to Jan'y 1, 1872," in NDR.)

[16] Secretary A. P. Usher to the Speaker of the House, Aug. 10, 1842, in Exec. Doc. No. 282, 27th Cong., 2d sess. vol. V. The Senate on July 29, 1842, on the urging of John C. Calhoun, passed an amendment to a naval enlistment bill restricting the use of Negroes to service as cooks, stewards, and servants, but this failed of final enactment.—Cong. Globe., 27th Cong. 2d sess., vol. XI, pp. 805-07. Note that the Navy did not keep separate records for white and Negro personnel.

[17] The Army, in 1820, had specifically forbade enlisting Negroes. This was

done in a General Order, Adjutant and Inspector General's Office, Feb. 18, 1820: "No Negro or Mulatto will be received as a recruit of the Army . . ." —Elon A. Woodward, compiler, "The Negro in the Military Service of the United States . . ." (MS), p. 348, located in War Records Office, National Archives, Washington, D. C. For comment on this Woodward collection, see footnote 8, p. 210 *ante*.

[18] Stringham to Welles, July 18, 1861, aboard U. S. S. *Minnesota*, Hampton Roads, Va., in ORN, VI, pp. 8-9.

[19] Welles to Stringham, July 22, 1861, *Ibid.*, p. 10.

[20] From reports of various naval officers, *Ibid.*, pp. 81, 85-86, 95, 107, 113-14.

[21] Welles to Flag Officer Goldsborough, commanding the Atlantic Blockade Squadron, *Ibid.*, p. 252. "Boys," or apprentices, formed the lowest ranks in the navy. There were 3rd, 2nd, and 1st class "boys" who received $8, 9, and 10 respectively. It is important to observe that *this restriction applied only to contrabands,* and, as will be shown, was shortly modified even as to them.

[22] See Special Order No. 72, Oct. 14, 1861, and General Order No. 37, Nov. 1, 1861, in *Exec. Doc. No. 85,* House of Rep., 37th Cong., 2d sess., pp. 2-3. For "unusual amount of labor" men might be given an extra fifty cents or one dollar. Those sick for less than ten days received half pay; over ten days, no pay. In addition, the workers generally were underfed. poorly clothed, and often cheated of what little pay they were supposed to receive.—*Ibid.*, pp. 4-13.

[23] Commission appointed by Maj. Gen. Wood, commanding Department of Virginia, on Jan. 30, 1862; its report dated March 20, 1862.—*Ibid.*, p. 9.

[24] Report of Secretary of the Navy, Dec. 7, 1863, serial number 1183, p. xi; Report of the Secretary of the Navy, Dec. 5, 1864, serial number 1221, p. xxiii; from 1861 to 1865 a total of 1059 vessels were commissioned by the Navy. These are listed by name in ORN, ser. II, vol. I, pp. 15-23.

[25] These conditions are complained of by the Secretary of the Navy in his Report of Dec. 7, 1863, *op. cit.*, pp. xxvi-xxvii.

[26] Stanton to Dix, July 4, 1862, in Woodward Ms. (see note 17, *ante*.), p. 889; Welles to Stanton, Jan. 7 and Jan. 12, 1863.—*Ibid.*, p. 1903. On April 8, 1864, Stanton ordered Maj. Gen. Lewis Wallace at Baltimore to transfer 800 Negro troops to the Navy—*Ibid.*, p. 2476. Welles ordered Commodore Charles Wilkes, commanding the James River Flotilla, Aug. 5, 1862 to "fill up the crews with contrabands obtained from Major-General Dix, as there is not an available sailor North."—ORN. VII, p. 632. For other complaints as to manpower shortage see ORN, XIV, p. 401; XXIII, pp. 246, 535; XXIV, p. 545.

[27] ORN, XIII, p. 209.

[28] MSS in NDR. Note that the remarks in the letter from the Superintendent are in conflict with the 1839 circular of the Navy Department, and the 1842 report of the Secretary, as given before.

[29] Muster rolls in NDR. In selecting these ships care was taken to see that they were of different types; otherwise the selection was entirely by chance. For a description of these vessels see ORN, ser. II, vol. I, pp. 37, 41, 159. The muster rolls, *after* 1862, contain columns for personal

descriptions, including hair and color, which make certain the identification, in terms of Negro and white, of the people involved. Occasionally, under the column, "occupation" will be found the word, "slave," and the columns for personal characteristics are then left blank. At times muster rolls prior to 1863 contain the entry "contraband" showing, only in this way, the presence of Negroes.

[80] Specifically, mention may be made of the following vessels—dates indicating muster rolls examined: *Monitor,* Nov. 7, 1862; *Kearsage,* Nov. 20, 1864; *Hartford,* Sept. 30, 1864; *Brooklyn,* June 30, 1864; *Oneida,* July, 1862; *New Ironsides,* Mar. 28, 1863; *Pensacola,* Dec. 31, 1863; *Stepping Stones,* Apr. 1, 1863.

[81] See ORN, XXII, p. 80; also VII, p. 324; XIII, p. 5. This order also directed that a monthly return "be made of the number of this class of persons employed on each vessel," but none has yet been found. These reports, when consolidated, were supposed to go to the Chief of the Bureau of Equipment and Recruiting, Rear Admiral Foote, but a search through the MS Letter Books of that official was unsuccessful. Occasional reports from individual ships are noted in this source,—as in vol. I, pp. 220, 312, NDR. On Jan. 1, 1863, Acting Rear Admiral David D. Porter informed Gideon Welles that there was "some irregularity" with these reports (*Ibid.,* I, p. 149); and on Mar. 3, 1863, he wrote to Capt. A. H. Pennock, Commandant of the Cairo Naval Station: "I have not received any report from any of the upper vessels about the contrabands. Please attend to this, as the Department seems to be very particular. Send me a list of them; also those you have employed on the station" (ORN, XXIV, p. 457). That some such records were forwarded is apparent from the following words—significant ones in terms of revealing Porter's thinking on the Negro—in a letter from him to Foote, Jan. 3, 1863: "Don't be astonished at the lists of niggers I send you. I could get no men, so I work in the darkies. They do first-rate, and are far better behaved than their masters" (ORN, XXIII, p. 603.)

[82] ORN, VII, p. 632.

[83] Porter to Bragg, Dec. 19, 1862, in ORN, XXIII, p. 639; for the facts on the *Glide* see ORN, XXIV, p. 308.

[84] Dated Cairo, Illinois, Oct. 26, 1862 in ORN, XXIII, p. 449. Since contrabands still were to be rated no higher than boys, their top pay would be $10 per month, while coal-heavers were supposed to receive $18, and firemen, $25 (2nd class), and $30 (1st class).—*Register of the Navy of the United States to Jan. 1, 1864* (Washington, 1864), p. 6.

[85] Dated July 28, 1863, in ORN, XIV, p. 401.

[86] Dated July 26, 1863, in ORN, XXV, p. 327.

[87] Circular dated Dec. 18, 1862, in ORN, XXIII, p. 639.

[88] Porter to Gen. Thomas, dated Cairo, Oct. 21, 1863, in Woodward MSS, p. 1049 (see note 17). Porter is, of course, referring only to his own Mississippi Squadron. The reader is again asked to remember that the total number of *contrabands* within a squadron was far from identical with the total number of *Negroes.* That, notwithstanding the Navy Department Circular of Dec. 18, 1862, just cited, Negroes were in some cases still under-rated is apparent from the postscript of a letter from

Commodore H. K. Thatcher to Commodore Bell, commanding the Western Gulf Blockade Squadron, dated Dec. 8, 1863. Thatcher, referring to an enclosed list of the strength of his vessel, the *Colorado,* added: "The coal heavers being all contrabands are rated as landsmen"—ORN, XX, p. 712.

[39] The pay of *white* pilots—about $250 per month—exceeded that of most commissioned officers; they were listed with officers; and were referred to as Mister. They were, however, technicians, not officers, holding a position analogous to the automotive experts employed by the Army during the Second World War. A trade union of pilots was largely responsible for their high wages and their success in maintaining these while serving the armed forces.—See ORN, XXI, p. 762; XXII, pp. 298, 404; XXV, pp. 153, 451, 557, 640, 714; XXVI, pp. 448, 725; XXVII, pp. 31-33, 132.

[40] The eight ships were: *New Hampshire,* June 7, 1864; *Argosy,* Dec. 31, 1863; *Avenger,* Oct. 1, 1864; *Pensacola,* Dec. 31, 1863; *Kearsage,* Nov. 20, 1864; *Brooklyn,* June 30, 1864; *Monitor,* Nov. 7, 1862; *Morning Light,* Jan. 1863. The source for the first seven is the original muster-rolls; for the *Morning Light,* see *Report,* Sec. of War, 1863, pp. 328-30. The excessive number of landsmen may be explained, in part, by the under-rating of Negroes, as already shown.

[41] J. P. Gillis to Du Pont, Jan. 3, 1862, in ORN, XII, p. 461. Gillis commanded the sloop, *Seminole,* and the naval force in Wassaw Sound, Georgia. There is no evidence that Du Pont objected to this act taken in plain violation of existing regulation, and Gillis' presuming that this would be the case appears to be significant.

[42] Welles' order of Dec. 18, 1862, had stated very clearly that contrabands "will not be transferred from one vessel to another with a higher rating than landsman."—ORN, VIII, p. 309.

[43] Du Pont to Welles, June 10, 1863, ORN, XIV, p. 251. No reply has been found.

[44] ORN, XII, pp. 647, 651; XIII, pp. 83-84.

[45] ORN, VIII, p. 735.

[46] Acting Ensign Miller to Commander Wolsey, dated New Orleans, Oct. 10, 1863, in ORN, XX, p. 451.

[47] Lt. Commander Weaver, dated "Off Suwanee River, S. C.," Mar. 25, 1864 in *Report,* Sec. of Navy, 1864, pp. 306-07. It is likely, though not certain, that the pilot of the *Cimarron* referred to as Prince, and called a "very reliable man" was Negro.—See *Ibid.,* pp. 317-18.

[48] A Court of Inquiry found that Small was partially responsible for the disaster because he had left his post in the course of the shelling.—ORN, XVI, pp. 192, 198.

[49] In addition to material given in note 31, *ante,* see ORN, XXIV, p. 678.

[50] Acting Rear Admiral Porter to Acting Volunteer Lieutenant R. K. Riley, Cairo, Dec. 9, 1862, in ORN, XXIII, p. 619.

[51] General Order No. 26, dated Off Vicksburg, July 26, 1863, in ORN, XXV, pp. 327-38.

[52] Porter to Commander W. A. Parker, dated Hampton Roads, Nov. 24, 1864, in ORN, XI, pp. 90-91.

[53] The quoted words come from an order given to a Lt. Collins by Flag Officer Du Pont, Nov. 10, 1861, in ORN, XII, p. 338.

[54] Commodore Hitchcock to Capt. Jenkins, dated Off Mobile, Feb. 3, 1863, in ORN, XIX, p. 599.

[55] J. S. Watson, Acting Master, U.S.S. *Juliet,* Off Ellis Cliffs [Miss.?], Mar. 15, 1864, in ORN, XXVI, p. 177. Similar action, however, was not always taken. In Sept., 1862, Lt. Truxton heard of an uprising of Negroes at Cumberland Island, Georgia. He dispatched men to the scene and nine armed Negroes were seized and brought to Truxton aboard the *Alabama.* They were put in irons, but when they requested to be allowed to serve as crewmen, and when their master released them—apparently glad to have such slaves off his hands—the officer "placed them on the ship's books as a portion of her crew."—Truxton to Du Pont, Sept. 6, 1862, in ORN, XIII, pp. 298-300. See also ORN XII, pp. 336-39.

[56] This occurred in Mar., 1865.—ORN, XVI, pp. 297-98.

[57] Du Pont to Gustavus Fox, Port Royal, S. C., Dec. 22, 1862, in ORN, XIII, p. 486. The *Vermont* was an ordnance, receiving, storage and hospital vessel.—*Ibid.,* p. 667.

[58] ORN, XXVI, pp. 249, 252; the *Petrel* was captured Apr. 22, 1864.

[59] *Ante,* note 48. The pilot, Stephen Small, had joined this ship two days prior to the disaster. The general remarks of Porter that Negroes could not be trusted as lookouts, and his rather contradictory one that his Negro sailors were doing "first-rate" have been noticed.

[60] Lt. Commander A. W. Weaver, dated Off Suwanee River, S. C., Mar. 25, 1864, in *Report,* Sec. of Navy, 1864, p. 307.

[61] This occurred in Nov., 1862.—ORN, XIII, pp. 430-33.

[62] *Report,* Secretary of Navy, 1864, pp. 338-44.

[63] Gen. L. Thomas to Stanton, telegram, dated Memphis, Apr. 4, 1863, in Woodward MSS, p. 1167 (see note 17).

[64] Recommendation dated Mar. 31, 1865 in ORN, XI, p. 488, and *Report,* Sec. of Navy, 1865 (serial number 1253), pp. 146-47.

[65] *Records of Medals of Honor Issued to the Officers, and Enlisted Men of the United States Navy, Marine Corps and Coast Guard 1862-1917* (Washington, 1917).

[66] Two men received Medals of Honor as a result of this engagement; one, white, was named Patrick Mullen, the other was Anderson. In the report of the fight nothing is said of Anderson's role except that he "assisted him [Ensign Summers] gallantly," while of Mullen some detail is provided. In the official *Record of Medals of Honor* (*op. cit.,* pp. 7, 79), however, this is reversed and that which is said of Mullen is cited for Anderson and vice versa. The report is in ORN, V. p. 535. J. W. Cromwell, *op. cit.,* p. 252, repeats the error of the official *Record.*

[67] *Record of Medals of Honor Issued . . .* p. 14.

[68] ORN, XIX, p. 437; *Record of Medals of Honor,* p. 68. These two sources do *not* indicate that Lawson was a Negro, but checking the original

muster roll of the *Hartford,* Sept. 30, 1864 (NDR) proves this to have been the fact. This same John Lawson had been severely wounded in Apr., 1862, while aboard the *Cayuga* in the attack on New Orleans.—ORN, XVIII, p. 181. The muster roll shows Lawson to have been 26 years old, born in Pennsylvania and a "laborer."

[69] ORN, Ser. I, vol. III, pp. 67-68.

[70] Daniels to the Rev. Mr. Huddleston of Wellington, Ohio, dated June 10, 1913, in file No. 11954, NDR. The precise source of Mr. Daniels' corrections of the official casualty figures is not indicated by him, but this must certainly have been his Bureau Chiefs and advisors.

[71] Lt. Comdr. K. R. Breese informed Rear Admiral Foote that the sickly season was approaching, that last year half the crews were prostrated, and since the ships were already short-handed, "God help us this year."—dated Yazoo River, Miss., May 5, 1863, in ORN, Ser. I, vol. XXIV, p. 653.

[72] ORN, ser. I, vol. XXVI, pp. 87, 167, 176; for another instance, see *Ibid,* IX, p. 436.

[73] The accounts do not name the Negro. An official report from Colonel W. S. Dilworth, C. S. A., to Major T. A. Washington, dated Tallahassee, Fla., Apr. 4, 1862, mentions the capture of the Negro "who had piloted the enemy into the inlet to [New] Smyrna, and who was to be hanged." An individual named George Huston boasted of having killed the Negro. He was himself killed in June, 1862.—ORN, ser. I, vol. XII, pp. 647, 651, vol. XIII, pp. 83-84.

[74] ORN, ser. I, vol. XV, pp. 158-61. Quoted words from report of Brig-Gen. J. H. Trapier, C. S. A., dated Georgetown, S. C., Dec. 8, 1863.

[75] ORN, ser. I, vol. XXVI, p. 419.

[76] For examples of this see: *Report* of Sec. of Navy, 1864, pp. 312, 317-19; ORN, XII, pp. 516-17; XV, p. 410.

[77] Dated Aug. 26, 1861, in ORN, VI, pp. 113-14.

[78] Reports dated June 23 and June 26, 1862, in ORN, VII, pp. 498, 506-07.

[79] Report dated Oct. 8, 1863, in ORN, XXV, pp. 452-56.

[80] Report dated Jan. 15, 1865, in ORN, XXII, pp. 8-9.

[81] All material on the *Planter,* unless otherwise indicated, is based upon official reports from Union and Confederate officers in ORN, XII, pp. 821-25.

[82] The names of several other participants in this remarkable adventure are known: John Smalls, A. Gridiron, J. Chisholm, A. Alston, G. Turno, A. Jackson, and two of the women referred to simply as Annie and Lavinia.

[83] Private Act No. 12, approved May 30, 1862, appraisal made July 9, money distributed Aug. 19, 1862, with Robert Smalls getting $1,500 of the total of $4,584.

[84] On Sept. 11, 1862, it was turned over to the Army's quartermaster department at Hilton Head, S. C.—MS log of U.S.S. *Planter,* Sept. 8-11, 1862, in NDR. No muster roll of the vessel appears to have been preserved, and the log for only the above four days is available.

[85] See ORN, XIII, p. 126; and *Official Records of Union and Confederate Armies in the War of the Rebellion,* ser. I, vol. XIV, p. 105.

[86] Charles Cowley, *The Romance of History in the 'Black County' and the Romance of War in the Career of General Robert Smalls,* (Lowell, Mass., 1882), pp. 9-10. Smalls was, of course, a South Carolina Congressman for ten years after the Civil War, and a General of the State's militia.

[87] *The Liberator,* Mar. 24, 1865, p. 48; Cowley, *op. cit.,* p. 11.

[88] See, as examples, ORN, XII, p. 353; XIII, pp. 257-58; XV, pp. 396-97.

[89] Examples of each of these items are in ORN, VII, pp. 87-89; IX, pp. 383, 420; XII, pp. 525, 584; XIII, pp. 199, 212; XIV, p. 121.

[90] See ORN, IX, pp. 383, 730; XII, pp. 468, 572-74.

[91] See report from Acting Rear-Admiral Porter to Secretary Welles, dated Mar. 26, 1863 and other documents and reports plus a map in ORN, XXIV, pp. 474-96.

[92] Report of Colonel John M. Stone, dated May 22, 1863, in ORN, VIII, p. 763. In addition to the accounts cited above, giving some more or less precise information as to the type of information supplied by Negroes, there are very many reports from officers in which mention is made of this, but in purely general terms. Almost the entire ORN is filled with this. See, as examples: VI, p. 695; VIII, p. 829; XII, pp. 50, 406; XIII, p. 342; XIV, pp. 190, 227; XV, p. 158; XVII, p. 818; XXIII, p. 523; XXV, p. 662.

## ORGANIZATIONAL ACTIVITIES OF SOUTHERN NEGROES, 1865

[1] See A. A. Taylor, *The Negro in South Carolina during Reconstruction* (Washington, 1924); *The Negro in the Reconstruction of Virginia,* (Washington, 1926), *The Negro in Tennessee, 1865-1880* (Washington, 1941); W. E. B. Du Bois, *Black Reconstruction* (N. Y., 1935); James S. Allen, *Reconstruction: The Battle for Democracy* (N. Y., 1937); M. Gottleib, "The Land Question in Georgia," in *Science & Society* (1939), III, pp. 356-88; Horace M. Bond, *Negro Education in Alabama* (Washington, 1939); Vernon L. Wharton, "The Negro in Mississippi 1865-1890," unpublished Ph.D. thesis, University of North Carolina, 1939; LaWanda F. Cox, "Agricultural Labor in the United States 1865-1890 with special reference to the South," unpublished Ph.D. thesis, University of California, 1941; Murray Greene, "The Negro Convention Movement in the Reconstruction Period," unpublished master's thesis, Columbia, 1946; Herbert Aptheker, "South Carolina Negro Conventions, 1865," in *The Journal of Negro History* (1946) XXXI, pp. 91-99. Note, also, F. B. Simkins, "New Viewpoints of Southern Reconstruction," *The Journal of Southern History* (1939), V, pp. 49-61; H. K. Beale, "On Rewriting Reconstruction History," *American Historical Review* (1940), XLV, pp. 807-27; T. H. Williams, "An Analysis of Some Reconstruction Attitudes," *Journal of Southern History* (1946), XII, pp. 469-86.

To this writer's knowledge there is no satisfactory narrative and evaluation of the Southern Negro's own activities, opinions, and desires during this period.

[2] There were meetings and the voicing of demands for full equality by Southern Negroes earlier than 1865, where conditions made this possible, —as, for example, in New Orleans in November, 1863, and February,

1864, and in Port Royal, S. C., in May, 1864. See Du Bois, *op. cit.*, pp. 155, 230; *The Liberator,* Mar. 11, 1864, p. 44.

[3] Sidney Andrews, *The South Since the War* (Boston, 1866), pp. 38-39; J. P. Hollis, *The Early Period of Reconstruction in South Carolina* (Baltimore, 1905), pp. 34-37; L. A. Kibler, *Benjamin F. Perry, South Carolina Unionist* (Durham, 1946), pp. 371-94.

[4] Complete text in Columbia *Phoenix,* Sept. 15, 1865 (in library of the University of S. C.). Compare with the remarks of another Johnsonian Provisional Governor, Patton of Alabama, in his inaugural address of Dec. 13, 1865: ". . . It must be understood that politically and socially ours is a white man's government."—H. Bond, *op cit.*, pp. 23-24. Virginia represents a special case for it had had a Union government, in Alexandria, from 1863 on. The pattern here too, however, is similar. In May, 1865, this government, under Pierpont, was recognized as the official state government. An extra session of the twelve members of the legislature met in Richmond in June and promptly suggested the enfranchising of the late rebels. At the conclusion of the session, the Speaker of the House, Downey, congratulated all concerned for having kept the state government out of Abolitionists' hands. He concluded: "Whatever they may do to other States, thank God, they cannot now saddle negro suffrage upon us."—H. J. Eckenrode, *The Political History of Virginia during the Reconstruction* (Baltimore, 1904), pp. 28-30. Governor Pierpont, in a speech at Norfolk on Feb. 16, 1865, addressing himself to the question, "What is to be done with him [the Negro]?" declared that most Negroes "are little better than nuisances" and hoped the military would continue, for the time being, in "charge of Sambo."—Francis H. Pierpont, *Reorganization of Civil Government . . .* (Norfolk, 1865), p. 5.

[5] To Professor D. D. Wallace, these laws "were sincere attempts of kindly paternalism to adjust appalling difficulties."—*The History of South Carolina* (N. Y., 1934, 4 vols.), III, p. 242. For a convenient summary of their contents see A. A. Taylor, *The Negro in South Carolina during Reconstruction,* pp. 43-49.

[6] Du Bois, op. cit., p. 456.

[7] A. A. Taylor, *The Negro in Tennessee 1865-1880,* pp. 2, 6-7. It may be mentioned here that southern Negroes throughout 1865 took advantage of all kinds of occasions to turn out en masse and to express their sentiments. For example: on Mar. 20, "upwards of 5,000" Negroes marched through Nashville celebrating the ratification of the revised state constitution outlawing slavery.—N. Y. *Tribune,* Mar. 21, 1865, p. 4; Raleigh Negroes met on Apr. 24 to express their devotion to the martyred Lincoln.—*Ibid.,* May 2, 1865, p. 1; New Orleans Negroes on May 10 thanked Gen. Butler for his efforts on their behalf.—*Ibid.,* May 31, p. 7; numerous parades of thousands of Negroes occurred throughout the South on July 4.—*Ibid.,* July 12, 1865, p. 1.

[8] It is altogether likely that this Hodges was related to the brothers, Charles E., John Q., and Willis A. Willis A. Hodges represented Princess Anne County in the Constitutional Convention, 1867-68; while the other two were members of the House of Delegates, for Norfolk County and Princess Anne, from 1869 to 1871.—L. P. Jackson, *Negro Officeholders in*

*Virginia, 1865-1895* (Norfolk, 1945), p. 21. There is reference to Willis A. Hodges attending a meeting of Negroes in 1879 in New York to which city he had been driven by violence.—N. Y. *Daily Tribune,* Feb. 28. 1879, p. 5.

[9] Thomas Bayne (1824-1889), was born a slave, in North Carolina, suffered severely, came to Norfolk in 1846 where he served as an apprentice to a dentist, and finally worked as a regular dentist himself. He helped slaves escape from Norfolk to the North, and, in 1855, fled himself. He then made his home in New Bedford, Mass., where he practiced dentistry, and was elected to the city council. Bayne returned to Norfolk early in 1865 and "became the most spectacular, the most radical, and one of the most hated of the Negroes in politics. In color and features he was a pure African." He was sent from Norfolk as a member of the 1867-68 Constitutional Convention.—See L. P. Jackson, *op. cit.,* pp. 2-3; and his testimony before a Congressional committee given in Washington, Feb. 3, 1866, in *Report of the Joint Committee on Reconstruction at the First Session Thirty-Ninth Congress* (Washington, 1866) pt. II, pp. 58-59. (Hereafter cited as Rept. Jt. Comm.)

[10] Calvin Pepper had lived in Norfolk since 1864, and prior to that had practiced his profession for six months in Alexandria. He was a native of Massachusetts and will appear again in the course of this narrative. See *Rept. Jt. Comm.,* pt. II, pp. 49-50.

[11] The members of the committees—every one of them, by this act, a hero—were: 1st ward—Albert Portlock, Thomas Wisher, Junius Fraser; 2nd ward —T. F. Paige, Jr. (probably a relative of Richard G. L. Paige, a well-to-do Negro lawyer, who represented Norfolk County in the House of Delegates from 1871-75 and 1879-82.—L. P. Jackson, *op. cit.,* p. 32), Joseph T. Wilson (Civil War veteran, later author of the still valuable *The Black Phalanx,* Hartford, 1888), Peter Shepherd; 3rd ward—E. W. Williams, G. W. Cook, William Southall; 4th ward—George W. Dawley, A. Woodhouse, the Rev. Mr. Lewis, A. Wilson.

[12] In a contest among three slates, that of Todd, De Cordy and Hall received an average of 93 white votes, the winners receiving 135, and the tail-enders, 60.

[13] The N. Y. *Tribune* said that this Norfolk election was dominated by secessionists, and that beatings of Negroes were common (June 28, 1865, p. 7). In the spring of 1865 the citizens of Fernandina, Florida, elected a mayor, and "the loyalists were very glad to be reenforced by the negroes" who, thus, did vote. The elected mayor was sworn into office by the visiting Chief Justice of the United States.—See Whitelaw Reid, *After the War: A Southern Tour* (N. Y., 1866), pp. 160-61.

[14] Negroes were urged to communicate with William Keeling in Norfolk in order to co-ordinate the Labor Associations. A similar function for Land Associations was to be performed by George W. Cooke, and it was urged that a Union of Virginia Colored Land Associations be formed. For the material on the Negroes of Norfolk see *Equal Suffrage. Address from the Colored Citizens of Norfolk, Va., to the People of the United States. Also an Account of the Agitation among the Colored People of Virginia for Equal Rights. With an Appendix concerning the Rights of Colored Witnesses before the State Courts* (New Bedford, Mass., 1865, copy in

N. Y. Pub. Lib.); the *Address* was printed in full (consuming over three columns) in *The Liberator* Sept. 8, 1865, XXXV, p. 144. Reactionary terror resulting in the killing of several Negroes was instituted at about this time in Norfolk.—See editorial, "The Reign of Terror in Norfolk," N. Y. *Tribune,* July 11, 1865.

[15] *The Liberator,* June 30, 1865, XXXV, p. 103.

[16] The five Negroes were: Joseph C. Jackson, George R. Dolly, Benjamin W. Roberts, Peter Duncan, and Joseph S. Tison. Their letter was dated June 15, 1865; Sumner's reply was cordial and stated that the petition had been forwarded as desired.—Wilmington, N. C., *Herald,* July 28, 1865, p. 1 (in library of University of N. C.). Mass meetings of Georgia Negroes in 1865 are mentioned but not particularized in W. Reid, *op. cit.,* pp. 147-48.

[17] Correspondence dated Newbern, May 10, in N. Y. *Tribune,* May 19, 1865, p. 6. Professor J. G. de Roulhac Hamilton cites correspondence from Wilmington of the same day, appearing in the N. Y. *Herald* of May 15, 1865 (this writer did not find the item in that paper), referring to a similar petition. He says this was due to "outside influences," but this is the unsubstantiated assertion of a far from objective writer.—*Reconstruction in North Carolina* (N. Y., 1914), p. 149.

[18] Prominent in these proceedings were: the Rev. William E. Walker, Miles Walker, Matthew Thomas, Thomas Scott (from 1872-74 an Overseer of the Poor in Petersburg), Thomas McKenzie, Sr. (there was a Lt. McKenzie on the Petersburg police force in the 1870's), Richard Kennard (later the city's Commissioner of Streets), John K. Shore (a barber, was a free Negro in slavery days, a member of the City Council, 1872-74), James Ford, John Brewer, the Rev. Daniel Jackson, Thomas Garnes, and James H. Jones.—The Petersburg *News,* June 9, quoted in N. Y. Tribune, June 15, 1865, p. 5. For the biographical material, see L. P. Jackson, *op. cit.,* pp. 59, 86.

[19] An editorial commending these resolutions appeared in the powerful N. Y. *Tribune,* June 20, 1865. In a book published in 1935 one reads: "In many cases [the Negro] had come to think of this 'freedom' he'd heard so much about as a material thing, an article which would be delivered to him, handed to him. In almost all cases he believed that it meant at least freedom from work. . . . What was the use of freedom, he said, if a nigger had to work *anyway?"*—Donald B. Chidsey, *The Gentleman from New York: A Life of Roscoe Conkling,* p. 57. Unlike Howard Fast's stirring fictionalized account of Thomas Paine's life, books with such obscenities are not only not banned from our schools, but are printed by the presses of our most distinguished universities—in this case that of Yale.

[20] See also the N. Y. *Tribune* of June 15, p. 1, and the Washington correspondence of that paper, dated June 16, in the issue for June 17, p. 1. The "Appeal" was signed by N. H. Anderson, Richard Carter, Madison Carter, Spencer Smithen, Robert W. Johnson, "and many others." Mr. Johnson was a shoemaker, and later served on the Richmond City Council. —L. P. Jackson, *op. cit.,* p. 57. Negroes found without a suitable pass were to be hired out, by the Provost Marshal, to whomsoever he wished, and to be paid $5 per month. For instances of brutality see the papers concerning this in the National Archives, Records of the War Department,

Bureau of Refugees, Freedmen and Abandoned Lands, State of Virginia, consisting of sworn testimony from several victims, as well as an eye-witness account by Alex. M. Davis, a N. Y. *Tribune* reporter, in a letter dated June 9, 1865, to Col. Brown of the Freedmen's Bureau. One Negro, Ned Scott, for having resisted the maltreatment of his wife and allegedly wounding two soldiers, was bucked, rolled on the street, beaten with a club, paraded through the town to the tune of the *Rogue's March,* and then placed, in an upright position, within a coffin, head and toes exposed, and face covered with flour and flies. He was informed that he was soon to be executed and was put on exhibit in a main thoroughfare. The Richmond *Times* (June 8, 1865) said it never witnessed "a more ludicrous and amusing scene" and that for two hours the encoffined Negro "was surrounded by hundreds of persons, who enjoyed the spectacle hugely. The black rascal was then, almost half dead with fright and heat, released. . . ." The Richmond *Whig* (same date) reported that during this ordeal Ned Scott "blinked his mealy eyes and said not a word . . . [but] some of the negroes [who passed by] seemed very indignant, and swore that was no way to treat a free black man."—Photostats in writer's possession.

[21] Washington correspondence, June 16, in N. Y. *Tribune,* June 17, 1865, p. 1. The delegation is referred to as "a fine-looking body of men." According to a North Carolina paper this address was written by a Mr. Van Vleet, a white man, and president of the Richmond Union League. The paper was a conservative one and whether this is true or not is not known. The assertion has not been seen elsewhere.—Washington correspondence, dated June 16, in the Wilmington *Herald,* June 23, 1865.

[22] Wilmington, N. C. *Herald,* July 7, 1865, p. 1. The paper wondered, with foreboding, whether the next step might not be conferring the suffrage upon the Negro.

[23] N. Y. *Tribune,* Oct. 28, 1865, p. 1.

[24] The names of some of the Negro leaders were: Pompey Ketto, Frank Rowan, George W. Walton, Alfred T. Jackson and M. H. Mason. The Memphis *Bulletin,* in N. Y. *Tribune,* July 1, p. 1; correspondence from Vicksburg in *Ibid.,* July 11, p. 7; J. S. McNeily, "War and Reconstruction in Mississippi 1863-1890," in *Publications of the Mississippi Hist. Society,* c. s., (1918), II, p. 297.

[25] N. Y. Tribune, Oct. 10, p. 4; *The Liberator,* Oct. 27, p. 169.

[26] Nelson Walker was elected president. Other leaders were: M. J. Gentle of Knoxville, T. J. Rapier of Maury, and Warner Madison of Sumner. See correspondence from Nashville in N. Y. *Tribune,* Aug 9, p. 1, Aug. 19, p. 7; and A. A. Taylor, *Negro in Tenn.,* p. 7; *Congressional Globe,* Dec. 21, 1865, 39 Cong., 1st sess., pt. 1, p. 107. The local press reported this convention quite fully.—Nashville *Daily Press and Times,* Aug. 9, 10, 12, 1865. See A. A. Taylor, *op. cit.,* pp. 7-9. The N. Y. *Tribune* correspondent from Nashville thought "The next session of the Legislature will be compelled to take some action in the premises."—Aug. 19, p. 7. But the suffrage law of May, 1866, ignored Negroes, and mass meetings and protests followed.—Taylor, p. 20. See also James W. Patton, *Unionism and Reconstruction in Tennessee 1860-1869* (Chapel Hill, 1934), pp. 127-28.

[27] Raleigh, N. C., *Daily Standard,* Aug. 10, 1865, p. 3 (in library of U. of N. C.). The editor of the *Standard,* J. S. Cannon, inserted his own "humorous" headlines above the reported speeches of each of the delegates, such as: "Mr. Kneeland Can't See That He Is Free Yet," or, "Mr. Smith, of Manchester, Walks Three Hundred and Eighty Eight Miles Without His Wife and Children." *The Liberator,* Aug. 11, 1865, p. 127, reported that "A call for a National Convention, to be composed of three delegates from each Congressional District in the country, to devise means for securing the voting privilege to the colored people, is being extensively signed and circulated in Norfolk, Portsmouth, and other parts of South-eastern Virginia." This paper's report of the Virginia State Negro Convention, dated Alexandria, August 4, is in the issue for Aug. 18, p. 131. See also, A. A. Taylor, *Negro in Reconstruction of Va.,* p. 14.

[28] The petition was signed by Nelson Hamilton and Cornelius Harris on behalf of "the colored citizens of Richmond," and was turned over, by the General, to his Provost Marshal for action.—N. Y. *Tribune,* Aug. 8, p. 1, Aug. 11, p. 5. The issue of Aug. 8 also reported the formation, in Richmond, of a Colored Loyal League for protection, education, and the securing of political rights.

[29] N. Y. *Tribune,* Aug. 25, p. 8; Sept. 16, p. 1.

[30] See the report, dated Raleigh, Oct. 15, 1865, of Col. E. Whittlesey, Ass't. Commissioner, Freedmen's Bureau, in *Rept. Jt. Comm.,* pt. 2, pp. 189-90. Col. Whittlesey remarks on the difficulties he had had in "disabusing" the Negroes of the idea "that they will be given land." See, on this subject, M. Gottleib, in *Science & Society* (1939), III, pp. 365-88.

[31] Galloway, a Civil War veteran, was from Fayetteville, and radical; Randolph was a carpenter and teacher from Greensboro and of more conservative views. No information has been seen on Price. See, Sidney Andrews, *The South Since the War: As Shown by Fourteen Weeks of Travel in Georgia and the Carolinas* (Boston, 1866), pp. 120, 125; F. A. Olds, "First Convention of Negroes in State," in *The Orphans' Friend and Masonic Journal* (Oxford, N. C.), Sept. 10, 1926, LI, no. 16, in Un. of N. C. library. Observe that this meeting was held in Wilmington. Several contemporaries referred to the very militant and highly organized character of the Negroes of that city and of New Bern.—See, N. Y. *Tribune,* Oct. 7, 1865; *Rept. Jt. Comm,* pt. II, p. 183; W. Reid, *op. cit.,* pp. 29*n.,* 51. Reid reported that in the spring of 1865 the Negroes of Wilmington already had a Union League "the object of which is to stimulate to industry and education, and to secure combined effort for suffrage, without which they insist that they will soon be practically enslaved again."

[32] Raleigh *Daily Standard,* Sept. 7, 1865, p. 3.

[33] Wilmington *Herald,* Sept. 22, p. 1, Sept. 23, p. 1 (Un. of N. C. Lib.). This paper was opposed to Negro suffrage.—See issue of June 9. Sampson and a William Smith were chosen as delegates to the State Convention. The paper remarked that Sampson's father had lived in Wilmington "and was looked upon as a man of more than ordinary intelligence and worth."

[34] Charlotte *Democrat,* Sept. 19, *Ibid.,* Sept. 22, p. 1. The next day students at the university who had been largely responsible for this assault found their own lodgings damaged, apparently by retaliating Negroes.

[35] Dated Raleigh, Sept. 29 in N. Y. *Tribune,* Oct. 7, 1865, p. 9. A month before a "reign of terror" was reported from Raleigh.—See *Ibid.,* Aug. 31, pp. 1, 4. On the last day of the Convention a committee of three was appointed for the purpose of seeing Gen. Ruger, the Federal commander, and requesting "protection for certain delegates returning home where bitter feelings exist against the colored convention."—Raleigh *Journal of Freedom,* Oct. 7, 1865; see also, Reid, *op. cit.,* p. 131.

[36] The memorial was the work of a committee of five—James Henry Harris, John Randolph, Jr., the Rev. George A. Rue, Isham Sweat, and John R. Gore. The "Official Proceedings of the Freedmen's Convention" was printed in the recently established Republican paper, the Raleigh *Journal of Freedom,* Oct. 7, 1865, pp. 1-2. A very full account is given in the N. Y. *Tribune,* Oct. 7, p. 9. Contemporary sources differ on some details, and the *Journal of Freedom* is followed here. A series of resolutions was also adopted hailing emancipation, the proposed 13th amendment, and the radical wing of the Republican party. One resolution set up a permanent Equal Rights League of North Carolina which affiliated with the national organization of the same name that had been formed in Syracuse in 1864. See *Proceedings of the National Convention of Colored Men, Syracuse, N. Y., October 4-7, 1864* (Boston, 1864, in Boston Pub. Lib.).

[37] The entire speech, a brief one, may be found in Andrews, *op. cit.,* p. 122; the press reported that it was received with prolonged applause. The press accounts differ from that in Andrews only slightly, except that according to it the Rev. Mr. Hood called for "the right of colored men to act as counsel in the courts for the black man" in addition to the other demands. —N. Y. *Tribune,* Oct. 7, p. 9.

[38] Raleigh *Journal of Freedom,* Oct. 7, pp. 1-2; N. Y. *Tribune,* Oct. 7, p. 9. Included in the appeal was this sweeping sentence: "We most earnestly desire to have the disabilities under which we have formerly lived removed; to have all the oppressive laws which make unjust discriminations on account of race or color wiped from the statutes of the State." Taken alone this would indeed be radical, but it must, of course, be considered in connection with the entire character of the paper.

[39] Extracts from editorials are reprinted in the Raleigh *Journal of Freedom,* Oct. 7, 1865, p. 3. The Raleigh *Sentinel* liked the petition but reported rumors that many of the Negro delegates were, privately, radical. Edward P. Brooks, editor of the *Journal of Freedom,* denied this at least so far as "the majority of the delegates" was concerned. The correspondent of the N. Y. *Tribune* reported considerable militancy among delegates from the eastern seaboard and said that one, from Wilmington, "even proposes to demand admittance [to the] White Convention, under instructions from his constituents." This, however, was felt to be "so absurd and foolish and likely to result so badly for the colored people [that] the Convention has already set its seal of condemnation upon the project." In the evening of Sept. 29, James H. Harris, of Raleigh, made the featured speech. He insisted that the Negro's best friends were the "intelligent white class in the South . . . counseled moderation, kindness. . . . The speech was in the happiest vein, and kept the house in a roar of merriment. . . ."—*Tribune,* Oct. 7, 1865, p. 9.

[40] Raleigh correspondence dated Oct. 5 in N. Y. Tribune, Oct. 10, p. 8; *Journal*

*of Freedom,* Oct. 21, p. 1. The last paper also carries a letter from "A Colored Man of Raleigh" denouncing this report as accomplishing nothing.

[41] Quoted in *The Liberator,* Oct. 6, 1865, p. 159.

[42] J. T. Trowbridge, *A Picture of the Desolated States* . . . (Hartford, 1888), pp. 230-31*n*.

[43] Trowbridge, *op. cit.,* p. 405. The strike occurred in December. In a divisive move the police arrested only Negro strikers.—R. W. Shugg, *Origins of Class Struggle in Louisiana* (Baton Rouge, 1939) p. 301. Compare with P. S. Foner, *History of the Labor Movement in the United States* (N. Y., 1947), p. 397*n*.

[44] The entire contemporary press and literature and such investigations as that by the Joint Congressional Committee on Reconstruction (1866) are filled with substantiation of these points. See also, M. Gottleib, *op. cit.,* and sources there mentioned. The traditional method of handling this epic resistance movement of the Negro people is to expatiate on an "ignorant race" who had "utter disregard for their obligations" and whose "insubordination" was insufferable. Quotations from a very recent example.—Lillian A. Kibler, *Benjamin F. Perry, South Carolina Unionist,* Duke Un. Press, Durham, 1946, pp. 401-02. The work contains an uncritical laudatory foreword by Professor Allan Nevins. See, on the other hand, the excellent treatment in Fred A. Shannon, *The Farmer's Last Frontier* (N. Y., 1945), pp. 78-83.

[45] N. Y. *Tribune,* Sept. 28, p. 4. What became of this movement, assuming it was able to continue, is not known.

[46] U. S. Senate, Jan. 5, 1866, *Cong. Globe,* 39 Cong., 1st Sess., pt. 1, p. 128.

[47] *Daily Phoenix,* Sept. 23, 1865 (in library of Un. of S. C.). The resolutions are quoted in full in Herbert Aptheker, "South Carolina Negro Conventions, 1865," in *Journal of Negro History* (1946), XXXI, p. 93. There had been a meeting of 4,000 Charleston Negroes, May 12, to greet the visiting Chief Justice of the nation, Salmon P. Chase. Speeches were made by Gen. Rufus Saxton, who urged the Negroes to petition for the ballot, Major Martin Delany, who decried the ill-will that he said existed between mulatto and Negro, a Mr. Tomlinson of the Freedmen's Bureau, who urged unity between Negro and poor white in order to "crush out the old oligarchy," and by Mr. Chase who urged patience upon the Negroes though assuring them that he personally would be happy to see them enfranchised at once.—N. Y. *Tribune,* May 22, 1865, p. 1. For other contemporary references to hostility between Charleston mulattoes and Negroes see correspondence from South Carolina dated July 4 and July 12 in *The Nation* (N. Y.), July 27, Aug. 10, 1865, I, pp. 106, 173.

[48] *Ms.* in Slavery File No. 3, "Petitions 1865," S. C. Hist. Comm., Columbia, S. C., quoted in full in Herbert Aptheker, *op. cit.,* pp. 93-95. The Charleston *Courier,* Sept. 26, declared in connection with this petition: "It cannot but be the earnest desire of all members that the matter be ignored *in toto* during the session."

[49] The four documents are given in full in the N. Y. *Tribune,* Nov. 29, 1865, preceded by a remark from the paper's correspondent in Charleston, himself a Negro. See issue of Nov. 30, p. 4, that "A candid world is bound to acknowledge its proceedings as the gravest exhibition of progressive

ideas the State has ever known." This convention was very extensively reported, and its proceedings, published in pamphlet form, were widely circulated. The documents, as published in this pamphlet (*Proceedings of the Colored People's Convention of the State of South Carolina . . .* Charleston, 1865), differ somewhat from those given in the *Tribune.* The difference represents a tightening and a certain toning down in the manner of expression. The original manuscript "Petition to the State Legislature," which differs in minor details from the contemporaneously published versions, is in the S. C. Hist. Comm., and was reprinted in Herbert Aptheker, *op. cit.,* pp. 96-97. According to the *Tribune* correspondent the Address came from the pen of Richard H. Cain, later a member of the State Legislature and of Congress, while the Memorial was written by Jonathan C. Gibbs, later school superintendent for the State of Florida. President of the Convention was Thomas M. Holmes; others who were prominent were Jacob Mills, John C. Des Verney, A. J. Ransier, Robert C. De Large (later a Congressman), Martin Delany, and Francis L. Cardozo. This convention is noticed in several secondary accounts.—See A. A. Taylor, *op. cit.,* p. 43; F. B. Simkins and R. H. Woody, *South Carolina During Reconstruction* (N. Y., 1938), p. 173; R. S. Henry, *The Story of Reconstruction* (N. Y., 1938), p. 173.

[50] In addition to material already presented, note the following: Brig. Gen. Charles H. Howard (brother of the Major-General Howard), an inspector in the Freedmen's Bureau with headquarters in Charleston, testified before a Congressional Committee on Jan. 31, 1866, ". . . there is a strong desire, amounting almost to a passion, on the part of a large number of the more enterprising of the blacks, to obtain land by lease, or to own land, and that there is a corresponding repugnance on the part of the citizens of South Carolina to allow them either to obtain land by lease or purchase. That is the case in Georgia also."—(*Rept. Jt. Comm.,* pt. III, p. 36.) Dr. George R. Weeks, an Army Surgeon who spent two and a half years in Arkansas, testified before the same committee: "I was with General Sanburn recently, who has charge of the negroes in the Indian territory, at Fort Smith. A negro walked up to him and said, 'Sir, I want you to help me in a personal matter.' 'Where is your family?' 'On Red River.' 'Have you not everything you need?' 'No, sir.' 'You are free.' 'Yes, sir, you set me free, but you left me there.' 'What do you want?' 'I want some land; I am helpless; you do nothing for me but give me freedom.' 'Is not that enough?' 'It is enough for the present; but I cannot help myself unless I get some land; then I can take care of myself and family; otherwise, I cannot do it.' "—*Ibid.,* p. 77, testimony dated Feb. 19, 1866. A correspondent reported from Orangeburg, S. C., on Sept. 8, 1865, that "The sole ambition of the freedman at the present time appears to be to become the owner of a little piece of land, there to erect an humble home, and to dwell in peace and security at his own free will and pleasure." A Negro asked him: "What's the use of giving us freedom if we can't stay where we were raised, and own our houses where we were born, and our little pieces of ground?"—*The Nation,* Sept. 28, 1865, I, p. 393.

[51] Mary Ames, *From a New England Woman's Diary in Dixie in 1865* (Springfield, 1906 pp. 96-103. The bracketed words are mine, condensing interpolations by the diarist; see also the testimony of Capt. A. P. Ketchum, of Gen. Howard's staff, who was present at this meeting, in *Rept. Jt.*

*Comm*, pt. II, p. 231. Capt. Ketchum remarked: "I have attended their political meetings . . . they have shown that they can organize . . . they are quite well informed . . . ."

Though Gen. Howard went ahead according to his orders and attempted to reinstate the planters, the Negroes' refusal to sign contracts resulted in no change in 1865. Congress in Jan. 1866, passed a bill validating land titles stemming from Sherman's Sea Island order of the previous year, but President Johnson vetoed this. In June, 1866, land titles at Port Royal, S. C., were validated but elsewhere force was used to remove the Negroes. That force would be needed was apparent from the greeting planters received from Edisto Island Negroes early in 1866: "You had better go back to Charleston, and go to work there the planters were told and if you can do nothing else you can pick oysters and earn your living as the loyal people have done—by the sweat of their brows."—Charleston *Courier,* Feb. 6, 1866, in Simkins and Woody, *op. cit.,* p. 229. These lands were not regained until Nov., 1868.

[52] Published in St. Louis, 1865, copy in Boston Pub. Lib. The committee consisted of H. McGee Alexander, chairman, J. Milton Turner, Secretary, and Samuel Helms, Francis Roberson, Moses Dickson, George Wedley, G. P. Downing and Jeremiah Bowman. On Oct. 19-21, 1865, there met, in Cleveland, the *First Annual Meeting of the National Equal Rights League* (Phila., 1865, copy in N. Y. Pub. Lib.) at which 41 delegates were present, including seven from Richmond, Raleigh, Knoxville, and Nashville. This Convention recommended to Congress the following constitutional amendment: "That there shall be no legislation within the limits of the United States or Territories, against any civilized portion of the inhabitants, native-born or naturalized, on account of race or color, and that all such legislation now existing within said limits is anti-republican in character and therefore void."—p. 20.

[53] *Rept. Jt. Comm.,* pt. II, p. 216.

[54] Saxton to Rep. G. S. Boutwell of Mass., Feb. 21, 1866, *Ibid.,* pt. III, p. 102. Of this Charleston Negro Union League one observer declared: "It was not to be supposed that they [the Negroes] initiated and prosecuted these undertakings without assistance from their white friends. Mr. [James] Redpath has been ever at hand with his suggestions and practical wisdom."—Henry L. Swint, *The Northern Teacher in the South 1862-1870* (Nashville, 1941), p. 86, citing the *National Freedman,* March 1, 1865. See, also, Horace M. Bond's remarks about the social distance between the mass of Alabama Negroes and many of their leaders.—*Negro Education in Alabama* (Washington, 1939), p. 27.

[55] Testimony of Charles A. Harper, in *Rept. Jt. Comm.,* pt. III, p. 74. Mr. Harper had come to Arkansas in 1862, after a residence of twenty years in Texas. See, also, the remarks of W. H. Gray, a Negro who had been a delegate at this convention, made, in 1867, as a member of the Arkansas Constitutional Convention, in J. T. Trowbridge, *op. cit.,* pp. 661-62.

[56] The Institute was opened in September. See a report of the ceremonies and the speech delivered there by Frederick Douglass in the *Journal of Freedom* (Raleigh), Oct. 14, 1865, p. 4; for reference to the convention see the N. Y. *Tribune,* Jan. 3, 1866, p. 7.

[57] Douglass was the son of Frederick and had fought as a non-commis-

sioned officer with the 54th Mass. Regt.; Matthews had also served in the Union Army, rising to the rank of a 1st Lt. in an independent battery of light artillery. For the Florida convention see *Cong. Globe*, Feb. 19, 1866, 39th Cong., 1st sess., pt. 1, p. 912.

[58] Rumors of Negro insurrection appeared everywhere in the South in December, 1865. Undoubtedly much of this was deliberately inspired for the reasons cited by the Norfolk Negroes, but whether or not there was any foundation for the rumors in any case is a moot point. Reports of the occurrence of actual violence recur, some with a highly dubious quality. Thus, from Milledgeville, Ga., it was reported on Dec. 22, that a squad of Negro soldiers and recent dischargees attacked the supposedly unprotected home of a widow, near Augusta, but they "met unexpected resistance," three Negroes being killed and two wounded, when Federal troops rescued the inhabitants of the house, among whom no casualties were reported. From New Orleans it was reported that on Christmas Day three policemen had been severely wounded by "a gang of excited negroes. Some forty of the negroes were arrested, most of whom were armed."—N. Y. *Tribune*, Jan. 1, 1866, p. 7.

[59] The others were Richard Hill and Cornelius Allen of Hampton, Robert Bailey of Old Point, Frederick Smith of Williamsburg, Dr. D. M. Norton of Yorktown, and George Chahoon, white, of Hampton. This material on Virginia is based on manuscripts in a box marked "Negroes" in Records of the Quartermaster Dept., War Records Office, National Archives. In addition the Rev. William Thornton came from Hampton, Alexander Dunlop and Edmund Parsons from Williamsburg, and Madison Newby from Norfolk. See their sworn testimony and that of Pepper, Norton, Hill and Bayne in *Rept. Jt. Comm*, pt. II, pp. 49-60. All, except Pepper, were natives of Virginia and had lived there most of their lives. Pepper asserted that he was acting not only for Negroes in demanding equal suffrage, but also two hundred and fifty white men of Norfolk and Portsmouth.

## MISSISSIPPI RECONSTRUCTION AND THE NEGRO LEADER, CHARLES CALDWELL

[1] C. H. Brough, "The Clinton Riot," in *Publications of the Mississippi Historical Society* (1902), VI, p. 55 [hereafter cited as PMHS]; J. S. McNeily, "Climax and Collapse of Reconstruction in Mississippi, 1874-76," *Ibid.*, (1912), XII, pp. 403, 428; D. Rowland, *History of Mississippi* (2 vols., Chicago, 1925), II, pp. 198-99. To the credit of J. W. Garner it is to be noted that he referred to Caldwell as "courageous" albeit "dangerous."—*Reconstruction in Mississippi* (N. Y., 1901), p. 384. Contemporaries rarely mentioned Caldwell without citing his daring.—See *The Testimony in the Impeachment of Adelbert Ames, as Governor of Mississippi* (Jackson, 1877), pp. 90, 93, 136, 145 [hereafter cited as *Impeachment Testimony*]; *Report of the Select Committee to Inquire into the Mississippi Election of 1875, with the testimony and documentary evidence*, Senate Report No. 527 (2 vols.), 44th Cong., 1st Sess. (serial numbers 1669, 1670), II, p. 1263 [hereafter cited as *Boutwell Report*].

[2] For his slave-time occupation see W. C. Wells, "Reconstruction and its Destruction in Hinds County," in PMHS (1906), IX, p. 101.

[3] The census of 1860 gave Mississippi 437,404 Negroes and 353,901 whites; that of 1870 showed 445,060 and 384,549 respectively, with no figures available for five of its counties. The census of 1870 was particularly poor, the Bureau itself estimating it had failed to count about 512,000 Southern Negroes.—*Negro Population in the United States, 1790-1915* (Washington, 1918), p. 27.

[4] A biography of Alcorn is urgently needed. See P. L. Rainwater, "Letters of Alcorn" in *The Journal of Southern History* (1937), III, pp. 196-209; sketch of his life by F. R. Riley in the *Dictionary of American Biography,* I, pp. 137-38; and his very revealing speech in the Senate, Dec. 20, 1871 in *Cong. Globe,* 42nd Cong., 2nd Sess., p. 246.

[5] C. S. Sydnor on Sharkey in *Dict. of Amer. Biog.,* XVII, pp. 21-22.

[6] Several of these officials reinstituted slave ordinances and in some counties the old slave patrols returned to duty, at times with the approval of Federal officers—see *Reminiscences of Carl Schurz* (3 vols., N. Y., 1908), III, p. 188, and Schurz's report to the President, made in Nov. 1865, in *Senate Exec. Doc.* No. 2, 39th Cong., 1st Sess (serial number 1237).

[7] Johnson in a telegram of Aug. 25, 1865 assured him this would be done. By May 1866 the last of the approximately 9,000 Negro troops had been removed leaving but one battalion of (white) infantry for the entire State. Even in 1867 when registration of voters was conducted under Federal auspices there were but some 2,000 white troops in Mississippi—Garner, *op. cit.,* pp. 104, 171; W. E. B. Du Bois, *Black Reconstruction* (2nd edit., N. Y., 1938), p. 433.

[8] *PMHS* (1918, c.s.), p. 313.

[9] In the words of a sympathetic chronicler: "Thus perished slavery in Mississippi, killed in the house of its friends, and by those who loved the institution most."—Garner, *op. cit.,* p. 90.

[10] Based on, *Journal of the Proceedings and Debates in the Constitutional Convention of the State of Mississippi August, 1865* (Jackson, 1865); *Ordinances, Resolutions and Constitutional Amendments, Adopted by the Mississippi Constitutional Convention, August, A. D., 1865* (n.p., n.d.).

[11] *Memphis Bulletin* quoted in N. Y. *Tribune,* July 1, 1865, p. 1; correspondence from Vicksburg, *Ibid.,* July 11, 1865, p. 7.

[12] The press reprinted this widely, at times adding editorial comment.—N. Y. *Tribune,* Oct. 10, 1865, p. 4; *The Liberator* (Boston), Oct. 27, 1865, p. 169. We have already referred to these meetings and have seen they were typical of the actions of Negroes throughout the South that year—see the previous chapter.

[13] *Canton American Citizen,* Oct. 29, 1865; *Natchez Courier,* Nov. 2, 1865.

[14] See Alcorn's speech in the Senate, Dec. 20, 1871, *Cong. Globe,* 42nd Cong., 2nd sess., p. 246. In the same election Benjamin G. Humphreys was selected as governor. He had been a Confederate general and *at the time of the election was still an unpardoned rebel,* an oversight quickly remedied by the President who, however, continued to deal with Sharkey as acting Governor until December, 1865—Garner, *op. cit.,* p. 94.

[15] *Laws of the State of Mississippi passed at a Regular Session of the . . . Legislature . . . October . . . December, 1865* (Jackson, 1866), pp. 254-55, 280-84.

[16] *Ibid.,* pp. 82-89, 115.

[17] U.S. Senate, Jan. 5, Feb. 13, 1866, in *Cong. Globe,* 39th Cong., 1st sess., pt. 1, pp. 128, 806. These petitions were referred to the Joint Committee on Reconstruction whose papers are missing so that examination of them in the original has not been possible—letter to writer from Mr. Thad Page, Director of Legislative Service, National Archives, Washington, April 17, 1947.

[18] *Report of the [U.S.] Commissioner of Agriculture for the Year 1867* (Serial No. 1347), (Washington, 1868), pp. 416, 417, italics added. In the spring and summer of 1865 the Freedmen's Bureau in Mississippi tried to institute a system of semi-annual wage payments. These were miserably low—from $6-10 per month for men; $5-8 for women; $2-3 for children under 14—but the press denounced them as exorbitant and obnoxious and hoped that "After awhile . . . our country will right up, and then negroes will receive such wages as their services are worth *and no more,* if the whole country was flooded with military orders."—*Canton Tri-Weekly Citizen,* June 11, 1865; R. H. Moore, "Social and Economic Conditions in Mississippi during Reconstruction" (unpublished doctorate, Duke University, 1937), p. 45. In the winter of 1865 planters formed organizations dedicated to employing Negroes only as sharecroppers and pledging to rent land to and hire none.—*Hinds County Gazette,* Nov. 25, 1865; Moore, *op. cit.,* pp. 54-56; V. L. Wharton, "The Negro in Mississippi, 1865-1890" (unpublished doctorate, University of North Carolina, 1939), p. 112. Wharton's work is particularly valuable.

[19] Moore, *op. cit.,* p. 357, citing *Jackson Daily Mississippi Clarion and Standard,* June 24, 1866.

[20] G. P. Sanger, ed., *The Statutes at Large . . . of the United States . . . Dec. 1865—March, 1867* (Boston, 1868), pp. 27-29.

[21] For the complete law see Sanger, *op. cit.,* pp. 428-29. On the same day Congress enacted a little-noted law, "to Abolish and forever Prohibit the System of Peonage in the Territory of New Mexico and other parts of the United States" (*Ibid.,* p. 546), which, had it only been enforced, would have been quite as revolutionary as the 13th amendment.

[22] For the total figure see *Journal of the Proceedings in the Constitutional Convention of the State of Mississippi 1868* (Jackson, 1871), appendix [hereafter cited as *1868 Proceedings*]; Garner, *op. cit.,* p. 181. The estimate of the Negro-White registration is based on the fact that in September the military announced that of about 106,000 registrants, over 46,000 were white and 60,000 Negro. This early and incomplete figure has led to some confusion in the literature.—as Du Bois, *op. cit.,* p. 434.

[23] For the boycott see especially J. R. Lynch, *The Facts of Reconstruction* (N. Y., 1913), pp. 18*ff.* There was by no means unanimity on this tactic. In addition to such characters as Alcorn and Campbell to whom reference has been made observe that men like former Senator Brown, ex-Governor McRae and Ethelbert Barksdale (before the war a rabid secessionist and after the war editor of the rather moderate Democratic *Jackson Clarion*) agreed with Campbell on the advisability of "cooperating" with the Negroes. See *Jackson Clarion,* May 16, 1867; J. B. Ranck, *Albert Gallatin Brown* (N. Y., 1937), p. 255; Garner, *op. cit.,* p. 179; Wharton, *op. cit.,* pp. 257-61. The story of Bourbon efforts to win over the Negro and make him *agree* to a subordinate position remains to be told.

[24] J. L. Power, *op. cit.*, p. 78; Wharton, *op. cit.*, pp. 265-66.

[25] Thus, on Dec. 9, 1867, Gov. Humphreys issued a proclamation referring to "serious apprehensions that combinations and conspiracies are being formed among the blacks to seize the lands and establish farms," and ending, "I warn you that you cannot succeed." Immediately thereafter Gen. Gillem notified all Negroes that they were expected to sign contracts "and go to work upon the best terms that can be procured, even should it furnish a support only" or they would be jailed as vagrants. A special committee appointed by the convention to investigate this declared it to be a hoax and a slander, while Gen. Gillem admitted he had "never shared in belief that insurrection was meditated."—*1868 Proceedings*, pp. 577, 579, 581; *American Annual Cyclopedia, 1867* (N. Y.. 1868), pp. 518-19.

[26] *1868 Proceedings*, pp. 3-5.

[27] Caldwell was absent one day and part of two others; he was a member of the Committee on Ordinance and Schedule.—*Ibid.*, pp. 37, 531, 711, 714.

[28] See the testimony of J. H. Estell, a white native of Alabama, long-time resident of Mississippi and a Jackson lawyer who participated in Caldwell's defense.—*Boutwell Report*, I, pp. 327-28. The jurors must have been white, as Negroes were not authorized to serve in that capacity until Gov. Ames so ordered in April, 1869.—*American Ann. Cycl, 1869*, p. 455.

[29] Only half the Negro vote was cast.—Garner, *op. cit.*, p. 217*n*. A Mississippi planter declared in 1868: "That in hiring freedmen for another year, we require them to expressly stipulate, to use their time and services for our own interest and advantage, and if they begin to neglect their duties and lose time by stopping their work during the week and attending 'club meetings,' without our permission, such hands shall be dismissed from our service and their wages forfeited. That when any freedman shall be thus discharged, we pledge ourselves not to hire or give such freedman employment under any circumstances."—*De Bow's Review* (1868), V, p. 224. See also Wharton, *op. cit.*, pp. 276-77. The disfranchising clauses created some division of feeling amongst Republicans as to the wisdom of supporting the constitution.—Lynch, *op. cit.*, pp. 21*f*.

[30] Before Gillem's departure a public meeting, presided over by a former Confederate general, thanked him for his courtesies and good-will.—See PMHS (1918, c.s.), II, p. 356. Grant's vigor is explicable when it is recalled that his election over Seymour in 1868 was made possible by a half million Negro votes; he received altogether 3,012,000 votes while Seymour received 2,703,000. Mississippi, of course, did not vote in that election.—C. H. Coleman, *The Election of 1868*, (N. Y., 1933), pp. 369-70.

[31] Grant, in a letter to Dent, Aug. 1, 1869, declined to support him—on political, not personal grounds, of course. See the exchange of letters in *Amer. Ann. Cycl., 1869*, p. 457. The official election returns are in *Boutwell Report*, II, Documentary Evidence, pp. 137*ff*. Caldwell's county went Republican by 3,819 to 1,415. Negroes ran on both tickets, but only some ten per cent of the Negro vote went Democratic. About 20,000 whites voted Republican. For a typical Democratic Negro of this period see the description of Henry House, "the faithful servant," as a result of whose efforts the planters "took up a collection and bought for him an excellent little home."—in PMHS (1912), XII, p. 165. With the pressures and dangers that existed and the rewards that were offered it is a tribute to

the Negro people that they were afflicted with so few Henry Houses.

32 One month later, Feb. 17, 1870, Congress admitted Mississippi into the Union.

33 Contemporaries agreed that while Caldwell was not a dramatic orator he was a very lucid and clear speaker.—*Boutwell Report,* I, p. 327, II, p. 1263. The Board of Police had had five members, two of whom were Negro. This Board not only performed the functions indicated by its name, but also was the county tax-levying body.—PMHS (1906), IX, p. 89. Lynch is in error when he says there were four Negro state senators in 1870.—*op. cit.,* p. 45. He names Hiram Revels, Robert Gleed, T. W. Stringer and Caldwell but omits William Gray.—see Wharton, *op. cit.,* p. 316.

34 These laws were enacted in the spring and summer of 1870.—*Laws of . . . Mississippi, passed at a regular session commencing Jan. 11, 1870, and ending July 21, 1870* (Jackson, 1870), pp. 1-18, 73, 95, 104*f.,* 132-43. Contemporary evidence shows that Jim-Crow habits were not, of course, abandoned overnight but they were, in many spheres, including marriage, dissolving. This requires and demands a study of its own, that is, a study of the actual functioning of the institutions of Jim Crowism throughout the South during Reconstruction. It is of interest to note that while there were eight negative votes on ratifying the 14th amendment, there was only one on the 15th, showing almost universal reconciliation to the idea of Negro voting.—PMHS (1918, c.s.), II, p. 382.

35 Acts passed April, 1873, in *Laws of . . . Mississippi . . . 1873,* (Jackson, 1873), pp. 78-79.

36 The published volumes of session laws, 1870-74, are filled with these acts of incorporation. The tax refund law was passed in April, 1872.—*Laws . . . Mississippi . . . 1872* (Jackson, 1872), pp. 65-67.

37 The growth in numbers of independent Negro business men, shop-owners, teachers, public officials (as a result of the 1873 election there were 64 Negroes in the state legislature alone out of a total membership of 152, while the Speaker of the House, the Lieutenant-Governor, the Secretary of State and the Superintendent of Education were Negroes, and hundreds of local offices were filled by Negroes), was very great and noted by contemporaries.—*Jackson Weekly Pilot,* Dec. 24, 1870; Garner, *op. cit.,* p. 288; Wharton, *op. cit.,* pp. 306*ff.* There is record of at least one Negro newspaper during this period—the *Vicksburg Plaindealer* but no copies have been seen.—Garner, *op., cit.,* p. 293*n.*

38 *Hinds County Gazette,* Sept. 16, 1869; *Jackson Weekly Pilot,* Nov. 26, 1870; Wharton, *op. cit.,* p. 111.

39 G. W. Wells to Attorney-General G. H. Williams, Holly Springs, April 10, 1872, and E. P. Jacobson to same, Jackson, Feb. 17, 1872, in House Exec. Doc. No. 268, 42nd Cong., 2nd sess., pp. 30-41. In July, 1870, Mississippi enacted an anti-KKK law which had a salutary effect for a brief time.—*Laws . . . Miss. . . . 1870 . . .* pp. 89-92.

40 See the two volumes of documentary material on KKK violence in Mississippi in Report No. 22, House of Representatives, pts. 11, 12, 42nd Cong., 2nd sess. (Washington, 1872, ser. nos. 1539, 1540); also Moore, *op. cit.,* p. 223.

41 Another precipitant of the break was Alcorn's policy of appointing as

few Negroes as possible to official positions and the desire of his wing of the Party to have few Negroes run for public office.

42 *Cong. Globe,* April 11, 1871, 42nd Cong., 1st sess., p. 571.

43 Figures from *Boutwell Report,* II, Doc. Evid., pp. 137-45. Here Alcorn is listed as a Democrat which is proper in fact if not in form. The split cut the Republican vote, for in the 1872 Presidential election Grant beat Greeley in Mississippi by 82,000 to 47,000 or by 35,000 votes. Grant carried Hinds County by 2,500 votes; Ames by 2,200.

44 The testimony before the Congressional committee investigating the Klan is filled with references to the Meridian affair.—See also *Amer. Ann. Cycl.* (*1871*), p. 523.

45 *Amer. Ann. Cycl., 1874,* p. 573; *Laws . . . Mississippi . . . December, 1874* (Jackson, 1875), pp. 5-7; Wharton, *op. cit.,* p. 350.

46 In addition to the violence, 1874 marked the highpoint in a taxpayers' strike, so that the *Greenville Times,* Oct. 10, 1875, said: "Last fall a majority of the taxpayers refused payment of taxes." Much of the *Boutwell Report* is concerned with this violence. See also Garner, *op. cit.,* pp. 357*ff*.; A. T. Morgan, *Yazoo . . .* (Washington, 1884), *passim.* While in Mississippi, Morgan had served in the 1868 convention and in the legislature as well as sheriff and tax collector of Yazoo County. He married a Negro school-teacher.

47 The Democrat invited was W. C. Wells. See his article in PMHS (1906), pp. 85-108. Wells admits that he himself went armed to the meeting, while Caldwell was unarmed. Caldwell's district—comprising Hinds and Rankin counties—was allowed two senators. His running mate, Henry Kerneghan of Brandon in Rankin county, had come to New Orleans as a boy from Ireland and lived there until settling in Mississippi in 1859. As a result of murder threats and Kerneghan's urging, Caldwell did not canvass in Rankin. See Kerneghan's testimony, *Boutwell Report,* II, p. 1243*ff*.

48 *Jackson Weekly Pilot, n.d.,* quoted by Wells, *op. cit.,* p. 96. No figures have been cited as to how many Negroes and white people were present. Some contemporary news accounts and later commentators say fifteen armed whites put to flight three hundred armed Negroes—who deliberately provoked a conflict. But such assertions are manifestly absurd, and such reporters on the activities of the Negro people are about as reliable as Mrs. Luce's quotations from Karl Marx. Clearly, the Clinton riot and aftermath were parts of a deliberately calculated policy of terror and repression. That is fundamental; the details are obscure and non-essential. On the same day as the Clinton riot an armed body of Democrats surrounded a group of about one thousand Negroes near Utica and forced them to listen to speeches—Brough, *op. cit.,* p. 55.

49 The name was taken from the Modoc Indians who had recently risen against the Federal government and been suppressed by the Army in a war lasting several months.—J. Curtin, *Myths of the Modocs* (N. Y., 1912).

50 Wells, *op. cit.,* p. 100. One of the white people killed was Wm. P. Haffa, a Justice of the Peace, whose wife taught at a Negro school.—*Boutwell Report,* I, 483*ff*.

51 Testimony of Mrs. Caldwell given in Jackson, Miss., June 20, 1876, in *Boutwell Report,* I, p. 439. Of these Modocs one historian has permitted

himself to write what they performed "valiant and vigorous work for the protection of life and property"!—PMHS (1902), VI, p. 61.

[52] PMHS (1902), VI, p. 61.

[53] PMHS (1912), XII, p. 390. James Zachariah George, Colonel in Confederate Army, Brigadier-General of Mississippi State Troops, Chief Justice of Mississippi's highest court, 1879-81; U. S. Senator, 1881-97; drafter of the disfranchisement clause of the 1890 constitution.—*Dict. Am. Biog.* VII, pp. 216*f.*

[54] Morgan, *op. cit.,* p. 475*f.* Pierrepont as Attorney-General in a Republican administration is indicative of the slight significance of party labels in critical moments of American history. In the late 'fifties he was a leading New York Democrat, and during the war was a Union Democrat. He favored Johnsonian Reconstruction and was a regular Democrat until 1868 when he campaigned for Grant. His later elevation to the Cabinet was one of his rewards for this.—*Dict. Am. Biog.* XIV, p. 587.

[55] PMHS (1912), XII, p. 391. Bruce, the second and, so far, the last Negro Senator, was elected to his position by the Mississippi legislature in 1874 after Ames' victory. He was much more militant than Revels.—See G. D. Houston, "A Negro Senator," in *Journal of Negro History* (1922), VII, pp. 243-56.

[56] *Amer. Ann. Cycl., 1875,* p. 576. According to Lynch, Grant decided against sending troops because he felt the state was already lost and because a Republican delegation from Ohio feared the political effect of such action upon the October elections there.—J. R. Lynch, *op. cit.,* pp. 150*ff.* The press, in accord with the decision of both political parties to restore Bourbon domination to the South, hailed Grant's action. This is true of such Republican papers as the N. Y. *Tribune,* Baltimore *Sun,* Philadelphia *Times,* and Chicago *Tribune.* The N. Y. *Times* in its typically pompous manner asseverated: "The country will receive the expressions of Mr. Pierrepont with entire satisfaction."—See *Boutwell Report,* I, pp. 376-77.

[57] *Hinds County Gazette,* Sept. 29, 1875; V. Wharton, in *Phylon* (1941), II, p. 368.

[58] General Order No. 7, State of Mississippi, dated Oct. 1, 1875. Caldwell's commission was dated Sept. 25.

[59] Morgan, *op. cit.,* p. 481.

[60] *Yazoo Democrat,* n.d., in PMHS (1912), XII, pp. 408*f.*

[61] Testimony of State's Adjutant General, in *Impeachment Testimony,* p. 131.

[62] *Ibid.,* pp. 19, 89-93, 131; Garner, *op. cit.,* p. 384; PMHS (1906), VI, pp. 67*f.*

[63] Thus, George received the following telegram from the Democratic leader at Edwards' Depot on Oct. 9: "We learn that Caldwell, with one hundred armed men are marching upon our town. What shall we do—submit or resist? We are able to do either." He replied: "We advise to avoid a difficulty, by all means. Escort is under orders."—*Impeachment Testimony,* p. 260; see also PMHS (1906), VI, p. 68.

[64] *Aberdeen Examiner,* Sept. 30, 1875; Garner, *op. cit.,* p. 384. On Peyton's background, see Donald, *op. cit.,* p. 448. Peyton resigned in 1876 and was promptly given an annual pension of $3,000 by the Democrats while his son received a juicy sinecure.—*Boutwell Report,* II, pp. 238*f.*

[65] Caldwell's own commission expired, officially, Oct. 21. There is some evidence that his company made no haste in disarming, but all its rifles were accounted for—except nine—by the end of October. *Impeachment Testimony,* pp. 137, 261-62; *Boutwell Report,* I, p. 36 .

[66] Text of treaty in *Impeachment Testimony,* pp. 230*ff*.; see PMHS, (1906), VI, pp. 65-77; (1912), XII, p. 409; *Boutwell Report,* I, p. 699.

[67] *Amer. Ann. Cycl.,* 1875, p. 516; *Boutwell Report,* II, Doc. Ev., p. 20; Garner, *op. cit.,* p. 376.

[68] *Boutwell Report,* II, Doc. Ev., pp. 160-69; *Greenville Times,* Oct. 30, 1875; Wharton, *op. cit.,* pp. 336-41. The bribery ran the gamut from a dollar bill to a yearly pension of $3,000 (as already indicated) and the position of a college presidency for ex-Senator Revels. Revels campaigned for the Democrats in 1875, and two days after the election wrote a letter to Grant assuring him of the fairness of the vote and hailing the result. In 1876 the Democrats reinstated him as President of Alcorn [!] College. Revels' letter to the President was probably the best single propaganda device the Democrats had and was widely reprinted—*The Nation,* Jan. 6, 1876, XXIII, p. 2; *Amer. Ann. Cycl., 1875,* pp. 517*f*.; W. L. Fleming, ed., *Documentary History of Reconstruction* (2 vols., Cleveland, 1907), II, pp. 402*ff*.

[69] *Boutwell Report,* II, Doc. Evid., pp. 160-69. The next day a mass meeting of Negroes in Jackson adopted resolutions of similar purport and forwarded them to the Governor, *Ibid.,* p. 31.

[70] Houston Burrus to Gov. Ames, Nov. 1, 1875 (received, Nov. 4), *Ibid.,* p. 99.

[71] *The Nation* (N. Y.), Oct. 28, 1875, XXI, p. 269. For an extraordinary piece of allegedly historical writing see the handling of this election in R. S. Henry, *The Story of Reconstruction* (N. Y., 1938), p. 544.

[72] See Wharton, *op. cit.,* pp. 345, 361-62; Wells, *op. cit.,* pp. 103-04.

[73] Welborne's testimony, Washington, July 8, 1876.—*Boutwell Report,* I, p. 496. Welborne fled a lynch mob in December, 1875.

[74] Thus, in Dec. 1875, six Negro leaders were lynched at Rolling Fork. The press continued to call for violence through Dec. 1875 and Jan. 1876.—see *Boutwell Report,* II, Doc. Evid., p. 167.

[75] Mrs. Caldwell's testimony is the basis for this.—*Boutwell Report,* I, pp. 435-40.

[76] This was Judge E. W. Cabaniss, another moderate Republican who reneged. He served as a minority of one Republican on a committee of three set up by the Democratic Party to investigate the Moss Hill riot. The report of this committee—a complete whitewash—was used for propaganda purposes during and after the 1875 campaign.—PMHS (1912), XII, p. 387.

[77] PMHS (1912), XII, p. 428.

[78] Quoted without date in *Appleton's Annual Cyclopedia. 1877* (*n.s.,* II), p. 231; quoted, in part, by P. S. Foner, *History of the Labor Movement in the United States* (N. Y., 1947), p. 464.

[79] Compare this account with that in Jesse T. Wallace's *A History of the Negroes of Mississippi from 1865 to 1890* (Clinton, Miss., 1927, Ph.D. Thesis, Columbia University); and in W. A. Cate, *Lucius Q. C. Lamar* (Chapel Hill, 1935), chapter XII, "Mississippi Redeemed."

# INDEX